Sun Turned to Darkness

Religion, Theology, and the Holocaust
Alan L. Berger, *Series Editor*

Sun Turned to Darkness

*Memory and Recovery
in the Holocaust Memoir*

David Patterson

1998

Syracuse University Press

Library of Congress Cataloging-in-Publication Data

Patterson, David, 1948–
   Sun turned to darkness : memory and recovery in the Holocaust
memoir / David Patterson. — 1st ed.
      p. cm. — (Religion, theology, and the Holocaust)
   Includes bibliographical references and index.
   ISBN 0-8156-0530-7 (cloth : alk. paper)
   1. Holocaust, Jewish (1939–1945)—Personal narratives—History and
criticism. 2. Autobiographical memory. I. Title. II. Series.
D804.195.P37 1998
940.53′18′092—dc21   98-24320

For Miriam and Rachel

David Patterson is Distinguished Professor and Director of the Honors Program at the University of Memphis and has taught courses on the Holocaust, Jewish thought, ethics, philosophy, and literature. He is the author of more than eighty articles on topics in philosophy, literature, Judaism, Holocaust, and education, and his books include *The Greatest Jewish Stories Ever Told* (1997), *When Learned Men Murder* (1996), *Exile* (1995), *Pilgrimage of a Proselyte* (1993), *The Shriek of Silence* (1992), *In Dialogue and Dilemma with Elie Wiesel* (1991), *Literature and Spirit* (1988), *The Affirming Flame* (1988), and *Faith and Philosophy* (1982).

Contents

PART THREE

The Open-Endedness of Recovery

Preface

In *One Generation After* Elie Wiesel returns again to his ongoing remembrance of the Shoah. There he asserts, "Whoever sees himself as a severed branch becomes other, the Midrash teaches us. Isolate yourself within time, and time itself becomes abstraction, and so do you. Time is a link, your 'I' a sum total. Your name has been borne by others before you. Your fate is not yours alone" (1970b, 217). Reading these lines, not only a Jew but especially a Jew must ask: What ties me to this tree of life, so that I do not fall prey to the death of the severed branch? So that, indeed, I do not impose this death on others—living, buried, and yet unborn? The Jewish response to this question and this quest is: memory. This is the link to the past that opens up for Jews the horizon of the future.

The Jewish people, said Franz Rosenzweig a generation before the Holocaust, "did not originate from the womb of nature that bears nations, but—and this is unheard of!—was led forth 'a nation from the midst of another nation' (Deut. 4:34). . . . And so only he who remembers this determining origin can belong to it; while he who no longer can or will utter the new word he has to say 'in the name of the original speaker,' who refuses to be a link in the golden chain, no longer belongs to his people" (1955, 81). Here memory links Jews not only to a past but to an origin that precedes the past, one that lays claim to them like a name borne before them. Such a linkage makes Jewish memory an essential part of sacred history. This study of the Holocaust memoir, then, is undertaken from just this premise, that Jewish memory belongs to a *sacred* history. As a Jew I approach these texts written by Jews. As a Jew I regard them as a new part, a new branch, of sacred tradition in their struggle to recover that tradition—so as not to become a severed branch.

"In Judaism," says Rosenzweig, "man is always somehow a remnant. He is always somehow a survivor, an inner something, whose exterior was seized by the current of the world and carried off while he himself, what is left of him, remains standing on the shore. Something within him is waiting. And he has something within himself. . . . But he has a feeling that both the waiting and the having are most intimately connected with each other. And this is just that feeling of the 'remnant' which has the revelation and awaits the salvation" (1972, 405). In the texts before me, written by a remnant, what the Jew has is a certain memory; what he awaits is a certain recovery. What he has and what he awaits are, moreover, intimately intertwined, for it is not only the past that was but a life yet to be that summons this memory, which in turn posits a recovery: the two are of a piece.

This truth uttered by Rosenzweig before the Shoah is one truth that, like a remnant, has survived even the Shoah. But the stakes have changed. "The tasks begun by the patriarchs and prophets," writes Abraham Joshua Heschel, "and carried out by countless Jews of the past, are now entrusted to us. No other group has superseded them. We are the only channel of Jewish tradition, those who must save Judaism from oblivion, those who must hand over the entire past to the generations to come. We are either the last, the dying Jews, or else we are those who will give new life to our tradition. Rarely in our history has so much depended upon one generation. We will either forfeit or enrich the legacy of ages" (1955, 420–21). The memory that one receives in the Holocaust memoir belongs to sacred history because it is the one thing standing between the Jews and the annihilation that the Nazis planned for them. Thus, from out of the ashes of Jewish mothers and fathers the question is put to Jews: Shall we become accomplices to those who sought to obliterate Jewish being, or shall we oppose that plot and preserve this being that affirms the dearness of all human being? It is in the light of this question that the investigation at hand is pursued. It is, therefore, with profound reverence, great trepidation, and an overwhelming sense of responsibility that I assume this task of determining the relation between memory and recovery in the Holocaust memoir. In those days of death and destruction the sun turned to darkness. In these days of response and remembrance the task is to return the light to the sun—not only for the sake of the Jews and Judaism but for the sake of the sanctity of human being that Jewish being signifies.

Both the vessel that bore the bones of Joseph from Egypt and the vessel that bore the Torah from Sinai were referred to as the Ark. Just so, these memoirs constitute an ark bearing both the bones of the dead unburied and the Word of the truth unrealized. It is my hope that the labor before me may be a part of a much greater endeavor to bring both a bit nearer to the place of the Promise.

I thank the National Endowment for the Humanities, which supported a portion of the research for this project.

Memphis, Tennessee   David Patterson
September 1997

Sun Turned to Darkness

Introduction

"Let Him remember," writes Elie Wiesel, "for He alone can make us remember" (1985, 1:114). Yet in nearly every discussion of the Holocaust memoir He is the first one forgotten despite the fact that in nearly every memoir He is there, either affirmed or denied, either silently or explicitly. For those outside the Event, standing at the abyss of ashes piled abysmally high under the massive concrete dome at Maidanek, it may be difficult indeed to sanctify and bless His Great Name; perhaps because, although one may be outside the Event, the Event is not outside of oneself. "We flounder," writes Terrence Des Pres, "in a torment having nothing to do with us yet felt in some strange way to be very much a part of our deepest, most secret being. The terror of the camps is *with* us" (1976, 170). As one plunges into page after page of these memoirs, voices alien to one's own creep into one's own and bring with them the silence of the One whom one cannot escape and yet who eternally eludes one. Of all the distinctive features of the Holocaust, this is perhaps the most distinctive: there is no memory of this Event in time without the eternal memory of the One who is eternally the victim, the One whose immortality lies in His ability to be murdered time and time again.

It is this murder of the immortal that makes "the essence of survival," as Des Pres expresses it, "a passage through death" (1976, 176). Lawrence Langer amplifies this statement by saying, "These memories are irreversibly fused with a kind of death that admits neither birth nor renewal" (1982, 13). It is not too much to say, however, that for those who undertake the memory of their own deaths, the act of remembrance is a matter of life and death. Nor is it inappropriate to recall the words of Pavel Florensky and to reiterate: "Without the remembrance of God, we die; yet our very remembrance of God is made possible through God's remembrance of us. . . . If it should be asked whether the phrase 'eternal memory' requires a *genetivus objectivus* or a *genetivus subjectivus*, then, on the basis of what has been said, it must be acknowledged that both meanings are included here; for my 'eternal memory' signifies God's 'eternal memory' of me" (1970, 195). And so one sees that couched in these texts of memory is the outcry of the Rav condemned to death in Elie Wiesel's *Twilight*: "Here is my prayer. God of Israel: *Listen to the people of Israel!*" (1987, 34). When people turn their backs on their fellow human beings, God folds His arms. How, then, is one to bring about this reversal of the *Shema* so that the One who speaks might hear? Only through one's own act of response.

In this book I offer a response to the many voices that speak from a world—or an antiworld—where the sun turned to darkness and the moon turned to blood. Among the questions that shape the endeavor are: Who is the *I* who speaks in the memoir, and who is the *I* about whom it speaks? What is the nature of the transformation experienced by the person who articulates such a memory? Who is the implied reader of the memoir, the one to whom and for whom the cry of "Hear!" is uttered? What is the nature of the response that the memoir seeks? How is a memory of the loss tied to a recovery from the loss? And what do such issues suggest about a method for examining these texts? All of these questions have as their point of reference the Jewish question of life and the return to a life lived in relation to the Creator of life. The response with which one wrestles, therefore, comes in a remembrance of the idea expressed in Elhanan's prayer in Wiesel's *The Forgotten*: "God of Auschwitz, know that I must remember Auschwitz. And that I must remind You of it. . . . Remember that only memory leads man back to the source of his longing for You" (1992, 11–12). Indeed, the seeds of recovery are planted in the soil of that longing, watered by the tears of Rachel, who weeps for her children and refuses to be comforted. But the questions outlined above and the longing that Wiesel invokes are conspicuously absent from the investigations of the Holocaust memoir accomplished thus far. It appears that the critics believe they can manage quite well without the One who is so critical to Elhanan's struggle with memory. Why?

One reason for this absence lies in the hermeneutic and historiographic methods that characterize existing studies, in which the interest lies either in the interpretation of texts or in the clarification of facts. In opposition to these methods I here adopt a phenomenological method much as it is described by Emmanuel Levinas. This method, he explains, "permits consciousness to understand its own preoccupations, to reflect upon itself and thus to discover all the hidden or neglected horizons of its intentionality. . . . Phenomenology is a way of becoming aware of where we are in the world, a *sich besinnen* that consists of a recovery of the origin of meaning in our life world, or *Lebenswelt*" (1986b, 14–15). What Levinas describes as "intentionality" I understand as the longing for life that distinguishes the authors' pursuit of memory and their attempted return to life. If I were to further amend Levinas's statement, I might change "origin of meaning" to "origin of questioning" because as Mikhail Bakhtin has pointed out, "meaning always responds to particular questions" (1986, 145). The word *origin*, however, remains central to one's concern, in all of its theological and ontological implications—in all of its *Jewish* implications. For the phenomenon of this particular remembrance and attempted recovery belongs to a sacred history that is particularly Jewish. In Jewish sacred history every Jew views himself as having stood at Sinai to receive the Torah or what Emil Fackenheim calls "the Jewish book." But after the rise of the Third Reich, argues Fackenheim, "a Jew, is able to keep the Jewish book only if he views himself as though he had personally been present at Auschwitz or Buchenwald as well" (1978, 250). And the act of remembrance situates the Jew in the place where he is summoned to stand. Here the declaration of "Here I am!" includes the affirmation of "I remember!"

In the light of the foregoing remarks I establish a basis for the exploration of the Holocaust memoir first by considering those previous efforts that create the context for the current endeavor; most prominent among these are works written by Terrence Des Pres and Lawrence Langer. Having identified certain difficulties with these approaches, I then examine the nature of memory as understood within the texts of the memoirs in question. Once this is determined, I outline a philosophical orientation and methodological organization for this study; especially important in this connection are ideas developed by Emil Fackenheim and Emmanuel Levinas.

Previous Approaches to the Memoirs

Let it be said at the outset that any success achieved in the endeavor at hand is indebted to the labor of others, both renowned and anonymous. The criticisms that follow, therefore, are not just intended to underscore the shortcomings of previous efforts. Indeed, whatever "shortcomings" they have are the result more of a stage in the development of thought than to any deficiency in the thinker. The point, then, is to establish a next step in the ongoing response to the voices that put to one the first question put to the first human being: Where are you?

Among the initial book-length attempts to engage the memoirs is Terrence Des Pres's *The Survivor: An Anatomy of Life in the Death Camp* (1976). The

general difficulty with this work—one that results in its particular problems—lies in the fact that Des Pres groups the texts of Holocaust memoirs
with the testimonies of other survivors, especially those who passed through
the Soviet Gulag. Although no one with a trace of humanity would minimize the suffering of Stalin's victims, one must make some distinctions to
understand the nature of the memory that calls from the depths of the
Holocaust memoir. In this instance it is a distinction between the political
and the ontological. One recalls, for example, an insight from Piotr Rawicz:
"I believe that the fate and condition of the Jewish people are the very
essence of the human condition—the furthest borders of human destiny.
And the fate of the 'Holocaust Jew' is . . . the ontological essence of that
ontological essence" (1975, 25). For the prisoners of the Gulag the crime lay
in an action performed or in an opinion held; the point was the elimination
of the act or the belief, not the extermination of the human being. To be
sure, many of these prisoners were not sentenced to death, and in every
instance time in the labor camp was viewed as a form of punishment. For
the Jewish internees of the death camps, however, the capital crime was
being. "For us," writes Primo Levi, "the Lager is not a punishment; for us,
no end is foreseen and the Lager is nothing but a manner of living assigned
to us" (1961, 75)—not a punishment but a category in the chain of being.
Resistance to the system, therefore, was not in the interest of any cause; it
was in the interest of essence. Thus, argues Fackenheim, "Resistance in that
extremity was a way of being. For our thought now, it is an ontological
category" (1989, 248). This distinction escapes Des Pres.

Because this fundamental distinction escapes him, Des Pres falls prey to
other misunderstandings. The Shoah, he asserts, "produced an endless scream
which, given time, has transmuted itself into the voices of many witnesses"
(1976, 33). True enough. But how does he read that scream? "Survivors do
not so much decide to remember and record, as simply find themselves
doing it, guided by the feeling that it *must* be done. Earlier I suggested that
this act can be compared to a scream, but perhaps it is a scream—a special
version of the social animal's call to its group—and thus a signal of warning
and appeal which on the human level becomes a process of establishing a
record and thereby transmitting information vital for both moral and practical reasons. We learn what to fear, what to call evil and therefore what to
call good" (1976, 199–200). Immediately after making this statement Des
Pres cites Irven DeVore's book *Primate Behavior* to point out that baboons
engage in similar forms of action and reaction, reducing the soul's endless
scream to an instance of social-biological stimulus-response. But in the

Holocaust memoir "transmitting information" has little to do with practical reasons, and surely one does not have to wait for the screams of the victims before one can recognize this torture and extermination as evil.

This misreading of the memoirs is the outcome of the premise that there is nothing more primary to survivors and their "social groups" than survival itself, that nothing sacred in a spiritual sense transcends the moral and practical needs of the herd to sanctify life from within and from beyond life. If that is the case, then what can one say about the suicides of Tadeusz Borowski, Paul Célan, Piotr Rawicz, and Primo Levi? Where does one situate in such thinking Levi's assertion, "I'd like to be [a believer], but I don't succeed. . . . There is Auschwitz, and so there cannot be God. I don't find a solution to this dilemma. I keep looking, but I don't find it" (Camon 1989, 67–68)? How is one to deal with the existential, theological, and ontological problems that arise not just from *what* occurred but from the fact *that* it occurred, not just from what is remembered but from the essence of this remembrance? In this study I seek a response to these questions to which Des Pres cannot respond.

Viewing human beings in strictly social and biological terms, Des Pres is saddled with a strictly materialistic view of humanity, which, of course, is antithetical to the Jewish outlook necessary for responding to this Jewish memory. Operating in a discourse that makes the human being into a social *animal*, and therefore *material*, Des Pres unwittingly plays into the hands of the executioners. "All forms of idolatry," Rabbi Nachman of Breslov teaches, "are rooted in materialism" (1983, 140). And once idolatry looms, Fackenheim points out, Auschwitz appears (1989, 7). Idolatry rules where power eclipses truth and right is determined by the might of the murderer. The same idolatry that makes the word of the Führer into law makes the Jew into an animal. Charlotte Wardi, for example, recalls the *Schutzstaffel* (SS) practice of calling "a dog 'man' and a Jew 'dog' " (1986, 51). From the animal state it is a short step to the material state, or the state of raw material: reduced first to animals and then to objects, the Jews became a source of matter for stuffing mattresses, making lamp shades and uniforms, manufacturing soap and fertilizer, and mining gold.

The embodiment of the human image made into an animalistic body devoid of the divine is the *Muselmann*. This figure, so symbolic of the Holocaust antiworld, is all but absent from Des Pres's treatment of "the survivor." Fackenheim, however, has understood the significance of the *Muselmann*, as far as it can be understood. Once the Nazis had transformed the rejection of the divine image into law, he writes, "the murder camp was not an accidental by-product of the Nazi empire. It was its pure essence. The divine image in man *can* be destroyed. No more threatening proof to this effect can be found than the so-called *Muselmann*" (1978, 246). In *To Mend the World* he elaborates further, saying, "The Nazi state had no higher aim than to murder human souls while bodies were still alive. The *Muselmann* was its most characteristic, most original product" (Fackenheim 1989, 100). There is no greater evidence that the memory dealt with here is not a memory of a world, a place, a time, or anything else that can be situated in being. It is not even a memory of hell although Des Pres would make it into that. "The typology of Hell," he asserts, "was everywhere evident in the world of the camps" (1976, 172). Des Pres comes by this misunderstanding innocently, perhaps, because some of the survivors themselves invite such comparisons. In *Playing for Time*, for example, Fania Fénelon writes, "I was no longer anything, not even a slave. For me there was no longer either code or law. I was alone, abandoned, consigned to the executioner. We had arrived at the journey's end: hell" (1977, 20). But when she encounters Block 25, where those selected for the gas chambers were kept, Fénelon asserts, "You couldn't even call it hell, there is no name for it" (1977, 160). There is no name for it because it is not a place but a non-place, a black hole torn in the fabric of being.

Even in hell one remains *something*; only individuals, people with names, are damned. Nowhere in Dante's *Inferno*, therefore, does one encounter the *Muselmann*. Even there, "High Justice, sacred mistress / of the First Father, reigns eternally / over the falsifiers in their distress" (1954, 244). The Jewish "typology of hell" fares no better as something that might convey the nature of the concentrationary universe. In the *Zohar*, for instance, "the angel presiding over Gehinnom is called Duma, and there are tens of thousands of angels of destruction under him. He stands at its door, but those who have carefully guarded the sign of the holy covenant he has no power to touch" (1984, 1:34). Once again an insight from Fackenheim proves helpful: " 'Abandon hope' are the words greeting those entering Dante's hell. Even so it cannot touch the innocent. The Holocaust-world touched *none* but the innocent. What is innocent if not birth? Who is innocent if not children? When the children were thrown into the Auschwitz flames hell was surpassed. When their screams could be heard in the camp hope was murdered. It was murdered for the little ones. It was murdered also for those hearing their screams. And as we re-hear these screams it is murdered again" (1990, 68). Where hope is murdered even for the innocent, even for those who have guarded the sign of the Holy Covenant, time is obliterated. Being itself goes blank. If not hell, one may ask, then what is one dealing with? Perhaps it is something akin to what Levinas calls the "there is." In *Existence and Existents* he explains that this concept does not derive from anything interior or exterior in being, saying, "We do not grasp it through a thought. It is immediately there. There is no discourse. Nothing responds to us, but this silence" (1978a, 57–58). Reading these lines, one may better understand what it means to say that the *Muselmann* is a *novum* in history (Fackenheim 1989, 100); the *Muselmann* is the *there is* incarnate.

Lawrence Langer appears to have some sense of the Holocaust's *novum*, of its breach, in history when in *Versions of Survival* he declares, "The women who died in degradation, the 40,000 Jewish children of Auschwitz, all those, in Martin Buber's words, whose deaths represent testimony without acknowledgment—and who continue to assault memory and imagination for that very reason—these exemplify a different version of survival, one that summons us back into the circumference of their past instead of liberating us into a boundless future" (1982, 88). Yet in this work Langer begins with a statement that contains more obscurity than insight, claiming that "for many, the existence of Auschwitz suspended the link between the human and the divine. But it went further, by shattering the bond between the human and the moral" (1982, x). If the relation to the moral exceeds the relation to the divine, then the social exceeds rather than derives from the ontological, and the imminent transcends the transcendent. Surely, this cannot be the case. "The relation between deed and motive," says Langer, "collapsed so often in the death camps that it ceased to represent an ethical bulwark for the victims" (1982, 98). But the *Muselmann* does not emerge as the result of a breakdown of the ethical. For the ethical belongs to action, and what one has here is not a rupture of action but a rupture of being, both human and divine. Alvin Rosenfeld has rightly pointed out that the Holocaust author's position is "analogous to that of the man of faith, who is likewise beset by frustration and anguish and, in just those moments when his spirit may yearn for the fullness of Presence, is forced to acknowledge the emptiness and silence of an imposed Absence" (1980, 14–15). The imposed absence is not the absence of the moral but of the meaningful, which is the ground of all moral concern. In Jewish terms it is the absence of the holy, the most extreme exile of the *Shekhinah*, which is the Indwelling Presence of God. The collision is not with the ethical void but with an ontological void, with the *there is*. What is thus beyond ethical discourse cannot be addressed in ethical terms.

Even though he tries to divorce moral relation from a relation to the divine, Langer's interest in the ethical is both admirable and needful. It leads him, however, to a preoccupation with *what* took place and not with *that* it took place. And because he is concerned with the *what*, he is concerned with the *image*. The problem facing the author of the memoir, he argues, "is to create a language and imagery that will transform mere knowledge into vision and bear the reader beyond the realm of familiar imagining into the bizarre limbo of atrocity" (1982, 12). Langer, of course, is not the first to link memory with image. Aristotle, for example, insists that "memory, even the memory of objects of thought, is not without an image" (1972, 49). This association, again, is born of a fixation on the memory of what occurred rather than a pursuit of the event and the essence of Holocaust memory. Langer is after *the thing itself* and this endeavor leads him to view memory strictly as testimony. Although I am willing to concede that there is an element of testimony in this memory, in the texts under consideration memory is not only testimony but, more importantly for an understanding of the assault on Jewish being, is part of a larger process of Jewish recovery. Viewed merely as testimony — that is, as offering evidence to explain and to confirm what happened — these memoirs are robbed of their transcendently Jewish element, of what Rawicz refers to above as their "ontological essence." Testament? Perhaps, if testament is understood as a bearing witness that bears implications for one's recovery of a relation to the Covenant. But testimony? Not exactly.

In Hebrew the expression "to make a covenant" is *karat briyt,* which literally means "to cut a covenant." This phrase clearly has its associations with the sign of the Covenant, which is circumcision, but it is also linked to an inscription of the Covenant, to a "writing" of the Covenant into the flesh and onto the heart. One recalls in this connection the epigraph to the "Afterword and Foreword" in Ka-tzetnik's *Shivitti:* "And subscribe the deeds, and seal them, and call witnesses (Jer. 32:44)" (1989, 105). This subscription, this inscription, this *scribere,* and its summons arise in the book, borne by the People of the Book. Yet in *Holocaust Testimonies* Langer goes to great lengths to demonstrate the illegitimacy of the book as a medium of memory. The written memoir, he argues, raises "issues of style and form and tone and figurative language that — I now see — can deflect our attention from the 'dreadful familiarity' of the event itself. Nothing, however, distracts us from the immediacy and the intimacy of conducting interviews with former victims or watching them on a screen" (1991, xii–xiii). Although it would be unfair to accuse Langer of voyeurism (he is not Lot's wife), one finds once more the key words that characterize his approach: *familiarity, immediacy, intimacy.* One may come closer to the suffering when one comes closer to the face and the gestures of the oral witness, but one does not come closer to the nature of the memory as either Holocaust or Jewish memory. The problem of familiarity as Langer presents it is a problem of knowing *what it was like* to be there so that, like Des Pres, he ignores what distinguishes the Holocaust memoir from other memories of catastrophe. In his effort to get closer to what it was like Langer avoids the more harrowing questions of what occurs in the process of re-membering the ontological rupture and of what the nature of *this* memory implies about a Jewish recovery of Jewish being.

Certainly such questions could be raised with the oral witnesses; it is not a matter of which is better, as Langer suggests, but of whether the written memoir reveals anything of value. In this study the written memoir is perfectly legitimate as a means of approaching these questions. To be sure, Edmond Jabès has argued very well that, to a large extent, "we have no other reality than the reality books confer upon us" (1990, 74). Hence, the "issues of style and form and tone and figurative language"—as well as such things as allusions to Jewish texts and traditions—may open up the portals of thought rather than veil the avenues of imagination. These and other issues surrounding one's relation to the written text characterize a specifically Jewish concern with the written word as Jabès has pointed out. "The Jew," he writes, "has understood that his truth lies in the book, in each word of the book. Remember that the name of God is the juxtaposition of all the words in the language. Each word is but a detached fragment of that name. 'Man' is only a word. All relations between man and God pass through the word. That's why the Jew, unable to bear the silence of the Book, has always busied himself with commentary on it. Every commentary is first of all a commentary on silence" (1990, 102). If oral testimony contains silences and pauses that the text cannot convey, the text itself is constructed upon a silence that eludes all conversation. It is a silence that situates the Holocaust memoir within a sacred history that is specifically Jewish.

Many of Langer's claims about written memoirs, moreover, are simply false. He maintains, for instance, that "in fashioning a consecutive chronicle survivors who record their accounts unavoidably introduce some kind of teleology, investing incidents with a meaning, be it nothing more than the value of regaining one's freedom" (1991, 40). Very often, however, the written memoirs do not follow a consecutive chronicle; Sara Nomberg-Przytyk's *Auschwitz* and Primo Levi's *Moments of Reprieve* and *The Drowned and the Saved* are good examples. Very often, also, one finds in the written memoirs lines such as this one from Moshe Sandberg's *My Longest Year*, "The days are so confused in my memory that I no longer remember the sequence of events" (1968, 76), and in *Return to Auschwitz* Kitty Hart declares, "I find it well nigh impossible to recollect things in proper sequence" (1982, 97). In fact, instead of following a chronological sequence, memory here is the memory of the breakdown of all chronology. As for the teleology ascribed to regaining one's freedom, this, too, is not borne out by the memoirs; indeed, the silence that Jabès refers to above, the silence that distinguishes the Jewish text, turns the teleological into an infinite open-endedness. Thus, many of these memoirs "end" with lines similar to those that one reads near the close of Miklos Nyiszli's memoir: "Now, home again, nothing. I wandered aimlessly through silent rooms. Free, but not from my bloody past, nor from the deep-rooted grief that filled my mind and gnawed at my sanity" (1960, 160). Such evidence supports Barbara Foley's correct observation in an article on Holocaust narratives that, unlike the traditional memoir, in the Holocaust memoir "the characteristic movement is from life to death. . . . Innocence, initiation, endurance, escape—such is the pattern repeated in memoir after memoir, a kind of negative mirror of the traditional autobiographical journey toward self-fulfillment. And after the description of escape, a silence" (1982, 338–39). Silence: once again Jabès's insight comes to mind and with it Levinas's comment on the *there is*, to which no teleology can be attached and of which Langer is unaware.

In addition to Langer and Des Pres other scholars' work on the Holocaust memoir is worth noting, and Barbara Foley is among them. What concerns her is the problem of testimony and mimesis in Holocaust narratives. As indicated by the citation in the preceding paragraph—and unlike Des Pres and Langer—Foley is sensitive to at least some of the distinctive features of the Holocaust memoir. Along with the pattern of innocence, initiation, endurance, and escape, for example, she points out another aspect of these memoirs that sets them apart from traditional forms. Traditional forms of autobiography, she explains, are an "elaboration of a unique individuality. . . . One goal of the Nazis' plan for the camp inmates, however, was precisely to obliterate such a sense of individuality; the goal of the Holocaust memoir is, accordingly, not to convey a rich and unique particularity, but to delineate that process of dehumanization and anonymity that aimed at producing in the victim a negation of self" (1982, 338). Nevertheless, Foley succumbs to the same misconception that hampers Langer's approach when she writes, "The memoir . . . speaks to us from across a seemingly unbridgeable gulf. The challenge facing both writers and readers is the need for imaginative empathy" (1982, 342–43). Although it is true that these voices speak from across an unbridgeable gulf, the significance of the distinctions that Foley outlines does not lie in the need to imagine so that one may empathize. The effort to know what it was like or how it felt does not bring anyone one whit closer to the process of a recovery of Jewish being and the sanctification of Jewish life. One may wince at every one of the twenty-five blows suffered by the victim; one may gaze into the mirror of the memoir and struggle to picture oneself cold and emaciated; one may weep at every description of mothers calming their children as they are forced into the gas chambers. But this brings one no nearer to the essence of the memory and the recovery it seeks.

At least one more scholar should be mentioned before I examine the nature of memory in the Holocaust memoir—James Young. Like Langer, Young's approach to the memoirs of the Event is more epistemological than ontological, but, unlike Langer, his approach leads him to the epistemological distinction between having evidence and having knowledge. "Narrative testimony," he argues, "documents *not* the experiences it relates, but rather the conceptual presuppositions through which the narrator has apprehended experience. If the diarists' and memoirists' literary testimony is evidence of anything else, it is of the writing act itself" (1987, 420). From this statement one may detect a certain similarity between Young's approach and the phenomenological method I adopt here. Anticipating the act of writing, he cannot—and does not—ignore the ontological element in the Holocaust memoir and in the reader's relation to the memoir. He maintains, for example, that the Holocaust scribe endows "his testimony with an ontological authority that verifies both the authenticity and—by extension—the facticity of his record" (1987, 409–10). But, he adds, "by imputing an ontologically *authentic* text an indisputably authoritative factuality, the reader confuses the kinds of privilege a survivor's testimony necessarily demands. For even though a survivor's testimony is 'privileged' insofar as it is authentic, the factuality of his literary testimony is not necessarily so privileged" (1987, 413; emphasis in original). According to Young, the only things that survive are the survivor and his or her memory. And even these, of course, do not survive indefinitely.

Quite the contrary, the survivor, in Young's view, does not even survive his own text. For in the act of writing, Young insists, the survivor is himself effaced. Once again, therefore, those who encounter the memoir need concern themselves only with "the conceptual presuppositions through which the narrator has apprehended experience." They are safe. And this is a difficulty with Young's approach despite the soundness and astuteness of the questions he raises. What Young makes safe in his focus on interpretation I would make dangerous through a shift toward transformation, that is, through an accent on the recovery cried out for in the Holocaust memoir: not a recovery of factuality but of being; not a retracing of the process that ends in the absence of the narrator but a pursuit of the human and divine Presence that summons this narration. One discovers, on further reflection, that what Young deems an ontological problem involving "facticity" is actually an ontic problem, that is, a problem concerning one's relation to the *fact* of the event. The interest here, however, lies not in a breach in factuality but in a rupture of being itself, which is the rupture of truth and meaning conceived not as something one knows but as something one is, or is becoming. "Some events do take place," Wiesel has written, "but are not true; others are—although they never occurred" (1968, viii). And so in *Against Silence* he says, "I know the facts, but I do not know the truth" (Wiesel 1985, 1:120). Why? Because truth belongs to the soul's coming into being, to a commencing, and not to a closure placed on the event by its factuality or by the effacement of the survivor in a text. When the word initiates this process of becoming, the matter exceeds the security of armchair interpretation and launches one into the dangers of accountability. For the memory that I encounter, the memory with which I collide, in the Holocaust memoir takes root in my own memory. There it grows, like a tear in the fabric of my being, and from the depths of that rupture I must somehow answer. I must become not an interpreter of texts but a mender of the world, a part of the recovery that this memory demands.

But what is the essence of this memory?

The Essence of Memory in the Holocaust Memoir

Undertaking this study of memory and recovery in the Holocaust memoir, one must first remind oneself that the investigation draws this memory into the core of one's own memory. If one is to bear this memory as one is summoned to do, then one must bear in mind what is at stake, what there is to hold dear, what is life's most ultimate concern. The approach to these texts far exceeds an exegetic or hermeneutic interest in texts and testimonies. Here is the life and death of the soul, which invariably translates into the life and death of men, women, and children. "The forgetful soul, then," to recall Plato's injunction in the *Republic*, "we must not list in the role of competent lovers of wisdom, but we require a good memory" (1961, 723). The foundation for the love of wisdom is a love for life grounded in a profound sense of the sanctity of life. For those entrusted with life, memory is as essential to wisdom as wisdom is to life, a notion that many Jewish thinkers share with

the Greek philosopher. "What man acquires through wisdom is called 'life,' "
writes the tenth-century Jewish thinker Saadia Gaon (1976, 330), and in a
text attributed to Maimonides one reads, "Wisdom and life are one and the
same in Him" (1990, 199). Here is a distinction between the knowledge that
concerns Young and the wisdom that distinguishes life. The former is something one acquires and is not necessarily related to who one is or the life one
leads; the latter is something one seeks to become and is an essential feature
of one's way of being. One takes on life in the search for life, or for the
wisdom of life, and memory is a necessary element in this search; "recollect-
ing," in the words of Aristotle, "is, as it were, a sort of search" (1972, 59). This
statement applies both to the recollection under examination and to one's
own recollection.

Similarly to his Greek predecessors, Saint Augustine associates the life
that belongs to memory with the very essence of the self or soul. Without
memory, he declares in the *Confessions,* "I could not even speak of myself. . . . The power of memory is great, O Lord. It is awe-inspiring in its
profound and incalculable complexity. Yet it is my mind: it is my self" (1961,
223–24). This utterance Augustine addresses to God in his search for the
God in whom wisdom and life are one. Although vastly different from
Augustine's *Confessions,* the Holocaust memoir also entails a search for the
God who is essential to the life of the self. The terrible cry of "Where is God
now?" resounds from the margins of every imprint on the pages of these
memoirs. At the end of the preceding section I suggested a distinction between fact and truth; here, in the longing for the Holy One, I perceive a
tension between matter and spirit. And with this discovery comes to light a
further confusion underlying much of the work done thus far on the Holocaust memoir. Preoccupied with factuality—that is, with what was seen, felt,
and experienced—many scholars to date have focused more on perception
than on memory. Their concern, therefore, has not been so much with the
spiritual as with the material, a conclusion one may draw from an insight
offered by Henri Bergson: "It is in very truth within matter that pure perception places us, and it is really into spirit that we penetrate by means of
memory" (1929, 235). But memory relies on perception in much the same
way that the soul relies on the body. Memory spiritualizes matter by giving
it form, which, in turn, opens up significance. Indeed, from a Jewish standpoint, as expressed in the eighteenth-century *Toldot* of Rabbi Yaakov Yosef of
Polnoe, "the principal purpose of the creation of man, who is made out of
form and matter, is that he should strive all his days to turn matter into form"
(Dresner 1960, 137) and in this way to impart meaning to life. With certain

important differences, the Holocaust memoir has this in common with other memoirs, that it strives to turn matter into spirit by imparting form to perception. It is memory that makes perception *matter.*

This process characterizes what Walter Benjamin calls "the weaving of remembrance" when he notes, "It is not what he has experienced that here plays the primary role for the author engaged in remembering; rather, it is the weaving of his remembrance" (1977, 311). Meaning lies not in the remembrance but in the weaving. In this creation of the text the self becomes significant; it does not offer signs but becomes a sign of what it seeks. Thus, what is at work in this weaving or *form*ation of remembrance is not the erasure of the self from the text, as Young claims (1988, 10), but the recovery of the living soul from the dead datum of experience. Benjamin's insight has an important bearing on the nature of memory as it unfolds in the written text of the memoir, for the text is what is woven from memory as the author imparts form to matter. Especially helpful in this connection is Bakhtin's insight that I remember a given experience "from the aspect of its to-be-attained meaning and object" so that "I renew the still-to-be-achieved character of every one of my experiences, I collect all of my experiences, collect all of myself *not* in the past, but in the future that confronts me eternally as a future yet-to-be. My own unity, for myself, is one that confronts me eternally as a unity-yet-to-be" (1991, 125–26). Memory's transformation of matter into form, therefore, is not the creation of an enclosure but the plotting of a direction, the opening of a horizon of time. Bakhtin enables one to see that the memoir is not about the past but about the future because memory is about a meaning that is yet to be revealed. Although the survivor may seal the deeds and summon the witness, memory and meaning *happen* when they remain forever unsettled.

Because memory operates with this orientation toward the yet-to-be-revealed, it is distinguished by a not-knowing; so distinguished, it addresses through the memoir the One who knows and who may, therefore, redeem or somehow heal the one who does not know. In *The Town beyond the Wall* Wiesel writes, "The essence of man is to be a question, and the essence of the question is to be without answer" (1964, 187); in Wiesel's *Twilight,* however, Pedro reminds, "What is important for man is to feel not only the existence of an answer, but the presence of one who knows the answer. When I seek that presence, I am seeking God" (1987, 197–98). It is before Him that the author stands with his or her memoir and to Him that the memory is offered, like a prayer. Prayer, in fact, "has the power to improve the memory and banish forgetfulness," according to Rabbi Nachman of Breslov

(1983, 277); prayer, he maintains, "is a *segulah* for developing a good memory" (1983, 106). In its Jewish manifestation, the greater the memoir's quest for a recovery of the soul, the deeper its ties to prayer. In his own way Bakhtin, too, adopts this view, as is evident when he says, "The deeper the repentance and the passing-beyond oneself, the clearer and more essential is one's referredness to God" (1991, 144); in the memoir, then, "there is no hero and there is no author. . . . Author and hero are fused into one: it is the spirit prevailing over the soul in the process of its own becoming, and finding itself unable to achieve its own completion or consummation, except for a certain degree of consolidation, that it gains through anticipation, in God" (1991, 147). What is prayer, if not a certain degree of consolidation, gained through anticipation, in God? If the essence of the Holocaust memoir shares some-thing with that of other memoirs, it lies in this fusing of author and hero in the relation to the God who forever abides along the horizon of the yet-to-be.

The essence of the Holocaust memoir, however, entails more than this, and, despite their depth, the insights derived from Bergson, Benjamin, and Bakhtin ultimately prove to be inadequate to the essence of this written memory that is in a category by itself. All of these thinkers, of course, wrote the texts I have cited before the Kingdom of Night descended upon the earth (although Benjamin was one of its victims). As a Jew who lived through the time of the Event and who has subsequently addressed the problem of the Jewish book, Jabès can help one see one's inadequacies when it comes to reading the written memoirs of the Holocaust. "One has to write out of the break [which is Auschwitz]," he insists, "out of that unceasingly revived wound" (1990, 62). One of Jabès's ontological metaphors for the wound is the desert. "In the desert," he writes, "one becomes other: one becomes the one who knows the weight of the sky and the thirst of the earth; the one who has learned to take account of his own solitude. Far from excluding us, the desert envelops us" (1990, 16). Memory in the text of the Holocaust memoir is situated not within a continuity but within the heart of a wasteland. The events that transpire in this desert do not belong to the coordinate system of other events. Bergson, by contrast, claims that "in the extreme plane, which represents the base of memory, there is no recollection which is not linked by contiguity with the totality of events which precede and also with those which follow it" (1929, 222). The Holocaust memoir, however, does not so much undertake a penetration of spirit in the light of contiguity as it seeks a recovery of the soul in the light of a rupture. "The rupture," says Jabès, "is primarily due to God who wanted to be absent, who fell silent. To rediscover the divine word means to pass through this rupture. Moreover, the implacable questioning this word is submitted to can only take place in the rupture; it is thanks to this rupture that the questioning acquires its true freedom and its deep meaning. Truth is always at the end of the questioning, on the other shore, behind the last horizon" (1990, 59). The passage through the rupture, through its questions, is what opens up this *novum* in history.

If I may join Jabès with Fackenheim in this connection, a distinguishing feature of the Holocaust memoir becomes more clear as one recalls Fackenheim's assertion that German resistance—and along with resistance one may add "memory"—"had to discover a true self to be respected. The Jewish resistance had to *recreate* Jewish selfhood" (1989, 222–23; emphasis in original). In the Holocaust memoir this task of re*creating* stands over against the re*situating* implied by Bergson. A further consideration of Jabès also renders inadequate to the Holocaust memoir Benjamin's claim that "where experience prevails in a strict sense, certain contents of the individual's past meet in memory with the contents of a collective past" (1974, 611). The ontological undoing of the Jewish position in history severs Jewish existence—at least in the first instance—from the collective existence of humanity. The Holocaust memoir recreates selfhood not to situate itself in the midst of a collective humanity but to mend a wound that has distanced the Jewish soul from humanity; it is not to once again be part of the nations but to once again become a light unto the nations as the other who puts a question to humanity by putting a question to himself. "It is precisely in that break," Jabès asserts, "in that non-belonging in search of its belonging, that I am without a doubt most Jewish" (1990, 64). For the Jew, Jabès shows, the result of this problem of having no place in the collective is that he moves into a position of "questioning himself and questioning '*the other*' " (1990, 77; emphasis in original) and "Every question is tied to becoming. Yesterday interrogates tomorrow, just as tomorrow interrogates yesterday in the name of an always open future. The famous 'Who am I?' finds its justification only in a universal questioning of which we would be but the persistent echo" (1990, 74). Questioning the other, the Jew is himself rendered other to the collective. In the process of mending that wound the Jewish memory makes heard the question most needful for all by becoming its echo before it is uttered. "Remember it before it comes and observe it after it has gone," one is enjoined in the fourth-century *Mekilta de-Rabbi Ishmael* (1961, 1:252). In the light of Jabès's remarks one sees that this ancient wisdom has a deep resonance in modern life.

Although Bakhtin brings out the profound search for God in "confessional self-accounting," he is unable to deal with the human self-accounting that profoundly implicates God's account of Himself. This, too, belongs to the essence of the Holocaust memoir. "The *first* performed act," says Bakhtin, "which is determined by the intrinsic purpose of the confessional self-accounting is praying" (1991, 149). And, as I have suggested, the Holocaust memoir bears the marks of prayer. "God is the place [*ha-Makom*] — as the book is," notes Jabès. "Bringing those two together is something that has always excited me. God, through His Name, is the book" (1990, 15); after Auschwitz, however, " 'God' is the metaphor for emptiness; 'Jew' stands for the torment of God, of emptiness" (1990, 57). Bakhtin takes no account of this emptiness; before Auschwitz it did not exist. But it must be kept in mind that this emptiness is not a void; if it were, it could have no metaphor. In the words of Wiesel, "The fact that I pray means someone is there to listen, that what I am saying is not uttered to a great void. But what I do say, I say with anger" (Patterson 1991, 83). If the Holocaust memoir is against silence, it is against the silence of God; if it is about the recovery of human life, it is also about the recovery of the life of the divine. In the memory of God's silence that silence takes on a voice heard in the memory's act of response. God speaks despite Himself. He speaks because the Jew will not allow Him to be silent, as if He were saying, in the words of the Talmud, "*Nitshuniy banay*, My children have defeated Me!" (Bava Metzia 59a). He speaks because the Jew remembers and, thus, refuses to remain silent. Despite himself.

The anger that Wiesel experiences is not simply the anger of someone who is bitter about having been cheated by life. His anger, like the anger of other authors of these memoirs, is the anger of one who has survived the loss of his own life fueled by the Hasidic outcry that "it is against the Creator of the universe and the Lord of history that accusation must be hurled. Ultimately, the exile — in body and in spirit — is His doing" (Dresner 1960, 239). It turns out that the peculiar essence of the Holocaust memoir does not lie merely in the endeavor to turn matter into spirit; more than that, it is the utterance of a soul that had been transformed into matter, that is, of one who has lived through his own death. "From the depths of the mirror," one reads in the closing lines of Wiesel's *Night*, "a corpse gazed back at me" (1960, 116) — *me contemplait*, as the French text states (Wiesel 1958, 178), "contemplated me," "studied me." And "the look in his eyes," he continues, "has never left me" (Wiesel 1960, 116). This memory of the death of the self, moreover, follows in the wake of another memory, the memory of the death of God. Rabbi Nachman says that "if you develop your memory in the right way, as we have explained, great *tikkunim* will be brought about in the upper worlds and the unity of God will be revealed" (1983, 107). If one applies this statement to the Holocaust memoirs, then one must dare to amend it: for what is sought in this mending, in this *tikkun*, is not just the revelation of God's unity but the recovery of God's life and with it one's own. To be sure, it is only through the memoir's resanctification and recreation of human life that the divine life can be restored. Wiesel makes this point when he declares, "Dostoyevski once said that if God does not exist, then everything is permitted; I say, no; if everything is permitted, then God does not exist" (1985, 1:371). And so, once more, a remnant of ancient wisdom belongs to the essence of the Holocaust memoir. For in the fifth-century *Pesikta* Rabbi Kahana cites the *tanna* Rabbi Shimon bar Yochai, saying, " 'Only when ye are My witnesses, am I God. But when ye are not My witnesses, I'—if one may speak thus—'am not God' " (1975, 232–33). Once again one sees what is distinctively Jewish in the Holocaust memoir and what distinguishes it from other memoirs; the One who is invoked in the memory needs that memory as much as the one who remembers.

Before the Holocaust—before this novum in history and in thought— the writer of the memoir gazed upon a life, not upon a corpse. For the authors of other memoirs, what Ludwig Wittgenstein wrote in his notebooks of 1914–16 is true: "Death is not an event in life. It is not a fact of the world" (1979, 75e); in the *Tractatus* Wittgenstein elaborates, "Death is not an event in life. Death is not lived through. . . . Our life is endless in the way that our visual field is without limit" (1922, 185). But for the survivor who undertakes the memory of God's death and his own the field of vision is limited to the narrow confines of the rupture. All other vision comes in the form of an evasion of this vision, as Alan Mintz points out: "When the survivor writes about the Holocaust it has the effect of an evasion interrupted or curtailed rather than an experience encountered or investigated; and when he writes of other things, the Holocaust seems to hover as an ontological condition" (1984, 259). The ontological condition determines the condition of the soul, and the condition of the soul shapes the essence of the Holocaust memoir. Hence, in the words of Wiesel, "the ultimate mystery of the Holocaust is that whatever happened took place in the soul" (1985, 1:239). Cast in an ontological category of its own, the Holocaust memoir is the soul's memory of itself and, through memory, the soul's struggle to recover itself. Similarly, it is the soul's memory of God and God's memory of Himself in a struggle to recover Himself. As in the recitation of the Eighteen Benedictions, it is God whom the survivor asks to open his lips—not, however, to sing His praise but to confront Him with what has become of His divine image once imprinted on the human soul. "What man did at Auschwitz," says Wiesel, "could not have been done outside of God; in some way He too was at work—was He questioning man? Was He showing His face? What a face! In a sense, at Auschwitz God was afraid—afraid of Himself" (1985, 3:309). In the Holocaust memoir the phrase "fear of God" requires both a *genetivus objectivus* and a *genetivus subjectivus*.

At this juncture a few lines from Yehudah Halevi's "A Camping Place" come to mind: "Lo, upon my heart is a thought from my God; / Yea, also upon my tongue is an answer from my Lord" (1924, 143). But what a difference these memoirs make in the reading of these lines! In the Holocaust memoir, if the answer comes at all, it comes in the silence that both frames and inhabits the memoir. Indeed, the written word of the memoir, the imprint on the page, conveys not only the memory written in black but the silence written in white. This is what makes the memoir "a moment of the wound, or eternity," to borrow a phrase from Jabès (1977, 28). Is inevitable failure, then, part of the essence of the Holocaust memoir? Is the survivor inevitably led to cry out with Sarah in Jabès's *Book of Yukel*, "Lord, I resemble You in my impotence to save You" (1977, 73)? To answer "yes" is too terrifying. To answer "no" is too cowardly. Here, too, the Jewish memory is ridden with the lament of Jewish antiquity. "Woe to me if I speak," cries Rabbi Yochanan ben Zakkai in the Mishnah, "woe to me if I do not speak" (Kelim 17:16). *Despite and because of* the rupture it represents, the Holocaust memoir, as an essentially Jewish text, must recover its link to a Jewish past if it is to open up a path to a Jewish future. Malkiel, the son of Elhanan in Wiesel's *The Forgotten*, understands this point. "For a Jew," he says, "nothing is more important than memory. He is bound to his origins by memory. It is memory that connects him to Abraham, Moses, and Rabbi Akiba" (1992, 71). One's link to one's origins is one's only link to one's future: in the Holocaust memoir memory is memory of the future. In that memory time takes on substance by taking one elsewhere, toward the absolutely other.

This last and most important point to be made about the essence of memory in the Holocaust memoir is that here memory moves from a perception of the past toward a recovery of the future, which is a recovery of time, through a relation to the other. "The other is the future," Levinas explains. "The very relationship with the other is the relationship with the future. It seems to me impossible to speak of time in a subject alone, or to speak of a purely personal duration" (1987b, 77). The essence of memory in the Holocaust memoir lies in the fact that, even though it is a memory of the void, it is not uttered in a void. Rather, it comes as a response addressed to another. "I felt under orders to live," one recalls Pelagia Lewinska's assertion upon her realization of the "motivating principle" at work in the death camp (1968, 150). In this responsive address time is recovered, for time, as Levinas notes, "is the very relationship of the subject to the Other" (1987b, 39). In the case at hand that relationship is made of memory. The injunction underlying the Holocaust memoir, moreover, is not only *zachor* but also *shamor*. "*Zachor v'shamor b'dibar echad*," writes Elie Wiesel. " 'Remember and observe' were given in one word. Just as all these days were created for one day alone, the Sabbath, all other words were created for one word alone, 'Remember' " (1977, 5). Indeed, for a Jew, that one word is the origin of all other words; as Rabbi Yitzchak Ginsburgh points out, "the word 'memory' (*zikaron*) itself, in Hebrew, means 'a source of speech' " (1991, 4). The linkage here lies in the fact that both time and the word constitute the substance of the self-to-other relation that distinguishes the essence of memory in the Holocaust memoir. And, in the light of Wiesel's remark above, one finds that this *Jewish* memory is tied to the Jewish Sabbath.

In the Mishnah one is taught that writing and letters were among the ten things created on the eve of the first Sabbath (Avot 5:6). It is at this point, and not with the six days of Creation, that time as the issue of Jewish memory enters existence. On the Sabbath one remembers and observes two primary events that infuse time with eternity: the Creation of the world and the Liberation from Egypt, which culminated in the Revelation of the Holy One at Sinai and the giving of the Torah. Commenting on the significance of the Sabbath, Abraham Joshua Heschel writes, "It is the dimension of time wherein man meets God, wherein man becomes aware that every instant is an act of creation, a Beginning, opening up new roads for ultimate realizations. Time is the presence of God in the world of space" (1981, 100). The summons to observe the Sabbath wherein human meets God is among the 613 commandments that came from God when He showed His face to Moses. At Auschwitz, too, God showed His face, as Wiesel suggests above. And so the parallel emerges: on the Sabbath one observes the interfacing of the Eternal One with time in a response to His commanding Voice, and in the Holocaust memoir one also encounters the remembrance and observance of a commanding Voice through a stepping before the Countenance. "No *redeeming* Voice is heard from Auschwitz," Fackenheim argues. "However, a *commanding* Voice is being heard, and has, however faintly, been heard from the start" (1978, 31). The Voice Fackenheim refers to is heard because the voices of these memoirs are heard; it is heard in the midst of those voices, and it belongs as much to the ontology of the Holocaust memoir as the observance of the Sabbath belongs to Jewish ontology. "To hear and obey the commanding Voice of Auschwitz," Fackenheim insists, "is an 'ontological' possibility, here and now, because the hearing and obeying was already an 'ontic' reality, then and there" (1989, 25). Once again one sees the essential role of time in the Holocaust memoir, and with the help of Fackenheim one sees even more—the essential role of the eternal in the Holocaust memoir.

Realizing the centrality of the Sabbath to Jewish life and its echoes in the essence of the Holocaust memoir, one is not surprised to find that the memory of the Sabbath is very often a part of the memoir itself. Leon Wells, for example, begins his memoir with a memory of his family's observance of the Sabbath before the Event (1978, 3), and in her memoir Judith Dribben recalls the lighting of Sabbath candles in Auschwitz. "I didn't know that Jews light candles in a concentration camp," she says to a fellow inmate. "What for?" And then she adds, "What I really wanted to say was that I was longing for the candles my mother used to light every Friday" (1969, 216). These memories of the Sabbath are an important part of the Holocaust memoir, but, of course, the memory in the memoir is not the same as the remembrance of the Sabbath. Indeed, the memory in the memoir ineluctably alters the remembrance of the Sabbath even as it summons that memory. This linkage with a difference comes out, for instance, in Nathan Shapell's *Witness to the Truth*, wherein the remembrance of the Sabbath in the Sosnowiec ghetto is characterized by the observance of the death of his father and of all his father symbolized, "When the Sabbath came I sat in our secret little place of worship and said Kaddish for him [his father] in the age-old prayers I had learned in another life, in a lost world" (1974, 50). Whereas the *zachor v'shamor* that pertains to the Sabbath reveals an essential feature of memory, Shapell's allusion to a lost world opens an essential aspect of recovery in the Holocaust memoir. Prayer is remembered in a text that is akin to prayer as a effort to regain what forever resides on an infinitely distant shore.

According to Jewish tradition, Rabbi Adin Steinsaltz notes, there are four crises in cosmic history: the Shattering of the Vessels upon the Creation, the Sin of the Tree of Knowledge, the Sin of the Golden Calf, and the Destruction of the Temple, whereupon the *Shekhinah* herself went into exile (1985, xxx–xxxi). All the 613 Commandments are intended ultimately to bring about a rectification of these crises in cosmic history. But the Shoah is a *novum* not only in history but in cosmic or sacred history. Thus, it represents a fifth crisis, one that necessitates a 614th Commandment, as Fackenheim has shown (1978, 19–24). The essence of memory in the Holocaust memoir, therefore, entails not just a recovery of time but a recovery of the eternal *in*

time through the observance of a 614th Commandment. This brings me to
the philosophical basis for an examination of memory and recovery in the
Holocaust memoir.

The Philosophical Foundation for the Investigation

When the Temple stood at the center of the world, only the High Priest was
allowed to enter the Holy of Holies, and he entered only on Yom Kippur, the
Day of Atonement—the day of the recovery of the human relation to the
divine. But even the Holy of Holies was occasionally in need of repair. When
such a need arose, workmen were lowered into the Upper Chamber in *tevot*,
or boxes, that would prevent them from feasting their eyes on this most
sacred sight. And from within the *tevot* they would repair the Holy of Holies.

In Hebrew *tevot* means not only "boxes" but also "words." Applying this
analogy to Holocaust memoirs, through the words—and the silences—of
their texts these authors descend into time to do the work of mending a
relation to the holy, the work of recovery, for the sake of human and divine
life. From the time when the High Priest entered the Holy of Holies on Yom
Kippur, this *tikkun*—this recovery or mending of the world—has been the
focal point of Jewish being. But from the time when that being became a
capital crime, the *tikkun* of Yom Kippur has assumed another aspect. "To
return the throne of judgment usurped by Dr. Mengele back to God," writes
Fackenheim, "has become a Jewish necessity, and the necessity does not
exist beside the Yom Kippur experience but is part of it" (1989, 324). This
movement of return and recovery is as much a part of the Holocaust memoir
as the memory of the Holocaust is part of Yom Kippur; the word *remember*,
in fact, appears more frequently than any word in the Yom Kippur service,
with the exception of the names of the Holy One. The importance of Holocaust memory to the Jewish liturgy signifies its importance to Jewish life
and to the recovery of that life. And, as Fackenheim demonstrates, that
recovery, that *tikkun*, is a possibility for the future because it was an actuality
in the past (1989, 300). With this in mind, then, Fackenheim outlines three
elements of *tikkun* confronting post-Holocaust Jewish thought: (1) the recovery of Jewish tradition; (2) the recovery from an illness; and (3) the open-
ended nature of the first two processes of recovery (1989, 310). Each of these
elements of a post-Holocaust *tikkun* is a definitive feature of the recovery
sought through the words and the silence that go into the Holocaust memoir. This study of memory in the Holocaust memoir, then, is organized
according to these three fundamental elements of recovery.

The Recovery of Tradition

If the Talmud is the struggle with the Angel, as Levinas has said (1982, 99), then, in the light of Fackenheim's invocation of Mengele—the Angel of Death—both the struggle and the Angel assume a different aspect after Auschwitz. The recovery of tradition that would restore a Jewish presence in existence no longer entails a battle of good against evil or even of life against death. The SS Angel of Death destroyed the Jewish death that had been part of Jewish life and robbed the victims of their graves. What must be recovered in this new struggle, then, are the frontiers between life and death, good and evil, holy and profane. It is the battle of a Jewish being deemed criminal against the Aryan nothingness that so deemed it. On the one hand, only in the being revealed by Jewish tradition are the distinctions that sanctify life. Planet Auschwitz, on the other hand, signifies the collapse of all distinctions of this kind. "There is no longer any difference," says Levinas, "between day and night, between outside and inside. Do we not smell here, more strongly than a while back, beyond all violence which still submits to will and reason, the odor of the camps? Violence is no longer a political phenomenon of war and peace, beyond all morality. It is the abyss of Auschwitz or the world at war. A world which has lost its 'very worldliness.' It is the twentieth century. One must go back inside, even if there is terror inside" (1990, 190–91). The movement back to the inside is the movement of memory back into tradition; it is memory's summons of tradition back into a present so that the present might once more be made of sacred history. If the sacredness of sacred history is derived from God's presence in that history, then the recovery of tradition is a recovery of God and of the *existence* of God. "The existence of God," Levinas argues, "is sacred history itself, the sacredness of man's relation to man through which God may pass" (1986b, 18). The recovery of tradition, therefore, entails a mending of that interhuman relation through which God may pass. When the one is lost, so is the other: Auschwitz signifies the single blow that works the double destruction of the human and the divine.

It has always been the case that a Jew cannot bear witness to the divine image within the human being unless he believes his own testimony. "In our time, however," Fackenheim notes, "he cannot authentically believe in this testimony without exposing himself *both* to the fact that the image of God was destroyed, *and* to the fact that the unsurpassable attempt to destroy it was successfully resisted" (1978, 251). The survivor's endeavor to recover the sacred tradition precedes the summons to that recovery; thus, it is through the survivor, through his memory, that the summons comes to us from beyond the survivor. Where is that "beyond"? It is couched in the texts and in the prayers of the tradition, which is itself a source of revelation as Jewish thinkers such as Saadia Gaon have maintained (1976, 336). To be sure, the sacred texts that form much of this sacred history are an explicit part of many of the memoirs; Wiesel's *Night* and Ka-tzetnik's *Shivitti* immediately come to mind. Even Primo Levi, the one who refused God in his refusal of Auschwitz, suggests that the tales of the Shoah might themselves be viewed as the tales of a new bible (1961, 59). If one concedes some sense to this notion, then one does so only through an embrace of the connection between the stories of the "new bible" and the texts of *the* Bible. Indeed, an encounter with the biblical text, Fackenheim maintains, has become a necessity for post-Holocaust Jewish thought (1989, 18); it is a key to any recovery of the tradition that has nurtured Jewish life for centuries. This existential necessity confronting the Jew—and anyone who would approach the Holocaust memoir as a Jewish memoir—lies in the nature of the Jewish relation to being. If being has meaning for the Jew, it is, in the words of Levinas, "to realize the Torah. The world is here so that the ethical order has the possibility of being fulfilled. The act by which the Israelites accept the Torah is the act which gives meaning to reality. To refuse the Torah is to bring being back to nothingness" (1990, 41). Either Torah or Auschwitz—that is the existential necessity confronting the Jew and underlying the recovery of tradition. And neither the Holocaust memoir nor a responsible reading of it can avoid this either/or.

Levinas confronts the reader with this inescapable decision when he asserts, "To renounce after Auschwitz this God absent from Auschwitz—no longer to assure the continuation of Israel—would amount to finishing the criminal enterprise of National Socialism, which aimed at the annihilation of Israel and the forgetting of the ethical messages of the Bible, which Judaism bears, and whose multi-millenial history is concretely prolonged by Israel's existence as a people" (1988b, 163). The absence of *ha-Shem* from the camps is an absence of the possibility of a *Kiddush ha-Shem*, or martyrdom from that antiworld. Those who were consigned to the crematorium were murdered not because of their Torah or their teaching but, again, because of their being. Whereas Hadrian made Jewish martyrdom by forbidding the teaching of Torah, Hitler did something quite different as Fackenheim has shown: "In making Jewish existence a capital crime, Hitler murdered Jewish martyrdom itself" (1978, 247). The recovery of tradition and with it the recovery of the inescapable either/or is a recovery of the possibility of martyrdom. Martyrdom can happen only where there is meaning, that is, where the holy is at stake in life. And the thing that subjects the martyr to destruction is the indestructibility of the holy texts and prayers of tradition. One recalls in this connection the story of the martyr Rabbi Chanina ben Tradion, who was wrapped in the Holy Scrolls and burned at the stake by the Romans for his teaching of Torah. As the flames rose, his disciples gathered around him and asked, "Rabbi, what do you see?" And he answered, "I see the parchment consumed by the fire, but the letters . . . the letters are flying up to heaven!" (*En Jacob* 1921, 5: 154). Fire could not consume the Torah, for the Torah itself is made of fire. The ascent of the Hebrew letters of the Torah to the Holy One, blessed be He, brings to mind an image of prayer. If the recovery of tradition includes a recovery of martyrdom, then tradition cannot be recovered without a capacity for prayer. Holocaust memoirs almost always include the memory of prayer in places where there should be no prayer. If the memoirs themselves cannot be viewed as prayers in a strict sense, they nonetheless represent a call to prayer.

One recalls the Hasidim in Buchenwald who sacrificed their bread— thus endangering their lives—to purchase *tefillin* for their prayers. What is remarkable about these prayers is neither that they can be explained nor that they explain anything but precisely that they appear without explanation as a kind of epiphany. In these prayers, says Fackenheim, "we have touched an Ultimate" (1989, 219). When one touches an Ultimate, the Ultimate touches us. From the heart of those prayers uttered in Buchenwald the hand of sacred tradition reaches out to one, and in its palm it holds a question: Where are you? The infinite speaks through the testimony one bears (see Levinas 1981, 151), and it speaks in the form of this question that arises from the depths of every affirmation and, thus, every memoir to come out of that Great Negation. The recovery of tradition is initiated in the demand for that recovery, and the demand speaks before it is spoken, in the prayers of the Hasidim of Buchenwald. But because these are Hasidic prayers uttered *in Buchenwald*, one cannot ignore a certain disjunction in their conjunction with sacred tradition. Along these lines Fackenheim comments, "In Ezekiel's image [of the dry bones], the dead have fallen in battle. The dead of the Holocaust were denied battle, its opportunity and its honour. Denied the peace even of bones, they were denied also the honour of graves, for they, the others, ground their bones to dust and threw the dust into rivers. To apply Ezekiel's image of Jewish death to the Holocaust, then, is impossible. The new enemy, no mere Haman, not only succeeded where Haman failed, for he murdered the Jewish people. He murdered also Ezekiel's image of

Jewish death" (1990, 67). This murder of Jewish death is just what necessitates the need for a recovery of Jewish life. Without a recovery of Jewish death Ezekiel's dry bones can never regain the flesh and blood of Jewish life. Yet those dry bones begin to take on flesh and blood in the utterance of memory in the Holocaust memoir. For that utterance is just as impossible and just as actual as the prayers of the Hasidim of Buchenwald.

This combination of impossibility and actuality shows that the tradition recovered is a tradition with a difference. One important element of Jewish tradition, for example, is Midrash, and Sidra Ezrahi, among others, has made note of midrashic elements in the writings of authors such as Elie Wiesel (1980, 117). But even though "Midrash was meant for every kind of imperfect world," Fackenheim points out, "it was not meant for Planet Auschwitz, the anti-world" (1978, 265). What, then, is the difference in the tradition with a difference? It is the insertion of a kind of madness into the tradition recovered, a madness that brings about the very recovery. For midrashic madness, Fackenheim explains, "is the Word spoken in the anti-world which ought not to be but is. The existence it points to acts to restore a world which ought to be but is not, and this is its madness. After Planet Auschwitz, . . . a Jew cannot do—with God or without Him—what a Voice from Sinai bids him do: choose life" (1978, 269). This is why Wiesel responds to the question of why he writes by saying, "Perhaps in order not to go mad. Or, on the contrary, to touch the bottom of madness" (1990b, 13). This is why his character Moishe in *The Town beyond the Wall* cries out, "These days honest men can do only one thing: go mad! Spit on logic, intelligence, sacrosanct reason! That's what you have to do, that's the way to stay human, to keep your wholeness!" (Wiesel 1964, 20). If the recovery of tradition is tied to a recovery from illness, then it cannot happen without a dose of this madness without which there can be no health.

The Recovery from Illness

The manifestation of the madness without which there can be no health comes upon the cry of "Here I am!" in response to the question "Where are you?" In that cry one discovers both an affirmation of the God of tradition and a healing embrace of the human other. "The witness," writes Levinas, "testifies to what was said by himself. For he has said 'Here I am!' before the other. . . . The glory of the Infinite reveals itself through what it is capable of doing in the witness" (1985, 109). With this statement one immediately goes to the rupture that distinguishes the illness from which one seeks recovery:

it is the illness of indifference toward the other. The Holocaust memoir entails a recovery from this illness because it refuses indifference in an act of response and responsibility. The memoir's recovery of tradition is a recovery of the sleepless gaze of God, and to be under the sleepless gaze of God is, as Levinas demonstrates, "to be the bearer of *another* subject—bearer and supporter—to be responsible for this other [human being]" (1990, 168). If one is to recover the Torah of tradition, then one must bear in mind, with Levinas, that "the Torah is given in the Light of a face. The epiphany of the other person is ipso facto my responsibility toward him" (1990, 47). One finds that this relation to the other person is a definitive feature of the Holocaust memoir and that the breakdown of the relation is the most profound symptom of the illness from which one must recover. Already one realizes that the illness in question is not just physical but is also spiritual. The recovery from the illness, however, is not simply a matter of isolating one from the other but of linking the two—the spiritual and the material—in the self-to-other relation as Levinas does when he notes, "The material needs of my neighbor are my spiritual needs" (1990, 99). Only in this form of the relation does the other, in his physical presence, signify the spiritual life constitutive of humanity—even in death. Wiesel's lament that the dead were robbed of their cemeteries (1985, 1:168) is a lament that they were robbed of their humanity.

Fackenheim states it more emphatically when he says, "That the dead had been human when alive was a truth systematically rejected when their bodies were made into fertilizer and soap" (1978, 89). This comes about not just when the human is reduced to the merely material—to raw material—but when there is a tearing of the material away from the spiritual, that is, a rupture of the human image born in human relation. "I have no spiritual needs, no accountability before the Holy," runs the logic of the illness. "Therefore, I have nothing to do with you, and you have nothing to do with me." When the other does not matter, the other is reduced to mere matter, and so is the self. This connection between the illness that destroys the other and the assault aimed at the self must be kept in mind when recalling Fackenheim's insight that Nazis not only loathed the Jews but set out to create within them a profound self-loathing. That, he explains, is the aim of "excremental assault" (1989, 209), a term that Fackenheim borrows from Des Pres. The purpose of covering the Jew with filth, in other words, is not to inflict the self with illness but to transform the self into illness through an isolation from the other. This obliteration of the self—this mutation of the self into illness incarnate—is just the opposite of the "despite-me" found in

Levinas's thinking when he declares, "All my inwardness is invested in the form of a despite-me, for-another. Despite-me, for-another, is signification par excellence" (1981, 11). Indeed, this relation is the basis of the Holocaust memoir, which always comes in the form of a despite-me, for-another. No survivor opens the wound of memory for the sake of self-gratification but in order to seek a recovery from an illness through a dialogical relation to another, for another, and in which the self signifies the dearness of the other.

The essence of Jewish tradition lies in loving God with all one's heart, all one's soul, and all the "more" that one is, *b'kol me'odekhah*. All the "more" takes one to one's neighbor so that, according to the tradition, there is no love of the Holy One without a love for the human other. Levinas makes this point by saying, "A relationship without correlation, love of the neighbor is love without eros. It is for-the-other-person and, through this, to God!" (1987b, 137). Jews are who they are to the extent that they express their love for God through their caring relations to their fellow human beings; that is the tradition and is what makes the tradition sacred. Therefore, the loss of the tradition is inextricably linked to the onset of the illness, and the recovery from the latter is tied to a recovery of the former. How is one to overcome the evil of the illness indicated by the loss of the self to indifference? Levinas answers, "By each taking upon himself the responsibility of the others. . . . Israel would teach that the greatest intimacy of me to myself consists in being at every moment responsible for the others" (1990, 85). The first faces of "hell and death" encountered by Eliezer in Wiesel's *Night* were not just among the Hungarian police; no, the face of Auschwitz first showed itself in the indifferent faces peeking out from behind their shutters (1960, 30). The Jews may have been threatened with starvation, torture, and murder, but the real threat, the ontological illness, lay in this indifference toward human being. Yet from the core of this being that had been deemed criminal the illness was resisted. The Holocaust memoir—and this is another unique feature of the Holocaust memoir—is an extension of that resistance and is, therefore, a struggle for a recovery from an illness that arises from the illness itself; once again, it is impossible, yet it is actual.

The being that the Nazis regarded as a disease thus became the being that resisted disease. "For all the resistance fighters inside and outside Nazi-occupied Europe, resistance was a doing," Fackenheim points out. "For Jews caught by the full force of the Nazi logic of destruction, resistance was a way of being" (1989, 223–24). Once again the ontological nature of the illness and of the recovery comes to light; once again one returns to Levinas's notion of the "there is" as the ontological manifestation of the illness. Only a "responsibility for the other, being-for-the-other," he writes, can "stop the anonymous and senseless rumbling of being" (1985, 52). From the Warsaw Ghetto to the Holocaust memoir the resistance that is a way of being is just such an act of response to the other and for the other, both death and alive. "If we still have you left," said one rabbi to the Warsaw Ghetto fighters, "from now on it shall be easier for us to die" (Lubetkin 1981, 159). For the fighters' very presence signified some recovery from the illness of indifference underlying and undermining a world that watched as the ghetto burned; the fighters' proximity to those who could not fight signified nonindifference in the midst of difference. Therefore, being had meaning despite the illness of meaninglessness. Here, too, Levinas opens one's eyes to the nature of a relation that marks a recovery from this illness. "The difference in proximity," he maintains, "between me and a neighbor, turns into non-indifference, precisely into my responsibility. Non-indifference, humanity, the one-for-the-other is the very signifyingness of signification" (1981, 166). This "signifyingness of signification," this capacity of meaning to be meaningful, characterizes the recovery from illness sought in the Holocaust memoir. As an act of response to another and for another, the very utterance of memory here ushers in the nonindifference that alone can open the path to recovery.

But it opens only the *path*, without completing the recovery itself. For in the act of response the self is restored to itself and is, thus, freed from the logic of self-destruction only to discover that to love with all the "more" is to be all the more indebted. Levinas explains, "It is I who support all . . . because I am responsible for a total responsibility, which answers for all the others and for all in the others, even for their responsibility. The I always has one responsibility *more* than all the others" (1985, 98–99). Here the Glory of the Infinite revealed through the witness opens up a dimension of the infinite within the witness. The return that makes possible a recovery from illness turns out to be an eternal return forever calling for *more* from the dialogical depths of memory.

The Open-Endedness of Recovery

"Two voices is the minimum for life, the minimum for existence," Bakhtin argues (1984, 252), because life cannot do without meaning, and meaning cannot do without dialogue. Dialogue is the stuff of the relation and the response to the other. In dialogue every word summons a response so that the final word is always relegated to the realm of the yet-to-be-uttered. In a sense, then, recovery—both of tradition and from illness—is consummated with the realization that it cannot be completed. Why? Because, in the words of Levinas, "the more I answer the more I am responsible" (1981, 93). Each act of response increases my capacity for response, so that I always have something more to offer that I fail to offer; I fall behind what my voice brings to bear from within myself. And so, Levinas concludes, "In approaching the other I am always late for the meeting. But this singular obedience . . . prior to all responsibility, this allegiance before any oath, this responsibility prior to commitment, is precisely the other in the same, inspiration and prophecy, the *passing itself* of the Infinite" (1981, 150). Here, perhaps more clearly than ever, one sees that the recovery from the illness of indifference is linked to the recovery of the God of tradition, of the *En Sof* or the Infinite One, for whom one expresses one's love through one's love for one's neighbor. "Man changes," writes Wiesel, "whenever he confronts his fellow-man, who, in turn, undergoes an essential change. Thus every encounter suggests infinity. Which means: the self is linked to infinity only through the intermediary of another self, another consciousness" (1973b, 88).

It is the infinity of God that makes the two forms of recovery forever incomplete. And it is the Promise of God, the Covenant with God, that makes the two forms of recovery forever needful. Here it proves helpful to recall André Neher's insight that "for the man of the Promise, God suddenly vanishes to the rear; but there is no purpose in seeking Him in that rear, . . . for God is already waiting out there in front, on the horizon-edge of a Promise which only restores what it has taken, without ever being fulfilled" (1981, 123). The horizon-edge that Neher invokes is the edge of time where, in the words of Levinas, "time means that the other is forever beyond me, irreducible to the synchrony of the same. The temporality of the interhuman opens up the meaning of otherness and the otherness of meaning" (1986b, 21). And once meaning is opened the God who had vanished to the rear, left hanging on the gallows of Buna, rushes to the horizon of time, invisibly "out there." Hence, Levinas insists, "time is the most profound relationship that man can have with God, precisely as a going towards God. . . . 'Going towards God' is meaningless unless seen in terms of my primary going towards the other person" (1986b, 23). The open-ended nature of the Holocaust memoir does not lie simply in the necessary miscarriage of any liberation for the survivor. Much more than that, it is rooted in the essence of this memory as a *movement toward* a humanity and a divinity that has "receded" to the horizon of the yet-to-be. The memory that has lost a sense of chronology, therefore, can regain it not through the proper reconstruction of a sequence in the past but through the time regained in the dialogical, human pursuit of the divine along the horizon of the future.

If recovery here entails a recovery of tradition, then the mound of ashes that traces the horizon contains not only the ashes of the victims of indifference but the ashes of time as well. Therefore, Fackenheim insists, *"Where the Holocaust is there is no overcoming; and where there is an overcoming the Holocaust is not"* (1989, 135). Overcoming of what? An overcoming of history, of the time that isolates the self from the event. If the self cannot overcome this time, then it cannot coincide with itself. Here, with the help of Levinas, one may see what characterizes the forsakenness of the survivor: it is the solitude of "a being that is as it were no longer in step with itself, is out of joint with itself, in a dislocation of the *I* from itself. . . . And this lag constitutes the present" (1978a, 35). Although Levinas would apply this statement to any I, it has a special significance for the I who speaks in the Holocaust memoir. One recalls, for example, Ka-tzetnik's comment on his first work, *Salamandra*, which he wrote while still wearing his Auschwitz stripes in an Italian hospital. He entrusted the manuscript to a Jewish soldier, who asked the writer whose name should go on it as the author. "The name of the author?!" cried the survivor. "Those who went to the crematorium wrote this book! Go on, you write their name: K. Tzetnik" (1989, 15–16). Thus, Ka-tzetnik became Ka-tzetnik. It is worth noting that the Hebrew word used for "author" here is *machber* (1987, 32), which also means "connector." In the original text the word itself suggests that the I who speaks from the page is not an entity unto itself but is a link—or a process of linkage— between two. Levinas declares that "subjectivity is the other in the same" (1981, 25); how haunting this statement becomes in the light of these lines from *Shivitti!* And how revealing! The one who awaits the author at the edge of his utterance is not only God or the other but the author himself. The splitting or fragmentation that the author of the memoir experiences is indicative of the fragmentary nature of any recovery that memory might attain. Yet there is an *I* who *feels* the split.

Memoir authors feel the split because they sense the urgency underlying their utterances, an urgency characterized by the impossibility of any liberation that would put a closure on the Event and by the necessity to bear witness to the Event. Operating from a stance of ultimate concern for the sanctity of a life that has been desecrated, these authors are on the track of an Ultimate that can be pursued but never captured. Distinguished by an allegiance to the Ultimate, to the absolute Other, the author here "does not give signs," to use Levinas's expression, but "becomes a sign" (1981, 49). As a sign, the author is continually conveyed elsewhere, outside himself, toward another. In this open-ended being-for-the-other the one who consigns his memory to the page imparts a profound significance not just to the subject matter of memory but to the one for whom the memory is invoked. This takes the self outside itself toward an eternal elsewhere, toward *ha-Makom*, the Place, where meaning is redeemed in a restoration of relation to another. Hence, says Levinas, "signification is the one-for-the-other which character- izes an identity that does not coincide with itself" (1981, 70). The disjunc- tion between the I who speaks and the I about whom it speaks in the Holocaust memoir, then, entails much more than the becoming-other-to-oneself that transpires in the split between the self as author and the self as character; it involves much more than making the self of the past into the object of concern for the self of the present. Beyond these divisions one has the frag- mentation that is incumbent upon the soul who would move toward the horizon of the yet-to-be from which the God of the Promise calls.

The realm of the yet-to-be, the horizon of time and eternity from which the summons arises, looms in the light of a history—or a breach in history— that would eclipse such a horizon. "God," Levinas suggests, "is perhaps nothing but this permanent refusal of a history which would come to terms with our private tears" (1990, 20). But the tears that stain the pages are not just private tears shed in a world whose sun has lost its shining. They contain a world, like the tears of truth in the legend about the Angel of Truth that Simon Wiesenthal relates in *The Sunflower* (1976, 12). The Angel opposed the creation of man, and so God cast him to the earth, banishing him from heaven. When he was finally allowed to return to the heavenly host, he brought along a clod of earth soaked with his tears. From that clod God created man, adding to the clod, perhaps, a tear of His own. Perhaps, then, the tears of these victims are the tears of God Himself, shed in His infinite longing for Himself. Because God longs for Himself in human longing for Him, "our desire for God," says Levinas, "is without end or term: it is inter- minable and infinite because God reveals himself as absence rather than presence" (1986b, 32). Yet the not-here of God's absence is the not-yet of God's presence, and the Holocaust memoir operates within this dialectic of time, which, Levinas points out, "is the very dialectic of the relationship with the other, that is, a dialogue" (1978a, 93). And, he adds in a later work, "time is essentially a new birth" (1987b, 81). That is what the Holocaust memoir is about: this memory of the death of the self is undertaken for the sake of a new birth—for the self, for the other, and for God. It vibrates on the edge of time and eternity where the already said breaks on the cusp of the saying it summons. And there is no engaging this dialogue *within* the memoir without being engaged in a dialogue *with* the memoir.

This task is as needful as it is difficult: needful because it is an essential past of the search for recovery that continues to confront the post-Holocaust world; difficult because this memory invades one's own memory and launches one toward the horizon of the question of life and death that recedes as one approaches it. The debt increases in the measure that it is paid. But without this approach one has no life; without this debt one is spiritually bankrupt. Let one, then, incur the debt.

PART ONE

The Recovery of Tradition

Context

Elie Wiesel writes, "The opposite of the past is not the future but the absence of future; the opposite of the future is not the past but the absence of past" (1990b, 239). This insight suggests that, insofar as the recovery of tradition entails a recovery of the past, it also includes the reawakening of a future. To the extent that the memoir accomplishes this task the memory here is not in time, rather time is in the memory or in the process of remembrance. To pursue the memory, therefore, is to pursue a trace of the eternal as that which transcends time. And that which transcends time — and yet permeates it — is the sacred. Hence, the recovery of tradition is a recovery of the sacred, of the holy, of the Holy One Himself. "Whoever kills," one recalls the line from Wiesel's *A Beggar in Jerusalem*, "kills God. Each murder is a suicide, with the Eternal eternally the victim" (1970b, 208). The attempt to exterminate not only the Jews but every trace of the Jews — every body, every book, every cemetery, every marker and signifier of Jewish being — is an attempt to obliterate the trace of the Eternal that is revealed through sacred tradition. One avenue through which the sanctity of tradition and with it the Origin of all sanctity might be retrieved is memory. Indeed, some portion of what is sought is already recovered in the act of seeking it: it is the sacred itself that summons the memory of the sacred. It lives even in the remembrance of its loss.

In the three chapters in part 1, then, I examine the memory of a loss as a process necessary to the recovery of what was lost. And the most precious of all entities lost was the family. Says Nathan Shapell, "The Germans obviously understood only too well the family structure of the European Jew. They knew that it was part of our heritage and training to feel a deep and abiding responsibility for one another — a brother for a sister, a daughter for a mother, a father for his children. . . . Our family devotion became a deadly weapon in their sadistic hands" (1974, 18–19). Because Jewish tradition holds the family to be the center of all relation to the Creator and His creation, the focus in the chapters that follow is on the primary origins of the family: mother, father, and God. As taught in the Talmud (Kiddushin 30b), these three are the participants necessary to the birth of a child, that event which is the highest of all human links to the divine. Hence, when the Nazis narrowed the circle of those family members whom the Jewish police of the Warsaw Ghetto could still protect, the mothers and fathers were the first to go in the effort to slay the Eternal. Zivia Lubetkin, for example, notes, "When the number of Jews available for deportation decreased from week to week the Germans informed them that they could still save their wives and children, but their parents must be sent off like everyone else" (1981, 105). In most cases, these memoirs are written by children who survived the deaths of their mothers and fathers—and God. The death of this third party in the creation of the child is what underlies Lily Gluck Lerner's question in her memoir, "How do other people live after their parents have gone?" (1980, 35). Yet, as these children speak, so do those who perished, those who above all signify the origin of life, the meaning of life, and all that is dear in life. As these children speak, tradition speaks—and is recovered.

1

The Loss of the Mother

If the Holocaust memoir is distinguished by the death of the self, the first signs of that death often come upon the loss of the mother. Mikhail Bakhtin points out that "the child receives all initial determinations of himself and of his body from his mother's lips and from the lips of those who are close to him. It is from their lips, in the emotional-volitional tones of love, that the child hears and begins to acknowledge his own *proper name*. . . . For the first time, he finds himself and becomes aware of himself as a *something*" (1991, 49–50; emphasis in original). Thus, when the mother is lost, the word that bespeaks the dearness of the human being is lost; the self or the soul of the human image is lost; the name that signifies the human essence is lost, transformed into the indifference of a number. In his commentary on the *Sefer Yetzirah* Aryeh Kaplan points out that the Feminine Essence belongs to the domain of Understanding, or *Binah* (1990, 16), a word that derives its root from *beyn*, which means "between." Understanding arises from the difference *between* two, and, as the highest manifestation of the Feminine Essence, the mother transforms the radical difference that characterizes understanding into the absolute nonindifference of love. The mother, then, is the closest tie that one has to the Creator, that absolutely Other who is revealed in the absolute nonindifference of love. Because this Other who is the Creator of the world is the one who is ultimately targeted for extermination in the Kingdom of Night, the obliteration of the mother is among the first principles that rule in the antiworld of that Kingdom.

Although she is not Jewish, Charlotte Delbo captures this idea with terrifying beauty when she writes, "My mother / she was hands / she was a face / They set our mothers before us naked / Here mothers are no longer mothers to their children" (1968, 15). With the removal of the hands that offered the embrace of love, with the erasure of the face that spoke the words

39

of love, the little girl is orphaned before she is orphaned; that is to say, she becomes an orphan not by the accidents of circumstance but *in principle*. A people and a world are ontologically orphaned, their essence redefined as the essence of the orphan. In many cases—and, from an ontological stand-point, in every case—these memoirs are the memoirs not just of survivors but of orphans. Sara Zyskind's memoir *Stolen Years*, for example, begins with the memory of the last Mother's Day that her mother enjoyed (1981, 11) before the destruction of all days. But soon she loses her mother to the slow death of ghetto life, and the memory of an outcry rises to the surface of her page: "I don't want to be an orphan, Mother!" (1981, 44). Her plea, of course, meets only with silence. Similarly, while standing at the window of a Nazi prison cell Paul Trepman looks out into a courtyard, where Jews stand na-ked, waiting to be murdered, and from the silent suffering of that crowd a terrible vision comes to him. "My mother," he writes, "had probably per-ished in the same way in the Warsaw ghetto, along with my sister, and the rest of my family. Now, for the first time, I felt truly orphaned" (1978, 130). Now, for the first time, he belongs to no one's memory.

The cry of "I don't want to be an orphan" is a cry of "I don't want to be forgotten." The orphan's memory is the memory of the loss of the one by whom the human being is always remembered. The bottomless void, the infinite emptiness, experienced by the orphan is the void and the emptiness of being forgotten—by force, by murder, not by an act of God, who remem-bers us even when He takes our mothers from us. Losing those hands and that face, the child loses her own hands and face, her own deeds and words, to become "the shadow of another shadow," as Ana Vinocur expresses it. "I felt an infinite emptiness in my mind and heart," she recalls. "They've taken my mother away. I'm nothing but the shadow of another shadow" (1976, 106–7). Once again the condition is not one of tragic mishap but of onto-logical obliteration. For in the original Spanish text the verb *I am* in this last sentence is not *estoy* but *soy* (1972, 215), indicating an essential condition rather than a transient condition. There is no getting over or overcoming this forsakenness, this *vacio infinito* (1972, 213), into which she is thrown. When the mother is turned to ash, creation is returned to the *tohu v'bohu*, the chaos and the void, antecedent to every origin. The first word in Vinocur's *Book without a Title* is *mother* (1976, 1). From this word arise all other words in the memoir; form this memory arises a large portion of the Jewish essence of the Holocaust memoir. "The greatness of Israel," one is told in the *Midrash Rabbah*, "is compared . . . to a woman bearing child" (1961, 9:327). If the Covenant that distinguishes the Jews is inextricably tied to the Creation—

briyt linked to *barah*, as Nachmanides argues in his *Commentary on the Torah* (1971, 1:112)—then the murder of the mother is inextricably bound to the extermination of the Covenant and of the children of the Covenant. When, upon their arrival at Birkenau, mothers are sent to the left and their children to the right, it is not simply the division of a transport into two groups, one condemned and the other yet to be condemned; what transpires is a rending of the Covenant itself and the tearing of a wound into the heart of Creation.

"Mama!" Isabella Leitner screams in the midst of this upheaval. "If you don't turn around I'll run after you. But they won't let me. I must stay on the 'life' side. Mama!" (1978, 19–20). No good-bye. No last look. Such things belong only to the world that comes from the hand of the Creator, only to the world where there are mothers, not to the antiworld where Mengele orchestrates the annihilation of the mother with a wave of his baton. And one knows why "life" is placed in quotation marks: there is no "life" side in this place where all that is sacred is turned inside out. The essence of the memory of Auschwitz is marked by the memory of this essence of Auschwitz, by this obliteration of the mother who signifies the obliteration of self and world. This point is devastatingly illustrated in the last of Ka-tzetnik's visions in *Shivitti* where he finally beholds the image of Auschwitz itself: "It's my mother... going to be gassed. I run after her. . . . 'Mama! Listen to me! Mama!' My mother naked. Going to be gassed. I behold my mother's skull and in my mother's skull I see me. And I chase after me inside my mother's skull" (1989, 100–101). The mother is the strength of Israel, Jewish tradition maintains. In that mass of Jews consigned to the flames it is she who is on her way to the gas chambers, every Jewish mother in every Jew and every Jew in every Jewish mother. For the mother is the embodiment of the origin, of the love, and of the home that constitute Israel.

The Obliteration of the Origin

To acquire a deeper sense of what is lost, from a Jewish standpoint, in the obliteration of the origin, one should first consider the Jewish view on the relation between the mother and the origin. The *Zohar*, in fact, clearly suggests a connection, declaring, "The [Supernal] Mother said: 'let us make man in our image'" (1984, 1:92). If one may allow oneself a moment of midrashic association, then one can see why the concept of the mother appears not just at the origin of the individual's life but in the midst of the six days of creation. Jewish tradition teaches, for example, that the Torah not only precedes the Creation (Midrash Rabbah 1961, 1:6) but is the basis of all that comes into being in the Creation. "As the Sages have said," notes Adin Steinsaltz, "before Creation, God looked into the Torah and made the world accordingly. By which it is implied that the Torah is the original pattern, or inner form, of the world: Torah and world are, inseparably, a pair" (1980, 88). Now the first letter in the Torah is the letter *beit*, which is also the word for "house," and the notion of a house is associated with the Patriarch Jacob as Yitzchak Ginsburgh points out: "At the level of Divinity, the house symbolizes the ultimate purpose of all reality: to become a dwelling place below for the manifestation of G-d's presence. 'Not as Abraham who called it [the Temple site] "a mountain," nor as Isaac who called it "a field," but as Jacob who called it "a house"' " (1991, 46). Because, according to the Talmud, "blessing is only found in a man's house on account of his wife" (Bava Metzia 59a), the sanctity of the house is linked with the Jewish woman, the wife and mother, who sees to all of the affairs of the house. Thus, the women, the wives and mothers, of Israel are known as the House of Jacob. This being the case, if the Torah is the foundation of Creation, the mother, through her tie to the beit in which the Torah originates, is the foundation of the Torah itself; she is the origin of the origin. Hence, the Hasidic masters maintain that "compassion is at the root of all Creation" (Aron 1969, 160) because the mother embodies compassion.

This position is further reinforced if one bears in mind the mothers who constitute the House of Jacob when in the *Midrash Rabbah* one reads, "The Holy One, blessed be He, said to His world: 'O My world, My world! Shall I tell thee who created thee, who formed thee? Jacob has created thee, Jacob has formed thee'" (1961, 4:460). The interconnections linking Torah, Creation, and women may explain why tradition holds that at Sinai "the Torah had to be accepted *first* by the women (the 'house of Jacob') before it could be accepted by the men (the 'house of Israel')" (Steinsaltz 1984, 8). If the Torah is the basis of Creation and the mother lies at the origin of the Torah, then one understands why the Torah enters the world through the women of the House of Jacob. First among those women are the mothers; according to Jewish tradition, the mother is the consummate form of woman. This point must be kept before one when Jiří Langer explains, "The souls of women come to this earth from higher worlds than the souls of men. The Law therefore sets women free from those commandments whose fulfillment is limited to a particular period, to a particular time of day or season. For the world in which the souls of women have their origin is raised above the concept of time" (1976, 136). To be sure, Rabbi Schneur Zalman identifies God with the Torah (1981, 15), inasmuch as a female, maternal element is part of His essence, which, of course, is above the conception of time. Levinas sheds light on these connections when he says, "*Rachamim* (mercy) . . . goes back to the word *Rechem*, which means uterus. *Rachamim* is the revelation of the uterus to the other, whose gestation takes place within it. *Rachamim* is maternity itself. God as merciful is God defined by maternity" (1990, 183). That this feminine element belongs to God is substantiated in the Torah itself when Moses addresses God as *at*, the feminine form of the pronoun "you" (Numbers 11:15). One also recalls that the Divine Presence, or the *Shekhinah*, is a feminine entity; it is, moreover, a maternal entity, as one may gather upon reading in Maimonides's *Commandments* that "Rabbi Joseph on hearing the sound of his mother's footsteps used to say, 'I will rise before the Divine Presence which is approaching' " (1967, 1:227; see also Kiddushin 31b). Examining the Holocaust memoir's account of the loss of the mother, one, too, must rise before the one who approaches in the memory of her loss. So rising, one may meet some small portion of one's responsibility for the recovery of this sacred tradition surrounding and sanctifying the mother's connection with the origin.

As the survivor enters into the memory of the mother, this one who had given him life becomes part of his life, in such a way that what survives is not the continuation of one life but a second life, one that now bears the trace of its maternal origin. In his memoir, for instance, Samuel Pisar writes, "My mother had given me life a second time on the night when we parted. This second birth had been much more painful for her than the first. My life, I felt, was no longer entirely my own. That part of her, of all the others, that was within me would have to live on too" (1979, 62). The life of the mother that lives on in the child does not consist of a genetic continuity; rather, it lies in this utterance of remembrance, in this sense of responsibility that characterizes Jewish memory and recovery. Initially, the man comes into the world as a Jew because his mother is a Jew; then he is reborn as a Jew through the memory of his Jewish origin, a memory manifested through a sense of Jewish responsibility. The process of memory, furthermore, entails a movement toward the womb of the origin that arises not afterward but from the depths of the Horror itself, from the first moment of the origin's obliteration. One example of the memory of that moment is found in Ka-tzetnik's *Star of Ashes* where he remembers the children who "push against their mother's belly as if seeking to get inside once more. Their scream, embryonic, unuttered, howls out of the mother's eyes" (1971b, 52). The root of the

Hebrew word rendered as "howl" is *shiv'a* (Ka-tzetnik 1971a, 52), which means to "cry for help" or to "implore"; seeking to merge with the *rechem* of the origin, the mute scream of the children rises up from within the origin, not in a howl of pain or despair but in a cry for help, for *our* help. It is we—those of us who have lived to know our mothers and whose mothers have thus lived—we are the ones summoned to the memory and the recovery denied to those little ones. Our relation to this origin is an essential avenue of any relation that we may have to ourselves. For once this relation to the origin is lost, the human image is itself undone, as Nathan Shapell suggests when, upon the death of his mother, he laments, "It was the end. My life had no further meaning. I had no function as a human being any more" (1974, 93). A cry rose up from the ghetto. It was the Jewish children weeping for their mother Rachel. And they would not be comforted. For she was no more.

In the Jewish tradition, as in most traditions, the mother is associated with the earth. Planet Auschwitz does not rest on the earth but on several feet of Jewish remains, on the mothers' ashes that now veil the Mother Earth. If one recalls the Hebrew phrase for "Mother Earth"—*ima adamah*, or simply *ha-adamah*—one immediately notes a link between the mother earth and the human image because the word *adam*, or "human being," is a cognate of the word for "earth," *adamah*. The loss of the human image of the self that Shapell experienced upon the loss of his mother is expressed in other memoirs as an eclipse of the earth. It is the earth—and, symbolically, the mother—of which Agnes Sassoon speaks in her memoir when she says, "My memories are of darkness and doom; heaviness, depression, desolation—everything enveloped in a shroud of grey gloom. I have no recollection of colors or texture. I cannot remember spring or summertime, or seeing flowers and greenery" (1983, 34). In short, she cannot remember the life that rises up from the womb of the earth because her every link to that origin has been severed by a darkness that the light cannot comprehend. In those days of destruction, in that destruction of days, the earth moved not with the stirring of life but with the throes of death. Donna Rubinstein, for example, recollects the mass graves at Krasnostav: "They covered up the graves but the soil heaved" (1982, 39). And, as though in a state of delirium, Judith Dribben writes, "They bury them half-alive . . . or half-dead . . . and the soil was moving . . . the soil was moving . . . they bury them half-alive . . . and the soil was moving" (1969, 85). The earth that heaves is not an earth that one can walk. With the annihilation of the *adam*, the *adamah* churns; the origin itself tosses and tumbles under the weight of the children forced back into her womb. This is the antiorder, the antiseason, void of spring and a place to belong. The ground itself literally crumbles in a mute, embryonic howl that reverberates throughout the pages of the Holocaust memoir.

Yet within the memory of the loss of the earth as mother springs a trace of the recovery of that earth. At times this recovery lies in the remembrance of a garden in a ghetto where there should be no garden, a sowing of the soil with life rather than death. Ana Vinocur was among those who planted such a garden and who remembers, "That dialogue in which the earth's answer was expressed so eloquently and in such a comforting way, brought to my mind that expression which is now so meaningful: Mother Earth" (1976, 45). The Spanish word translated as "meaningful," *sentido* (1972, 96), also has connotations of "direction" and of "hearing" (one meaning of the verb *sentir*). The act of sowing and, thus, affirming life at its origin enables the human being to hear the eloquence of the origin and, thus, to determine a direction toward the origin; the movement of return, or *teshuvah*, is, perhaps, most poignantly symbolized by the planting of a tree or some other sowing of the land. One sees this symbol, for example, in the Jewish tradition of planting a tree in the Promised Land and, thus, signifying the remembrance of a life and in the observance of *Tu B'shvat*, or the fifteenth of Shevat, which is the New Year for trees. Vinocur's characterization of her relation to the earth as a dialogue (*dialogo*) is also significant: the divine aspect of the mother imparts to the dialogue with the mother an aspect of prayer, which is essential to the recovery of tradition. Although the father never appears in the Holocaust memoir as an interlocutor in prayer, the mother frequently assumes that role. Eugene Heimler, for instance, writes, "If I was in trouble, all I had to do was to close my eyes, imagine my mother's face hovering before me — and pray to her" (1959, 102). Here the maternal aspect of the divine, the divine *Rachamim*, presents itself as an intermediary or a pathway to the divine. God may have turned away His countenance, but the prayer can still find its way to the mother's ear.

One sees this more clearly in Saul Friedländer's *When Memory Comes*. Hidden in a Catholic school during the Shoah, he was isolated from his mother and father. There, in the image of the Holy Virgin, he "rediscovered something of the presence of a mother" (1980, 122). If it should be objected that the Virgin is a Christian figure, one may reply that it is a Jew who utters the prayer and it is as a Jew that Friedländer invokes the memory. His rediscovery of the presence of a mother, moreover, lies not in the plastic image of the Virgin Mary but in the linkage to the divine opened by a prayer to the maternal. If, as Levinas indicates above, *rachamim*, or mercy, is tied to a maternal aspect of the Divine, then prayers of supplication are not only tied to that aspect of God but also include it; here one recalls the tradition that maintains that in the utterance of the *Amidah* (the daily Prayer of the Jews), it is the *Shekhinah* who speaks through one's lips. For Sara Zyskind, this linkage is revealed in the form of intervention when her father was ill in the Lodz Ghetto. When he is finally allowed to enter the hospital, she writes, "I ran to the cemetery to tell Mother about what happened. There was no doubt in my mind that the miracle had taken place thanks to Mother's intervention with the Divine Powers" (1981, 61). Here the dialogue with a mound of earth becomes a pathway to the Heaven of heavens; the one who signifies the human tie to the divine origin—precisely *because* she signifies that bond—has the power to intervene with the Divine Powers. Donna Rubinstein also expresses this condition when, upon her liberation and return to her hometown of Krasnostav, she cries, "O, my dear mama, did you intervene for me? Is it you who helped me survive the war? Please, mother dear, guide me in my future the way you have until now" (1982, 90). Even as she lies on the other shore the mother who is the origin of life is also the origin of the future. To be sure, according to the Jewish mystical tradition, the *Sifrah* of *Binah*, which is identified with the Supernal Mother, signifies the future (*Sefer Yetzirah* 1990, 240). The obliteration of the origin, then, entails not only the destruction of the past but, in that very destruction, it includes the murder of the future. The recovery of tradition, therefore, is a recovery of the future without which there can be no life, just as there can be no life without the mother.

The mother's intervention with the Creator is a manifestation of the compassion that lies at the root of Creation. But this intervention did not always occur; or, if it did occur, it did not always succeed. In many cases all that was experienced was the terrible absence of the mother and an infinite isolation from her compassion. While imprisoned with a group of women in Stutthof, for example, Sara Nomberg-Przytyk recollects, "We felt that we . . . could not even succeed in raising a trace of compassion. That was how it remained until Liza started singing a song about a Jewish mother, and we, who had lost our mothers so cruelly, could not keep ourselves from crying" (1985, 6–7). In the Polish text the term corresponding to "deaf" is *próżnię* (n.d. 3), a word that means "empty" or "void"; upon the obliteration of the origin from which arises the word of love from the mother's lips, the void overtakes the origin and swallows up every word. The emptiness in which the words of these women die is the emptiness that emerges with the loss of the mother and of the love that makes the mother who she is. The song about a Jewish mother is, after all, a song about love in its most sacred form. The recovery of tradition includes a recovery of the maternal love that is the basis of all creation. The memory of this love belongs to the essence of the Holocaust memoir.

The Annihilation of Maternal Love

In the sixteenth century Rabbi Yitzchak Luria, also known as the Ari, asked the question, "If *Binah* or Understanding, which is associated with the Mother, is a mental process, why is it said to be in the heart, and not in the head?" To which Aryeh Kaplan answers, "The heart is actually the Personification of Imma-Mother, which is Binah-Understanding, where She reveals herself" (*Bahir* 1979, 127–28). In the *Shema's* injunction to love God, the first thing with which one is called upon to love is the heart, *b'kol levavkhah* (Deut. 6:5). One also recalls that the *lamed* and the *beit* of the Hebrew word for "heart," *lev*, are the last and the first letters of the Torah. The heart, therefore, contains all of the Torah: it is on the heart, indeed, that the Teaching is to be inscribed (Deut. 6:6). The mother whom the *beit* situates at the origin of the Torah thus includes the sum of the Torah in her personification as the heart, or the *lev*. Personified as the heart, then, the mother signifies not only the origin of life but the center of life. In this connection Pavel Florensky points out, "The Hebrew word *lev* comes from the verb *lavav*, signifying something *covered*, *surrounded* by the organs and parts of the body and thus *hidden* in the depths of the body, something central, the *center* of the body, the middle organ of the body" (1970, 271; emphasis in original). Linking the Russian word for "heart," *serdtse*, with the Russian word for "middle" or "center," *seredina*, Florensky also notes, "The heart signifies something central, something internal, something in the middle—that organ that is at the core of the living being" (1970, 269). The heart bears this significance because it is the seat of the love and the teaching of God. And the loving-kindness shown by one human being toward another is the highest expression of that love and teaching centered in the heart and personified by the mother.

Hence, Rabbi Ginsburgh reminds, "loving-kindness is the means through which G-d's presence is ultimately revealed" (1991, 88), and it is originally revealed through the mother. In the *Tanya*, moreover, Rabbi Zalman maintains that loving-kindness in the form of charity is feminine and, by implication, maternal, for "it receives a radiation from the light of the *En Sof* that [like a womb] encompasses all worlds" (1981, 593). From a Jewish perspective, therefore, maternal love is not just a feeling or a state of mind but is the manifestation and revelation of the Most High. When that love is targeted for extermination, the light of all there is to hold dear, the light that was in the beginning, is assailed. Hence, the ontological assault that is manifested in the assault on the mother moves to a metaphysical level in the annihilation of maternal love. Like the light created upon the first utterance of God, the mother's love is the mainstay of life, even and especially during the reign of death; she is the one who reveals to the individual that he is still a human being and that his life *matters*. One sees this in Leon Wells's memoir when he says, "I began to observe to my disgust that I, too, was coming very near to developing the indifference and apathy of so many others. I was saved from succumbing to these feelings only by the thought of those at home, and the determination that my mother should see me alive" (1978, 74–75) . . . "Nothing could disturb me. I had seen my mother again. It had been the happiest day in my life for a long, long time" (1978, 86). Representing love in its holiest aspect, the mother embodies the opposite not only of human indifference but of ontological indifference, the opposite of what Levinas calls the "there is" or "the phenomenon of impersonal being" (1985, 48). Maternal love, in short, represents a loving non-indifference that comes from beyond the human being to awaken a non-indifference within the human being. If, as Olga Lengyel declares, "inhumanity was the natural order of things at Birkenau" (1972, 94), it is because Birkenau is the phenomenological manifestation of an imposed ontological indifference. For in Birkenau motherly love was carefully eliminated from the order of being; in Birkenau motherly love was a capital crime.

Where motherly love does exist, therefore, it signifies not only that someone cares about the human being but that she stands in a loving and, therefore, meaningful relation to other beings. "My one consolation was being with Mother," Ana Vinocur recalls of her days in Auschwitz (1976, 65). Why? Because through her love the mother opens up a small portal through which the Divine reveals itself in the form of an embrace of the other human being. "Mothers never thought of themselves," writes Vinocur. "They were sublime, special beings, divine!" (1976, 88). Levinas enables one to perceive why Vinocur makes such a remark: "Commanding love signifies recognizing the value of love in itself. . . . Faith is not a question of the existence or nonexistence of God. It is believing that love without reward is valuable. It is often said 'God is love.' God is the commandment of love. . . . God is the one who says that one must love the other" (1988a, 176–77). The memory of the mother's love is a memory of this commandment to love, regardless of reward, regardless even of the presence of the loved one who might return the look of love. The memory of the mother lost and of the love annihilated is also altogether gratuitous, and it arises from the heart of the love for the mother. The act of remembrance characteristic of the Holocaust memoir is an act of love, sometimes mirrored inversely in the memoir itself, as in *And the Sun Kept Shining* by Bertha Ferderber-Salz, where one reads, "Young mothers, who had lost their children, continued to sing lullabies" (1980, 117). And so those who witnessed the annihilation of maternal love continue to sing their song of love in the writing of these memoirs.

If one of the aims in writing the memoir is to recover some link with life, it should come as no surprise to find that the child's tie to her mother is an essential aspect of her memory. In a statement reminiscent of Leon Wells's remarks cited above, Kitty Hart writes, "One thing I needed very much: regular visits to my mother" (1982, 104). Why? Because every other image and entity she encountered in the concentrationary universe declared to her that she was a nonentity, not a child or a person at all but a mere shadow about to be swallowed up by the Night. Through her mother's eyes, however, she could retrieve some trace of herself as someone who was loved and who was, therefore, alive. When she fell ill with typhus, in fact, Kitty once again received life from her mother. "Mother talked to me," she relates, "though all she got in return was rambling nonsense. I did not even recognize her. But she persevered, slowly and steadily drawing me back to life" (1982, 106). In these lines one understands that maternal love is as unconditional as it is deep, absolutely unconditional, and, therefore, a reflection of the Absolute. The mother speaks, which is to say, the mother loves, without the reinforcement of response or recognition. She loves, then, without ground or limitation, infinitely and eternally, as God loves. And so she summons from the child a love that also transcends the boundaries of time and death as one may see from a memory recorded by Sara Nomberg-Przytyk: "A young girl whose mother was assigned to the gas did not want to be separated from her. She wanted to die with her mother. They tore her from her mother by force" (1985, 35). Here the assault on maternal love takes the form of an assault on the love for the mother, even unto death. Not only are the mother and child consigned to death, but the love between them is also condemned through the elimination of the embrace that arises *between* them. The space *between* the two, where this love abides, is obliterated by forcing each to die separately, in isolation from one another: no more visits, no more look, no more being together—not even in the gas chamber.

Yet the memory of the mother reestablishes a certain between space where the visitation of maternal love comes from beyond the grave, from the other side of the sky that became her grave. For Isabella Leitner, this visitation assumes the form of an epiphany of the face. "My mother's face," she writes in the present tense, "her eyes, cannot be described. . . . She knows that for her there is nothing beyond this. And she keeps smiling at me, and I can't stand it. I am silently pleading with her: 'Stop smiling.' I gaze at her tenderly and smile back" (1978, 6). One reels at this silent exchange. "The face speaks," as Levinas says. "It speaks, it is in this that it renders possible and begins all discourse" (1985, 87–88). But the mother's face does more than speak. The mother's face *loves*, silently because it is absolute, transcending all the limits of discourse, beyond words, silently and despite all pain. Hers is the face of the origin, for it is maternal love that constitutes the mother as the origin of life; inasmuch as her face conveys that love, it contains all the power of begetting. "Her face has an otherworldly look," Leitner continues her memory of her mother. "She wants us to live, desperately. All these years I've carried with me her face of resignation and hope and love" (1978, 16). The commandment to love that signifies the divine here becomes a commandment to live. Like the Good that chooses one before one makes any other choices, maternal love beckons the memory and recovery of life even as that life is about to be consumed. If memory is able to traverse time, it is because maternal love is able to transcend time, not only during but despite "all these years." More than the remnant of a life, the survivor is the bearer of a life. For she bears the loving gaze of the mother who bore her.

Because maternal love is of such a transcendent nature, the image—no, the *presence*—of the mother manifests itself despite death. Eugene Heimler, for example, lost his mother just before his deportation. Yet, while riding the train to Auschwitz with his wife Eva, he notes, "Everybody to whom I belonged was either unconscious or dead. Eva, too, was lying in a coma by my feet. And then I saw my mother's face approaching from the distance" (1959, 31). Once more the epiphany of the face announces the maternal love that overcomes all loneliness and isolation. Once more the memory of maternal love invokes a moment in life over which death has no power; it is a memory, therefore, that has the power to recover a life, as fertile as the mother herself. Saul Friedländer also recalls an instant of horror and panic during the time when, as a child, he was hiding from the Nazis. It, too, happened on a train; although the train was not bound for the death camps, the incident took place after his mother and father had been deported. "I screamed in terror," he writes. "But suddenly, by a miracle, my mother, who had set out in search of me, appeared. I ran to her, threw myself in her arms sobbing. . . . I opened my eyes: it was Madame Chancel stroking my forehead to calm me" (1980,

101–02). Here, too, one finds the language of apparition and the image of a loving caress reaching across the chasm of death as though his mother moved the hands of his protector Madame Chancel. But before one sinks too deeply into sentimentality, one must remind oneself that Heimler's mother is dead, that Friedländer's mother was not the one whose fingers were laid upon his head. If they experienced a few seconds of maternal love's embrace, it was not because the enemy had relaxed his efforts to annihilate it. The memory, although instilled with a sense of that love and originating from that love, remains the memory of a loss. If one may speak of a "cause" underlying the Holocaust memoir, then, it is a "cause" present by its absence.

What, then, does memory recover? Among other things, it recovers a word and, with the word, a world in which the human being may belong. Permeated with the sense of an abiding maternal love, the memory draws the word out of exile and, if only for a moment, rejoins the word with its meaning and returns it to the place where *it* belongs. Which word? Thomas Geve tells us in his memoir, where he recalls receiving a certain message from the women's camp in Birkenau: "News of my luck spread quickly and soon I was surrounded by dozens of roommates who, claiming to be my best friends, wanted to hear details—but above all to see the word 'mother.' There was a double reason for rejoicing: someone had found a mother, the being dearest to all of us" (1981, 82–83). Here the word *mother* is itself a message, a conveyor of meaning and of love, that appears in the midst of an antiworld dominated by everything that is opposed to love and the meaning it fosters. Just as young Geve's fellow inmates gather around this word, so does one gather around this memory rendered through the word. Just as they see in this message not just his mother but the mother, so does one seek in the memoir a trace of maternal love as such. For if this love succumbs to the annihilation aimed at it, then this word loses its meaning and one loses one's life. But if the word is there, if a life is risked to transmit this word, if memory can smuggle it into the present through the veils of the past—then the center of life might be recovered. As soon as this word overflowing with meaning appears in the prison block, the block is itself transformed, if only for an instant. Suddenly, these orphans lost in an orphaned world have a mother. Suddenly, the block assumes the air of a home. But only for an instant.

The Devastation of the Home

If, according to Jewish tradition, the letter *beit* situates the mother at the origin of all life, the meaning of the letter *beit* ("house") places the mother

at the center of the home. "The feminine aspect of the soul," Rabbi Ginsburgh
points out, "and, in general, the woman in Judaism is symbolized by the
house" (1991, 45). The reverse is also the case: the home, which houses life
within its walls, is symbolized by the woman, who also houses life within her
womb. Other associations and explanations also come to mind; one recalls,
for example, Rashi's commentary on the Torah, where he writes, "The decree consequent upon the incident of the spies had not been enacted upon
the *women*, because they held the Promised Land dear. The men had said,
(Numbers XIV.4) 'Let us appoint a chief and return to Egypt,' whilst the
women said, (XXVII.4) 'Give us a possession in the Land' " (1972, 4:131).
It is the women, in other words, who seek out the home and who, thus,
signify the home. The House of Jacob, whose reception of the Torah made
it possible for the House of Israel to receive the Torah, embraces the promise
of a place to dwell. The sum of the Torah lies in the commandment to love,
and the commandment to love opens up a dwelling place, a place where
children and families may come into the world. The mother is the incarna-
tion of that love; hence, the mother is the personification of the home. And
the Nazi Reich is precisely the opposite of the home.

The Kingdom of Night instituted by the Nazis is the Kingdom of Exile.
If, as Martin Buber has said, " 'Good' is the movement in the direction of
home" (1965, 78), then one perceives that this height of evil is the movement away from home and into exile. It was not for nothing, then, that the
language of extermination included terms such as *resettlement*. It was not
enough to kill the Jews. Waging an ontological war, the Nazis had to annihilate their homes and their concept of home; they had to drive them from
their homes and, thus, render them homeless before killing them because
the ontological onslaught was aimed directly at the destruction of all being
that inheres in dwelling. It may be noted that, according to the "Protocol of
the Wannsee Conference," Poland was targeted as the first site for the imple-
mentation of the Final Solution to the Jewish Problem. Why? According to
Dr. Josef Bühler, it was because "there in particular the Jew as a carrier of
epidemic spelled a great danger, and, at the same time, he caused constant
disorder in the economic structure of the country by his continuous black-
market dealings" (1981, 260–61). But there is another, deeper reason: of all
the lands of Eastern Europe Poland was the most closely tied to the notion
of a Jewish homeland. "So closely did the Jews associate themselves with this
new homeland," Harry Rabinowicz points out, "that its name was etymologi-
cally interpreted in Hebrew either as *Polin* (here ye shall dwell) or *Polaniah*
(here dwells the Lord)" (1988, 1). In the Nazi assault on the mother one sees

the fundamental human problem of dwelling manifested in its most extreme form: the murder of the maternal love that distinguishes the origin of life is engineered by the devastation of the home. Once the mother is eliminated, the reign of exile and homelessness is inaugurated. And the mother herself, the very one who had symbolized the home, becomes the symbol of exile. Even here, however, one finds a link to tradition, as Adin Steinsaltz helps one to understand: "Rachel weeping for her children is suited to see the tragic future of exile and suffering. . . . For many centuries during the First and Second Temple periods, and certainly after the destruction of the Temple, Rachel came to symbolize the Shekhinah in exile" (1984, 51). The memory of the loss of the mother is a memory of exile that initiates the movement of return from exile. For, as noted, in the Holocaust memoir it is very often her children who weep for Rachel.

The Nazi project aimed at the devastation of the home took a variety of forms. There were times, for example, when the house initially lost the sanctity and the sanctuary of a home by the mere appearance of the Nazis, who would come and go as they pleased. Such was the case in the Polish town of Bielitz, where before being forced out of her home, Gerda Klein recalls the loss of her home: "The sanctity of our home was gone, the chain of tradition broken, the shrine built by love and affection desecrated" (1957, 31). In just a few words Klein articulates the scope of the loss: an entire history, the time of tradition, was destroyed by the violation of this small space. Epitomized by the mother, the love that distinguishes the family is the love that constitutes the tradition. And the center of the life nurtured by tradition is the home. What Gerda Klein invokes with these words Lily Lerner conveys by means of an image. After being forced out of their home in the Hungarian town of Tolcsva, she and her family were forced to find shelter in Miskolc. "We no longer sat around the kitchen table," she writes. "The kitchen in Miskolc was too small to have one. In a strange sense, the family had lost a little of its magnetic core when it lost that table" (1980, 55). The sense of this loss is not so strange when one recalls that "R. Jochanan and R. Elazar both said: 'As long as the Temple was in existence, the altar was [the means of] atonement for Israel, but now [because there is no Temple], each man's table is [the means of] atonement' " (*En Jacob* 1916, 1:85). Thus, the Code of Jewish Law compiled by Rabbi Joseph Caro in the sixteenth century is known as the *Shulchan Arukh*, or (The set table). The table is where the family members join with one another and with Creation in the act of breaking and sharing a piece of bread. The life of the family has its origin in the mother, both literally and symbolically; from her womb come the children and from her hands the bread on which the blessing is said at the table. It is she who sets and orders the table, she, then, who creates the place of *dwelling*.

So one understands why Jean Améry insists that "there is no 'new home.' Home is the land of one's childhood and youth. Whoever has lost it remains lost to himself" (1980, 48). A man can have no new home any more than he can have a new mother or a new identity. The "new" one is always a counterfeit and invariably leads to the alienation experienced by Saul Friedländer when, as a child, he and his parents tried to find a new home in Paris after they had fled from Prague. There, he remembers, he could find a place neither among the Christian nor among the Jewish children: "I was tied to a tree and beaten . . . by Jewish children because they thought I was different from them. So I belonged nowhere" (1980, 45). The violence done to the home translates into violence done to the child. Here the Jew becomes the one who, by definition, belongs nowhere, forced into the situation that Edmond Jabès describes when he says, "I feel that I exist only outside of any belonging. That non-belonging is my very substance. Maybe I have nothing else to say but that painful contradiction: like everyone else, I aspire to a place, a dwelling-place, while being at the same time unable to accept what offers itself" (1990, 29). Jabès enables one to see that the beating suffered by the one who remembers results not only in bruises to the body but in an absence imposed upon the soul. Thus, when Friedländer recalls his mother's words, "we can no longer exist legally" (1980, 78), he articulates the memory of being cast outside the parameters of life itself. And that memory is articulated in the words of the *mother*: it is she who expresses the child's loss of being and belonging, because it is she who embodies the home that makes possible all belonging and that is rendered illegitimate *by law*, or by a kind of antilaw. Here one discovers a most insidious aspect of the ontological evil that national socialism represents: once it becomes a crime for a Jew to have a home, it is a crime for a Jew to be. And the archcriminal in this scheme of things is the mother.

If the concentrationary universe has been deemed an antiworld, it is because, among other reasons, it is antithetical to the home. Like the child whose "being" consists of not belonging, the home appears in this antiworld as the absence of the one thing needful, the absence of an entire world. Charlotte Delbo makes this point when she relates the story of how she and some of her fellow prisoners found shelter in the remains of a house while out on a work detail one rainy Auschwitz day. As the women dried themselves in the half-demolished structure, they imagined how they might have made it into a home complete with furniture, wallpaper, curtains, plants, and a radio (1968, 87–88). Although this talk brings them a moment of relief, it also accentuates the realization of where they are not. All the fixtures and furnishings that constitute a life in the world are absent from their antiworld; indeed, the whole of that antiworld seemed to be gathered into those ruins that had once been a home. For Filip Müller the devastation of the home is signified not by the ruins of a house but by the ruins of memory itself. "The memory of my parents," he writes, "my family and my early youth in my home town had faded" (1979a, 17). If, as Elie Wiesel has said, the Churban "was essentially a war against memory" (1990a, 155), it was a war against the memory of home and all the home symbolizes: mother, father, tradition, sanctity, meaning, love, life. The human being has no being without the home; and he has no home without the mother.

This linkage between home and mother is quite explicit in Kitty Hart's *Return to Auschwitz*. After she and her mother were completely shaved upon their arrival at the camp, she relates, "When I turned to look for my mother I couldn't make her out at first. . . . Had we come here straight from home? Home: the word had ceased to mean anything" (1982, 62). In Thomas Geve's memoir one finds a similar failure of recognition; upon seeing his mother for the first time in Auschwitz-Birkenau, he asserts, "I hardly recognized mother. Still in her early thirties, she looked as harsh as her companions" (1981, 83). In both instances the failure of the recognition of the mother is directly tied to the loss of the meaning of the word *home*; it is in her face, overflowing with maternal love, that the meaning of *home* is inscribed. Again, the mother is the sign of the home; when the sign is defaced to the point of nonrecognition, the thing it signifies, the home, is erased from being. And yet in the act of remembrance the sign is recovered; indeed, the Holocaust memoir is characterized precisely by this recovery of a sign or of the trace of a sign. Here remembrance entails recognition, the re-cognition that constitutes the face of the one defaced and the word drained of its meaning. Although his family may have faded from Müller's memory, the memory of the fading regains a trace of the family. Although Hart and Geve may have failed to recognize their mothers, a remnant of recognition—and with it a trace of the mother—is regained in the memory of its loss. For the memory of the loss as a loss entails an affirmation of the dearness of what was lost. And the recovery of tradition begins with that affirmation.

The reconstitution of recognition effected by memory points toward a reunion with the family that was often impossible during the time remembered. The devastation of the home includes the breakup of the family so that the longing for a trace of home frequently expresses itself as a longing for the family. When Moshe Sandberg and his comrades, for example, were transported from a Hungarian labor crew to Dachau, the first thing they asked the inmates of Dachau was how they might be rejoined with members of their families who had been sent there. They met only with cynical laughter, however, because those in Dachau knew, says Sandberg, "that we would also go the way of our families with whom sooner or later we would be reunited, yes, reunited in another world, in the world of the dead" (1968, 59). In the original Hebrew text "another world" is *'olam acher* (1967, 44), a phrase ridden with many connotations and associations. The word for "world," *'olam*, for instance, can mean "humanity," "community," "existence," "eternity," "distant future"; and *acher* may mean "different," "strange," "after." In the assault on the home the family becomes the alien humanity relegated to a realm that is eternally *after, later, not yet*. Thus, the memory of the family—and, by implication, the memory of the mother—becomes a memory of the future, of an *'olam ha-bah*, or a "world to come"; in the act of remembrance what *was not then* becomes what is *yet to be*. Why? Because once memory affirms the dearness of what was lost, the thing lost becomes the thing *sought*. One finds an illustration of this point in Zivia Lubetkin's memoir where she remembers a memory that came to her during the darkest hours of the Warsaw Ghetto Uprising: "My imagination drew my thoughts away to our ancestral Homeland, to my many friends there" (1981, 151). The ancestral homeland is the home where she has yet to arrive, *ancestral* not because she has already come from there but because it is the origin that summons her toward a future where a new life forever awaits. Here, too, one finds the mother, for in the Hebrew text the word for "homeland" is *arets* (1978, 107), a term that also denotes the earth; and I have already explored the associations between the mother and the earth.

Not long after the Nazis established a ghetto in Bielitz, Gerda Klein's parents arranged for her to go into hiding in another Polish town, Sosnowiec. Recalling the moment of their parting, she writes, "The picture of Papa's and Mama's mute farewells—those two faces suffering without uttering a cry—was imprinted on my heart forever" (1957, 95–96). The imprint of the memory of the mother—and, in this case, of the father as well—is the imprint of a face. In the movement of remembrance a face speaks. And when the memory is the memory of the loss of the mother, it is the face of the mother that speaks, the face of the origin, of love, and of home. The mother, who abides at the origin of life, is herself the origin of this memory: in a very important sense, the mother writes the memory of her loss. In that writing, then, a trace of the mother, who is antecedent to the utterance, is present in the utterance. From Gerda Klein's remark, one sees that the imprint on the heart, on the center and core of her being, finds its way into the imprint on the page. There the mute farewells become a silent summons. From the page—from the words and from the silence between the words—the voice of the mother calls to all who come before this page to a recovery of the origin, the love, and the home that were lost. It is not just Gerda Klein, the one who suffered the loss, who is called to recover and, thus, to uncover the traces of tradition. The utterance of the memory brings that summons to all who encounter the utterance so that the imprint that moves from the heart to the page now moves from the page to the heart.

There the little girl who cries out in Livia Jackson's memoir cries out to *me*. I am the one called to listen, the one whom she addresses when she screams, "Oh, Mommy! Oh, God, they are killing my mother!" (1980, 70). Can the heart endure this memory? Can it endure the words and the memory of Isabella Leitner when she says, "The air was filled with the stench of death. Unnatural death. The smoke was thick. The sun couldn't crack through. The scent was the smell of burning flesh. The burning flesh was your mother" (1978, 94)? Note the shift from the third person to the second person: "your mother," she addresses me. *My* mother!? Suddenly I am the one who must do the work of re-cognition that characterizes memory and recovery. Because the mother is definitively linked to the origin, the love, and the home that belong to a tradition, the memory of her loss is a memory that becomes part of a tradition and, therefore, part of a common memory. Thus I, too, am the one who, in an act of response and remembrance, must affirm the dearness of what was lost. Else I, too, am lost.

2

The Loss of the Father

In chapter 1 I explored what was lost and what is remembered in the memory of the mother. Now I begin an investigation of what was lost and what is remembered in the memory of the father. The mother embodies the origin of life, the love of what is most dear in life, and the home that establishes a center for life. In the father is the truth that provides a ground for life, the wisdom that underlies all thinking about life, and the order that constitutes the reality and substance of life. From an ontological standpoint, then, when the father's existence is rendered illegitimate, truth, thought, and reality come under attack. In Jewish terms these entail the truth of tradition as an avenue of revelation; the wisdom and the intellect that thinkers such as Maimonides (1956, 74) and Gersonides (1984, 1:157) identify with God; and the order of reality as it continually issues from the hand and the mouth of the Creator. All of this is lost in the loss of the father so that the memory of the father entails far more than a mournful reminiscence surrounding the head of a household. The attack on the father is, in fact, an attack on memory itself, and the memory at work in the Holocaust memoir arises as a remnant of the father and all he signifies. For, according to Jewish tradition, memory belongs to the father, who is responsible for handing down the tradition, just as the nurturing of life belongs to the mother. Regarding the *zachor v'shamor* that pertain to the Sabbath, for example, the *Bahir* teaches that " 'remember' (*zachor*) refers to the male (*Zachar*). 'Keep' (*shamor*) refers to the bride" (1979, 70). The male is the bridegroom, he who is to become a father in the observance of the first of all the commandments, namely to be fruitful and multiply (Gen. 1:28). And, insofar as the father is part of the essence of the Holocaust memoir, the memoir is itself an observance of that commandment.

58

Perhaps, then, the writing of the Holocaust memoir comes not only in the observance of what Fackenheim calls the "614th Commandment" (1978, 19–24)—the refusal to allow the Nazis a posthumous victory by allowing the Judaic tradition to die—but also in the observance of the very first commandment, the one from which all the others issue, including the 614th. In the project to exterminate the Jews, the Reign of Nothingness begins with the undoing of the first commandment, and it is the first commandment that makes the father who he is. Thus, Filip Müller, for instance, begins his *Auschwitz Inferno: The Testimony of a Sonderkommando* with the murder of a father. The memoir opens by relating an account of how the block clerk, Vacek, was the first to be singled out for death one Sunday in May 1942. He "was a father of four," writes Müller. "Before he became an inmate of Auschwitz he had scraped a living by reciting the Kaddish, the prayer for the dead, in the synagogue of his native town" (1979a, 1–2). The saying of the Kaddish is itself an act of remembrance and recovery, an affirmation of the sanctity of life and of the Creator of life. The memory of the murder of the father is a refusal of that murder and a recovery of a trace of all that is murdered in the slaying of the father—not a denial, be it noted, but a refusal, that is, a choosing of one structure of being over against another. Fania Fénelon expresses this act of choosing in the midst of remembrance by assuming the name of her late father upon her deportation to Auschwitz: "If I was going to die, I preferred to die under my father's name, Goldstein" (1977, 15). To retain the name of the father is to retain the truth, the wisdom, and the world signified by that name. Israel's center for the remembrance of the Holocaust is called Yad Vashem, which means "a memorial and a name," and in the Holocaust memoir the name attached to the memorial is the name of the father.

In the memory of the survivor, of course, the name not only signifies a long line of those who have held the name throughout Jewish tradition but it also conjures up an image that embodies that tradition. In many instances, then, the memory of the loss of the father begins with a memory of the crumbling of that image. Sara Zyskind, for example, recalls a moment of gazing upon her father as he prayed, wrapped in the *tallis* of ancient tradition. "It struck me," she relates, "that there was something very strange about Father's praying form, as if it were an apparition from another world. Another world? What am I thinking? I mustn't think of such things. Father was still part of this world, and he was all that I had left here. I gazed at him again. There was nothing about him that recalled the image of my once young and exuberant father" (1981, 100–101). In the Hebrew text there is an additional line that does not appear in the English translation: *leviy hitkavuts l'meraho*, "my heart shrank at the sight of him" (1978, 85), suggesting that with the collapse of the father's image there comes a breakdown within the core of the self. The father contains the seed of Israel, and what befalls him reverberates throughout the nation. This point becomes especially clear if one recalls Gerda Klein's description of her father's reaction on the occasion when her brother Arthur was forced to leave their home: "Now he was as helpless as I. An overwhelming feeling of pity and pain swept over me. I embraced Papa. The touch of my arms made him shiver, and a suppressed and terrible sobbing cry rose from his throat, a cry which I will never forget, which had no resemblance to the human voice; it sounded rather like the cry of an animal when it has been stabbed and is dying" (1957, 20). One cannot help but note the reversal of roles in this account: the child becomes the comforter of the father. He who had been the heir to the word—who had conveyed the word to his children—loses the word in the loss of his image. For the word, the human voice, is just what constitutes that image. Gerda Klein remembers that her father "had changed so much" (1957, 8). Leon Wells notes that his father's hair "had turned gray and he was very thin" (1978, 103). And in the opening pages of her memoir Livia Jackson recalls, "My father seemed to grow somewhat slack as winter wore on. His silences became longer" (1980, 3–4). In the ontological assault on Jewish being it is not enough simply to murder the father. The killing of his body must be preceded by the annihilation of his image, for in his image lies the Jewish being that the father symbolizes.

The attack on being is effective only if it is felt. And it is felt only if it is introduced as an imposed absence, that is, as a sense of having been abandoned. The tradition of truth, thought, and reality that is symbolized by the father and that underlies the movement of memory in the Holocaust memoir is something *living*. It moves among the living and fosters "life's attachment to life," as Henri Bergson calls it (1954, 210), which is essential to the structure both of Jewish being in particular and of human being in general. Thus, looking again at Livia Jackson, one sees that the loss of the father's image is soon followed by a feeling of abandonment when he is forced to leave his family: "Oh, Daddy! . . . How could you leave me?" (1980, 34). A similar outcry rises up from the pages of Eugene Heimler's *Night of the Mist*, "Father, my father, . . . do not forsake me" (1959, 186). In both instances it is as if the father himself were behind his elimination. And 'this *as if* is carefully engineered. No *father* would ever abandon his children. Yet the ontological image of the father is undone to the point of making him into precisely the one who abandons his children. Indeed, under the Nazis the world had been reordered to such an extent that the fear of abandonment became part of the child's being long before there was any immediate question of his father's forced departure. "I see my father once again," recall the lines from Saul Friedländer's memoir, "reading beneath the light of a tall standing lamp, the library in the background. . . . I would get up out of bed, tiptoe along the hall, and assure myself by glueing my eye to the keyhole that he was there, in his usual place" (1980, 13–14). When the father is in his place, the child has a place; being is itself in place, for truth, thought, and reality are in place. And the sacred tradition is alive.

The memory of the loss of the father is definitively tied to the recovery of tradition. As part of the process of that recovery, it is a memory that reconstitutes a reality by regenerating a process of thought that is grounded in truth. Here truth is not simply a matter of accurately attesting to the facts of what took place. It is an avenue of return to the Most High. For, as Adin Steinsaltz points out, truth is "the middle line from infinity to all that is below in the world, and everything has its point of contact with it" (1988, 91–92). In this examination of the memory of the loss of the father, then, I begin with the loss of truth.

The Disintegration of Truth

As the linkage between all that is above and all that is below, truth transcends the factual and extends to the holy. It lays claim to one before one stakes any other claims. In a parallel and symbolic manner the memory of the father in the Holocaust memoir is a memory of the one who has chosen the individual before all of his choosing. This pre-originary *having been chosen already* links the one who remembers—by way of the father—to the Good that distinguishes truth. An example of this relation comes from the Jewish tradition in the *Pirke de Rabbi Eliezer,* where one finds a comment on Joseph, "In all his wisdom a certain woman enticed (him), and when he wished to accustom himself to sin, he saw the image of his father, and repented concerning it" (1970, 305). From a third position between the self and the other the father emerges as the figure of the Good and, therefore, as a figure of truth. In modern psychoanalysis Jacques Lacan describes this arrangement by saying, "The Other with a big 'O' is the scene of the Word insofar as the scene of the Word is always in third position between two subjects. This is only in order to introduce the dimension of Truth" (1968,

269), and in his *Écrits* Lacan writes, "This Other, which is distinguished as the locus of Speech, imposes itself no less as a witness to the Truth" (1977, 305). In the murder of the father this Other is targeted for extinction. And the eclipse of this Other—the disintegration of truth—characterizes the condition of absolute evil, which, according to Jewish tradition, occasions the coming of the Messiah. In the *En Jacob*, for instance, one is taught that in the generation of the Messiah, "the wisdom of the scribes will be corrupted. Men fearing sin will be hated. The leaders of that generation will have the nature of dogs. And the truth will be lacking" (1921, 5:39). In short, the father will be annihilated. Thus, it came to pass. And yet one continues to await the Anointed One. That wait, however, is sustained by the memory of the father.

The memory of the father that sustains the wait and, therefore, the life of the self may manifest itself through memories of the sages or the human pillars of civilization and tradition. In the case of Primo Levi, for example, they are memories of Dante, which, he says, "made it possible for me to reestablish a link with the past, saving it from oblivion . . . in short, a way to find myself" (1988, 139–40). In the Italian text the word for "oblivion" is *oblio* (Levi 1986a, 112), the root of which is the same as the root for *obliare*, or "to forget": the figure of Dante is a figure of memory, the source and substance of the memory that comprises the substance of the human being. The phrase "to find myself," moreover, is a translation of *ritrovare me stesso* (1986a, 112), which has connotations of recovering one's bearings in relation to something or someone outside of oneself. The human being arrives at himself by way of a relation to another, and in this instance the other is the father, or the father image of Dante. In *Survival in Auschwitz* we find an illustration of what Levi is talking about on the occasion of his reciting a passage from the *Inferno* for his friend Jean, the Pikolo: " 'And three times round she went in roaring smother / With all the waters; at the fourth the poop / Rose, and the prow went down, as pleased Another.' I keep Pikolo back, it is vitally necessary and urgent that he listen, that he understand this 'as pleased Another' before it is too late; tomorrow he or I might be dead, or we might never see each other again, I must tell him, I must explain to him about the Middle Ages, about the so human and so necessary and yet unexpected anachronism, but still more, something gigantic that I myself have only just seen, in a flash of intuition, perhaps the reason for our fate, for our being here today" (1961, 104–5). What Levi refers to as "Another" is the Other who, from a third position, is the witness and judge of the truth that reveals itself between two. And this, again, is the position of the father.

That the father appears not only as a witness but also as a judge becomes clear when one recalls Paul Trepman's comment on being forced to teach the atheistic party line in a communist school while he was hiding from the Nazis: "I had never been what one might call extremely Orthodox but as I bombarded my young charges with atheistic propaganda that they did not know how to challenge, I felt that I was a traitor to the memory of my late father, to my family, and to everything I had been taught in my childhood" (1978, 45). And in Filip Müller's memoir one reads, "What could I have said to [my father] who, sickened by the plots of the fascist Hlinka Guards of Slovakia, had volunteered for one of the transports to the East as early as February 1942? And why had he done so? In order, as he said with the true ring of conviction, to help create a new life for his family there" (1979a, 47–48). In both instances the memory of the father is far more than an indication of psychological guilt feelings over having failed to obey the inner voice of the superego. Once more the memory of the father is a memory of truth that lends meaning to a present in the light of a meaningful past. Because the father is the bearer of truth, the family he heads can become the object of betrayal. The father places the voice of judgment outside the human being to situate it within a family and, therefore, within a tradition that alone makes truth part of life's essence. Through the father an entire world summons the response and responsibility that determine the direction that the man must pursue. He may choose to honor the father or to betray him, but he can neither choose nor refuse the accountability to which the father summons him any more than he can choose the world into which he is born.

In the tractate Avot of the Mishnah, Rabbi Shimon ben Gamaliel teaches that truth is one of the foundations of the world (1:18). "Speaking falsehood, then," writes Moshe Chayim Luzzatto, "is comparable to removing the foundation of the world; and, conversely, if one is heedful of the truth it is as if he maintains the world's foundation" (1990, 147–49). In keeping with this tradition, the Holocaust memoir often articulates the disintegration of truth associated with the murder of the father in terms of a crumbling of the ground. In the concentration camp, says Thomas Geve, for example, he and his comrades "felt as if the ground had receded from under our feet. . . . The refined city manner, the studying of Greek and Roman achievements, the strivings of democracy, the neutral nations' eagerness to help the oppressed, the many impressive churches I had seen, the beauty of art and progress I was to have understood, the trust in my parents' judgment—it all seemed to have been a disgusting farce" (1981, 51–52). Similarly, in *The Holocaust*

Kingdom Alexander Donat writes, "We could feel the ground slipping out from under our feet" (1978, 25). And: "A new kind of life began to take shape over the mass grave of the past" (1978, 94). In these passages and others like them one notices a connection between the parents—particularly the father—and the civilization upon which the world is structured. The father, who precedes one, signifies a past that precedes one and would lay claim to one as a truth given in the form of what one terms *civilization.* The ground that gives way to be transformed into a mass grave, then, is not to be confused with the earth that is associated with the mother. In the earth is planted the seed of life; on the ground are erected the symbols of truth. As a womb nurturing the seed, the earth is linked to the future, to a life *yet to be* born from the seed; as the foundation of truth that has established a world, the ground is tied to the past, to a tradition. "Chakhmah-Wisdom," notes Aryeh Kaplan in his commentary on the Bahir, "is said to represent the past, while Binah-Understanding is the future. Wisdom is similarity and unity, and there is only one past. Understanding is dissimilarity and plurality, and there are many possible futures" (1979, 107). And, as Kaplan notes in the *Sefer Yetzirah* (1990, 13), tradition holds that Wisdom belongs to the father, whereas Understanding is the realm of the mother.

As the thing handed down by the father, however, tradition itself collapses upon the disintegration of truth. The Jewish tradition in Sara Zyskind's *Stolen Years* where she recalls, "My childhood memories of my father are particularly strong. . . . From my father's lips I learned not only the story of his life but also the history of the Jewish people, which he narrated in a vivid manner" (1981, 12–13). This tradition, this history of the Jewish people, is just what crumbles when Donat relates, "The very bases of our faith had crumbled: the Polish fatherland whose children we had always considered ourselves; two thousand years of Christianity, silent in the face of Nazism; our own lie-ridden civilization" (1978, 100–1). It is the disintegration of truth that makes it possible to introduce the term *lie-ridden* to Donat's discourse. The Reign of Death that necessitates the death of the father is the Reign of the Lie so that in the movement of memory and recovery truth becomes an issue when it becomes absent signified by the inverted sign of the lie. Once again, from an ontological standpoint it is not enough to kill the father; a father killed is still a father, still the one who signifies the truth affirmed in the saying of the Kaddish. In the ontological assault not only the person of the father but all the father signifies must be destroyed. The father who signified the truth—who said to Leon Wells, "Trust in God as you have done so far, and all will end well" (1978, 105)—this father must be made into a liar. Yet the very existence of the memoir gives lie to the lie and, thus, initiates a recovery of the disintegrated truth. For the memoir affirms that the memory of the father *matters*, that there is a truth to be resurrected from the lie, and that this truth is to be found precisely in the father's memory. The tension between truth and lie is coupled with the tension between the past and the separation from the past. The father, therefore, announces the meaning of the separation and the disintegration as Friedländer suggests when he says, "It was my father who unwittingly revealed to me the real meaning of our separation: he hugged me to him and kissed me" (1980, 87). The kiss here is the kiss of truth that the separation would make into a lie. But the memory of the kiss refuses that mutilation; the memory of the kiss is a recovery of the meaning of the relation in which truth inheres.

In many instances one discovers that memory functions in this manner even in the midst of the horrific Event itself. In Vladka Meed's *On Both Sides of the Wall*, for example, we find just such a memory of a memory, as she recalls what went through her mind while hiding in a Polish church: "During the murmured prayers my imagination would carry me back to a world now gone from me . . . to my father, who had died of pneumonia in the ghetto. I saw him standing, his prayer shawl draped over his head" (1973, 216). In this example the memory of the father in prayer is precisely the memory of the Jewish tradition that the father represents. For the Jewish tradition represented by the father is a tradition of prayer (the father, after all, is the one who is obligated to observe the prayers), and the tradition of prayer is a tradition guided by the light of truth. Once the father and all he stands for are murdered, memory becomes the only link to the tradition, the stuff of the tradition itself and of the truth it embraces. In the Holocaust memoir, then, the utterance of the memory is not the narration of a life but, beyond that, it entails a movement into the truth of Jewish tradition. Other examples of the Holocaust memoir, however, are more problematic than Vladka Meed's text, for there the accent falls more on the disintegration of truth than on its affirmation. Yet here, too, the affirmation of truth is dialectically at work, for here, too, the father lies at the heart of the memory. Recalling the face of her dead father, for instance, Sara Zyskind writes, "His eyes were wide open as if frozen in the midst of a fearful question" (1981, 145). The Hebrew verb rendered as "wide open," *pekochot* (Zyskind 1978, 130), has connotations of insight and understanding, but this shade of meaning is immediately undercut by the phrase *sheelah v'pachad* (1978, 130), or "a question and a fear." The very one to whom insight belongs is the one whose vision is clouded by a fearful question. And when his vision is so clouded, all insight, all thought, is subject to collapse.

The Collapse of Thought

Sara Zyskind's memory of her dead father's face brings to mind a passage from Elie Wiesel's *Legends of Our Time* wherein he recalls, "In dying, my father looked at me, and in his eyes where night was gathering, there was nothing but animal terror, the demented terror of one who, because he wished to understand too much, no longer understood anything. His gaze fixed on me, empty of meaning" (1968, 18). As the father, however, it falls to him to understand, that is, to comprehend and to *think* what the world poses for thought. According to Jewish tradition, *Chakhmah*, or wisdom, is associated with the father; further, among the connections between the ten *Sefirot* and the parts of the body, the *Sefirah* of *Chakhmah* belongs to the skull or to the mind (*Bahir* 1979, 145), that is, to the seat of thought. The night that gathers in the eyes of the dying father darkens the mind that constitutes the father, darkens not only the mind of this particular father but the mind as such. From a philosophical standpoint the love of wisdom that is philosophy itself is the key to every concept of the human being and his world. Looking to the Jewish tradition, one finds that Bachya ibn Paquda, for example, expresses this notion by saying, "Sages declared that philosophy is man's knowledge of himself, that is, knowledge of what has been mentioned in regard to the human being, so that through the evidence of divine wisdom displayed in himself, he will become cognizant of the Creator" (1970, 1:151). But the cognition that characterizes one's thinking about creation is obliterated upon the murder of the father, for the father is the embodiment of that cognition. "Philosophy," Ka-tzetnik once said to me, "is a shabby word." Why? Because any meaning that it may have had lies buried in the ashes of the father.

Yet it is just in those ashes that memory seeks the recovery of the human image through a recovery of the image of the father. To the extent that human beings struggle to remain human, they struggle to understand; one cannot decide not to understand any more than one can decide not to have a father. Having taken on the name of the father given to her before the assumption of anything else, Fania Fénelon declares, "To understand—it was a mania with me. I continued to believe that there was something to understand, that this desire for extermination was motivated by reasons which simply escaped me" (1977, 91). That the longing to understand might be termed a "mania" is indicative of the ontological nature of the assault on the mind and, therefore, on human being itself. It is not that the reasons for the extermination are obscure or complicated; rather, the "reasons" do not belong to reason or to the rational and the thinkable, for, again, that is just what the evil of the antiworld sets out to destroy. In the words of Charlotte Delbo, those sent to the anti-world "expect the worst—they do not expect the unthinkable" (1968, 6). They do not expect the nullification of thought itself, which defines the parameters of expectation and the operations of the mind. Thus, among the first memories that Isabella Leitner calls to mind is the memory of incomprehension: "It is Sunday, May 28th, my birthday. . . . Tomorrow is deportation. The laughter is too bitter, the body too tired, the soul trying to still the infinite rage. My skull seems to be ripping apart, trying to organize, to comprehend what cannot be comprehended" (1978, 3). Once again one recalls the Jewish association of the father with *Chakhmah* and of *Chakhmah* with the skull. The ripping apart of the one amounts to the annihilation of the other. The collapse of thought is not just concurrent with the loss of the father, it is the consequence of that loss.

Despite the onset of mental cramps, however, one must remind oneself that this matter concerns neither comprehension nor incomprehension. With the loss of the father and the consequent collapse of thought such categories are null and void, even though the process of thinking may itself continue. Indeed, the fact that thinking does continue, which is something that ordinarily enhances life, now serves to further undermine the life of the human being. Jean Améry makes this point when he asserts, "It was not the case that the intellectual . . . had now become unintellectual or incapable of thinking. On the contrary, only rarely did thinking grant itself a respite. But it nullified itself when at almost every step it ran into its uncrossable borders. The axes of its traditional frames of reference then shattered" (1980, 19). It is worth noting that the term *intellectual* is a rendition of the German phrase *der geistige Mensch* (Améry 1977, 43), which suggests an image of the human being, or *Mensch*, as a creature of *Geist*, that is, of mind, spirit, or intellect. The very qualities that define the human being as human—mind and spirit— are perverted into the contraries of his "humanity," into a kind of antihumanity determined by the antiworld. This perversion is exactly parallel and is directly tied to the perversion of the father into the one who abandons the family or into the one who signifies the lie rather than the truth of tradition. The traditional frames of reference that are shattered in the self-nullification of thought are the frames of reference and reason signified by the father of tradition. Nevertheless, inasmuch as it is formulated according to the spiritual and intellectual aspects of the human mind, the memoir recovers some facets of *der geistige Mensch*. What was deformed is re-formed in an act of re-membering: Améry's examination of the collapse of thought is ruled by a carefully ordered pattern of thought.

Although other memoirs may not reflect Améry's intricate organization and highly intellectual approach, they do address the same point. Kitty Hart, for example, writes, "You might think an intellectual ought to have been able to cope better than a bewildered peasant, but it was often the other way round. The well-educated man . . . tried to find some rational, philosophical way of coping with the incredible situation; and just because it was so foul and incredible, his mind cracked" (1982, 79). Similarly, Filip Müller insists, "Neither intelligence nor education was a bulwark against the distortion of a man's personality" (1979a, 45) where "distortion" is a translation of the German *Deformierung* (1979b, 72) or "deformation," once again linking the obliteration of the human form with the collapse of thought. One can see more clearly why the intelligence becomes the enemy if one turns again to Jewish tradition itself. As a tradition of thought, the Jewish tradition is a tradition of commentary not only on the text of the Torah but on the world created from the blueprint of the Torah. Here the function of thought is to read the text of the world, as one might read the letters of the alphabet. Yitzchak Ginsburgh explains, "Each of the twenty-two letters of the Hebrew alphabet possesses three different creative powers, which in the teaching of *Chassidut* are termed: energy (*koah*), life (*hayot*), and light (*or*). . . . In the creative process the Hebrew letters appear at each of these three levels: as the energy building-blocks of all reality; as the manifestation of the inner life-pulse permeating the universe as a whole and each of its individual creatures ('pulsing' every created being, instantaneously, into and out of existence); and as the channels which direct the influx of Divine revelation into created consciousness" (1991, 2–3). Just as the father teaches his child the *alef-beit* by which the Torah is read, so does he signify the reading of the world and its symbols through a process of thought. In the antiworld, however, the alphabet of the world is erased, so that energy, life, and light are swallowed up rather than released in the effort to read the revelation. "The symbol," as Karl Jaspers expresses it, "catches what would otherwise stream out of us and be lost in the void" (1959, 38). With the collapse of thought the symbol is obliterated and the void overflows.

The father is the symbol of the symbol. He is the measure of thought, and thought is the measure of the world. The collapse of thought, then, is a collapse of measure and distinction, of limitation and delineation: the object of thought can no longer be *grasped*, for it recedes beyond the limits of measure. One recalls, for example, Fania Fénelon's assertion that "death, life, tears, laughter, everything was multiplied, disproportionate, beyond the limits of the credible. All was madness" (1977, 70). The word from the French text translated as "disproportionate" is *démesure* (1976, 102), which implies the absence of measure, excess, inordinance. The distinctions and limitations by which thought differentiates between A and *not-A* are completely undone: death is something else, life something else, tears and laughter something other than tears and laughter, all of it unthinkable—not because it is terrible but because it is *démesure*. And, just as thought extends beyond the confines of space and time so does the collapse of thought extend beyond the barbed wire. "The whole world had lost its reason," says George Topas. "What good was it to believe that the retribution would be so severe that it would prevent any possibility of a recurrence? In the meantime the burning bush to which Israel had been likened was being consumed" (1990, 151). Once again the selection of an image or a symbol is an expression of the collapse of all symbols and categories of thought. The burning bush of Israel—which, according to tradition, burns with the light of the Holy One and is not consumed—now burns with the dark, all-consuming flame of unreason. "Thought is present in the symbol," says Jaspers. "The symbol is never without thought" (1959, 51). Hence, with the undoing of the symbol thought is itself undone. There is no burning bush. There is only the burning, by which the symbol itself goes up in flames. Yet, like the Torah that is fire and, therefore, cannot be consumed by fire, the symbol arises once more . . . in the utterance of the memoir.

As the symbol of the symbol, the father is the symbol of the giving of symbols that distinguishes the saying of memory in the Holocaust memoir. He is the teacher who guides the memory. He is the ground for the reality that the memory would restore. "Reality itself is immediately present in the symbols," Jaspers explains. "It is more than I see and experience, but I experience it in the degree that I, on the basis of my Existenz, appropriate the symbols as my own" (1959, 56–57). The remembrance of the father is an appropriation of the symbol, or better, a recovery of the symbol, undertaken in a process of thought that would recover from a thinking that was void of thought. Thinking that is void of thought—that has lost the truth and the categories of thought signified by the father—is void of any experience of fate or love or vision. The breakdown of reality that follows in the wake of the collapse of thought, then, is not a problem posed for the imagination as many have claimed (e.g., Ezrahi 1980, 2–3; Langer 1975, 43; Wardi 1986,

41). On the contrary, once thought collapses—and with it the measures and limitations of reality—imagination itself becomes unlimited; after all, everything the Nazis did was imagined before it was done. If Ana Vinocur declares, "The more I thought, the more unreal everything seemed to me" (1976, 53), it is not because her imagination failed her. No, the problem of reality posed by the Shoah and addressed in the Holocaust memoir is the result of the collapse of thought, not of imagination. I consider, then, this final and perhaps most devastating consequence of the loss of the father.

The Breakdown of Reality

"A disproportion between suffering and every theodicy," says Levinas, "was shown at Auschwitz with a glaring, obvious clarity. Its possibility puts into question the multimillenial traditional faith" (1988b, 161–62). Elsewhere he elaborates. "In the appearing of evil, in its original phenomenality, in its *quality*, is announced a *modality*, a manner: not finding a place, the refusal of all accommodation with . . . , a counter-nature, a monstrosity" (Levinas 1987a, 180; emphasis in the original). The father signifies, among other things, the theodicy of Western thought and the multimillenial traditional faith. This tradition is not the invention of the father but determines and defines the father as such. The father is the opposite of disproportion and monstrosity. To oppose the father, then, is to impose "what is foreign itself": the unreal, manifested not simply by suffering but by the *disproportion* of which Levinas speaks. "For sheer demented horror," Samuel Pisar states in his memoir, "Treblinka, Maidanek, and Auschwitz were in a class of their own: the end of the world, the end of creation" (1979, 66)—the end of reality, the *dementing* of reality, infinitely removing it from the parameters of *mens* or "mind."

Thus, says Améry, "Existence as such became definitively a totally abstract and thus empty concept. To reach out beyond concrete reality with words became before our very eyes a game that was not only worthless and an impermissible luxury but also mocking and evil" (1980, 19). The phrase rendered as "concrete reality" appears in Améry's German text as *Realexistenz* (1977, 43), a term that could be translated as the "existence of the real." And the verb "to reach out," *herauszulangen* (1977, 43), is not so much a reaching out *beyond Realexistenz* as a reaching out *to* the existence of the real. Again, the problem does not lie with the imagination; indeed, the *images* are all too indelibly imprinted on the memory, like the number tattooed on the arm. The difficulty is that the existence of the real cannot be *thought* in the antiworld of Auschwitz; it is demented. "Everything for us was unreal and insubstantial," Simon Wiesenthal recalls (1976, 41), *irreal* and *unwirklich*, as the German text reads (Wiesenthal 1970, 43), the former term also meaning "incorporeal" and the latter "untrue" or "inactual." Does this mean that nothing was felt or experienced? No, on the contrary, what was felt and experienced surpassed all measure and proportion. Is it necessary to note that to deem the concentrationary universe unreal is not to say that it did not happen? Does one need to remind oneself that there is a distinction between what transpires in being and what can be accommodated by the categories of reality? Where reality happens, to borrow again from Levinas, "the *appearing* of a phenomenon is inseparable from its *signifying*. . . . Every phenomenon is a disclosure or a fragment of a discourse" (1987a, 112; emphasis in the original). But in the antiworld of Auschwitz, where existence *as such* becomes an empty concept—that is, where there is no signifying of anything, where the phenomenon does not speak but rather overwhelms with indifferent silence—there unreality *happens*. And it happens because the father, who is the sign of giving signs, no longer happens. If it is true that the appearing of a phenomenon is inseparable from its signifying, it is because the father has made an appearance and has, thus, rooted the human being in the real.

The breakdown of reality, then, is linked to a fundamental, existential uprooting. Levi makes this point quite explicitly when he writes, "This is the most immediate fruit of exile, of uprooting: the prevalence of the unreal over the real. Everyone dreamed . . . of improbable paradise, of equally mythical and improbable enemies" (1965, 107–8). The Italian word translated as "uprooting" is *sradicamento* (Levi 1989, 233), which also means "eradication" and suggests not just a removal from home but the annihilation of any place of belonging, of the home as such. One sees how the breakdown of reality is tied to the disintegration of truth and to the collapse of thought: all grounding in the soil of tradition and reason is obliterated so that disconnected dreams and categorical confusions overtake the structures of signification that constitute the real. In the words of Levinas, "for pure suffering . . . a beyond takes shape in the inter-human" (1988b, 158)—a beyond that is beyond truth, thought, and reality. It was not kilometers, says Filip Müller, "which separated them from their homes, but simply this world"—and this pain—"so alien and so far from their own familiar homes" (1979a, 76). Locked into the beyond of absolute suffering, the denizen of the Kingdom of Night confronts a distance that is not a distance between here and there but between the real and the unreal; it is not a spatial distance but an ontological distance. "Our tragedy," as Elie Wiesel expresses it, "was that children were old and old men were as helpless as children, so that there was a confusion, a total confusion of concepts and virtues and powers" (Patterson 1991, 21). Fathers are not fathers, sons no longer sons; the real is not real, the world is not world. It is not that one world has replaced another, as one might infer from Müller's remark; rather, the real has broken down so that there is no place where a world can make its appearance. That place, or that space, emerges in the midst of the relation that makes the father who he is. With the loss of the father all relations that go into the structure of the real are overturned.

One finds numerous examples of this confusion throughout the Holocaust memoirs. Moshe Sandberg, for instance, recalls, "The horse, pig and dog got more and better food than we did. Life became topsy-turvy. It was not the pig and the dog that ate man's leavings, but the reverse" (1968, 87). Gisella Perl writes, "The healthy, the talented, the beautiful were ruthlessly exterminated, but everything abnormal was a source of constant amusement and enjoyment to our jailers" (1948, 131–32). And Zivia Lubetkin remembers, "Absolute darkness reigned within the underground kingdom of the main bunker of the Jewish Fighting Organization on Mila 18. Outside a beautiful spring day must certainly have been shining brightly, but the order of life had been reversed in the bunker. Day had turned into night, and night into day" (1981, 206). In this last passage "had been reversed" is a translation of the Hebrew *nithafakh hagalgal* (Lubetkin 1978, 144), literally, "the cycle was inverted," once again underscoring the confusion of the categories of reality. These examples of how the unreal manifests itself have more in common than it may seem at first glance. Sandberg's memory of the reversal of the human and the animal, Perl's recollection of the confusion between the hale and the abnormal, Lubetkin's observance of the inversion of the cycles of light and dark—all of it comes to a breakdown of height, which, as Levinas has noted, "introduces a sense into being" (1987a, 100). As sacred history, tradition is not behind but above one. When reality breaks down the sky cracks; the structure of reality is a vertical structure; the father is situated in this structure as the one one looks up to. Here the relation is more clear between the memory of the father and the recovery of tradition in the Holocaust memoir. In the memoir the movement of remembrance is a turning inward that is an ascent upward. Memory's refusal of the breakdown described by Sandberg, Perl, and Lubetkin is a recovery of height in the order of being. It is a reinstatement of the sky that had been turned—or overturned—into a cemetery.

One understands, then, how certain memories of the sky might reflect the memory of reality's breakdown. "One evening at dusk," Fania Fénelon relates a very telling moment, "Florette commented on the magnificent sunset. But the distant red glow wasn't the sun" (1977, 144). No, it was not the sun: it was the glow of the ditch aflame with the burning corpses of the Hungarian Jews. Both the sun that sets and the sun that rises are eclipsed by the glow of the Auschwitz sky, as noted in Kitty Hart's memory of her arrival at Auschwitz: "Dawn was breaking. Or was it really the dawn? A reddish glow through the mist was flickering in the weirdest way, and there was a sickly, fatty, cloying smell" (1982, 60). Reality breaks down in these instances with the realization that the sun is not the sun above but another flame brought low where it consumes the earth and the mothers, fathers, and children of the earth. Just as the father needs the mother so that both may be who they are, so the earth needs the sky, needs the sun in the sky, in order to be the earth. The sun, moreover, shines not only in the sky but also on the earth, a point made evident in a refrain from the Maidanek Anthem as recalled by Paul Trepman:

> There has never been,
> Nor will there ever be,
> Anywhere on earth,
> A sun like that which shines
> Upon our Maidanek. (1978, 137)

In the light of this perversion of the sun Rudolf Vrba remembers, "Barracks, barbed wire and beyond that, nothing. Not a tree, not a shrub. Desolation. Maidanek had been set apart from civilisation" (Vrba and Bestic 1964, 58). Without a sun there can be no tree, no shrub—no reality. Once again, what sets Maidanek apart from civilization is not kilometers but the absence of the sun, of the height, of the tree, of all coexistence with these things that would constitute reality. "Reality," says José Ortega y Gasset, "is not the existence of the wall alone, and by itself—as realism wished—but neither is it the existence of the wall in me [idealism], as my thought, my existence alone and for myself. Reality is my coexistence with the thing" (1969, 147). But the light of the sun is needed to perceive the thing. The breakdown of reality in the Kingdom of Night did not lie in the fact that walls were erected to isolate the human being from the world; rather, it lay in the fact that all walls, all borders and limitations, were erased. One function of memory, then, is to reconstitute the frontiers according to which reality is delineated: the thing is recovered as the thing lost, yes, but it is not lost to memory.

Memory speaks, and the word seeks to recover its contact with its meaning—even if it is a word unuttered. Especially if it is a word unuttered. So
Charlotte Delbo remembers, "Some have not seen anything and ask questions. Others wonder if they did see and say nothing" (1968, 78). One need
not ask what might have been seen, for the vision of unreality is not an act
of seeing. What vision could be more unreal, more invisible to the eye of
understanding, and more expressive of the unreality of the antiworld than
the vision of those who dug up bodies and burned them as recalled by Leon
Wells? He writes, "The *Untersturmführer* . . . orders the three leather crafts-
men in the brigade to make the fire chief and his assistant two hats with
horns, like those of a devil. From then on, we march to work with the fire
chief and his assistant leading us, wearing their horns and carrying their
hooks they used to stir the fire" (1978, 187). This example of the Nazi
imagination provides still more evidence for the position that the difficulty
in approaching the borders of this Kingdom lies not in the lack of imagination but in the collapse of thought and the subsequent breakdown of reality.
A scene from Dante's *Inferno?* Hell? No. To situate this scene even in hell
would be to order it in a vertical reality that the scene itself undermines. The
bodies are piled high. The flames ascend on high. But there is no "high," for
these are the bodies of mothers and fathers who call out to their children-
turned-to-devils. "Many bodies," Wells relates, "are lying around with open
mouths. Could they be trying to say: 'We are your own mothers, fathers, who
raised you and took care of you. Now you are burning us.' Maybe they would
forgive us" (1978, 141–42). Here the memory becomes a plea, "Father, forgive me." As soon as the plea for forgiveness is introduced to memory, the
father once again becomes a father. For, like a monument atop a grave, the
memory signifies the one lost to the murder of reality. And the man made
into a devil or a dog becomes a child once more—or rather, one who was
once a child.

"Nothing," Vladka Meed closes her memoir. "Nothing was left of my past,
of my life in the ghetto—not even the grave of my father" (1973, 335), where
"of my past" is a translation of the Yiddish *fon meyin kiyndheyit* (1948, 358),
meaning "of my childhood." The human being's past, as a human being, is
precisely her childhood, and her childhood is couched first in her mother
and then in her father. This is where the loss of the father leads: to the loss
of the child. It is a child robbed of childhood who weeps at the grave of

which her father was robbed—now the grave of memory. When, in the movement of remembrance, the grave that is nowhere becomes the grave of memory, a summons rises up from the edges of that grave. In *Night* Elie Wiesel reveals what that summons is, when, describing the death of his father, he writes, "There were no prayers at his grave. No candles were lit to his memory. His last word was my name. A summons to which I did not respond" (1960, 112–13). Yet this memory from the child whose childhood was consumed by the Night is a response, a *yartseit* candle, a prayer said here over the one lost there. In the midst of the memory is the summons that calls it forth. Assuming the aspect of a prayer said for the father and summoned by the father, the memoir becomes a link to God the Father. I have already noted that, according to Jewish tradition, the father is associated with the *Sefirah* of *Chakhmah*, or Wisdom. Here, according to the same tradition, "Wisdom is the conduit of God's essence" (*Bahir* 1979, 92). As the guardian of tradition, the father is the guardian of one of the avenues of God's revelation. There is no murder of the father, then, that does not entail a murder of God the Father. And there is no memory of the loss of the father that does not include the memory of God.

3

The Memory of God

According to Jewish tradition, the mother and father are who they are inasmuch as they take a direct part in the Creator's creation of life. Any memory of their loss, therefore, entails a memory of God. This is an essential feature of the Holocaust memoir, for there can be no Jewish memory of the attempted annihilation of the Jewish people without this memory; transcending all linguistic, cultural, national, and racial divisions, a certain relation to *ha-Shem* is what makes a Jew a Jew. There is nothing of nostalgia or reminiscence, however, surrounding the memory of God. Rather, it is an agonized engagement with the Eternal One as one who is repeatedly, eternally, lost and recovered, as one whose immortality and infinity lie in His capacity to be murdered an infinite number of times only to return time and time again, eternally. "Loss of faith for some," Elie Wiesel remembers, "equalled discovery of God for others" (1968, 20). In either case, denied or embraced but not ignored, God dominates the memoir. This aspect of the Holocaust memoir then, is the first thing that I consider. Because, according to the Talmud (Kiddushin 30b), God is a third participant in the creation of a child, I next examine how the memory of the Holy One is tied to the death of this sacred little one. His eyes overflowing with the wonder of life, the child is the one closest to the God who commands one to choose life. Further, I explore the presence of prayer in the memoir, for God's presence in the memoir manifests itself as prayer and as the memory of prayer. " 'I am the prayer,' speaks the Shekina" in Martin Buber's *Legend of the Baal-Shem*. "Men believe they pray before God, but this is not so, for the prayer is itself divinity" (1969, 27). The Oneness of God so central to Jewish tradition lies in this idea that God is never the object of worship but is all subject. In prayer it is God who addresses God; it is He who opens the lips of the one who invokes Him, as affirmed each day in the opening utterance of the *Amidah*, the daily prayer of the Jews. And it is He who remembers in the memory of this memory. Thus, I close this discussion with a discussion of the memory of memory, which at times manifests itself as the memory of memory's loss. There can be no recovery of Jewish tradition without this recovery of God and memory. Addressing the Holy One, memory in the Holocaust memoir addresses memory itself. The One of whom one says, "Blessed be He," is the One who confers His blessing on the Jewish movement of remembrance in the Holocaust memoir—because and in spite of the one who remembers.

Refused or Affirmed But Not Ignored

The attempted genocide of the Jews was also an attempted deicide, as in Judith Dribben's memoir, when, upon the burning of a synagogue, a Nazi declares, "The Jewish God is burnt to ashes" (1969, 24). He is the One whom the enemy sets out to murder in the destruction not only of the Jews but of every trace of Jewish tradition. "He who kills," as Elie Wiesel has said, "kills God" (1976, 58). Yet Wiesel also insists, "God is one; He is everywhere. And if He is everywhere, then He is in evil and injustice too, and also in the supreme evil: death. It is man's task to free God of this evil" (1990a, 25). God abides not only in the victim but in the executioner as well. Ka-tzetnik expresses this notion with terrifying eloquence when he recalls a moment from the death camp and cries out to God, "Who is the being within me now delivered to the crematorium—and why? And who is the being within him delivering me to the crematorium—and why? For you know that at this moment the two of us, dispatcher and dispatched, are equal sons of man, both created by you, in your image" (1989, 11). This is a condition undreamt of in philosophy. As Fackenheim has noted, although Nietzsche and Sartre may have found some exhilaration in the idea that God is dead or absent, there is only terror in a God who is still present but has become an enemy (1989, 250). Here God becomes the absolutely Other—Other to Himself— implicating not only His creation in an undoing of the pronouncement that it is "very good," but also the human being created in his image. "It is impossible to believe anything in a world that has ceased to regard man as man," Simon Wiesenthal expresses it. "One really begins to think that God is on leave. Otherwise the present state of things wouldn't be possible. God must be away. And He has no deputy" (1976, 14–15). Where the translation has the word *deputy*, in the German text one finds the word *Stellvertreter* (Wiesenthal 1970, 13), which means "representative," that is, one who may signify God's presence; and the primary representative of God in His creation is the one created in His image. The images of creature and Creator, then, are inextricably linked, even—or especially—in their undoing. "At last you must admit, Rabbi," one reads in the first of Ka-tzetnik's visions in *Shivitti*, "that God of the Diaspora himself is climbing into this truck—a mussulman" (1989, 7). And so the ontological assault on the human becomes a metaphysical assault on the divine.

As one might gather from Wiesenthal's remarks, the effectiveness of the assault initially manifests itself as a loss of belief in God and everything else that belongs to the Good. One finds it also in Wieslaw Kielar's *Anus Mundi* where he writes, "If He existed—and it is in this belief that I was brought up—how could He allow these murders of helpless human beings, carried out by other human beings whose soldiers wore on the buckle of their belts the words 'God with us'?" (1980, 177). And, gazing upon the "forlorn and stupefied women" surrounding her, Sara Zyskind confesses that she "began to doubt the existence of God. . . . Perhaps God himself had begun to despise His own people" (1981, 195–96). The Hebrew word rendered as "existence" is *keyam* (Zyskind 1978, 181), which also means "permanence," "everlastingness," and "statute." God's existence lies in His abiding presence in the form of His Law; when the interhuman relation that reveals the truth and the holiness of the Law is lost, so is God. Yet in both of these instances God remains in the form of the terror over the prospect that He is not simply lost but has become the enemy: Kielar remembers the belt buckles of the murderers that read "God with us," signifying Zyskind's fear that perhaps He has come to hate the Jews. Only a believer can lose his belief; only one who is filled with the piety that itself bears the imprint of the divine can insist on his nonbelief. This point comes to light very starkly in Primo Levi's *The Drowned and the Saved*: "The experience of the Lager with its frightful iniquity confirmed me in my non-belief. . . . A prayer under those conditions would have been not only absurd but blasphemous. . . . I rejected that temptation" (1988, 145). The word from the Italian text translated as "non-belief" is *laicita* (Levi 1986a, 117), whose root is *lai*, meaning "lamentation": the nonbelief in this case is not so much the absence of faith as the presence of an outcry rooted and raised in the name of the holy. Levi refuses belief because he refuses the blasphemy and impiety of the nonbeliever. God cannot be ignored.

"Faith stands upon itself," one will recall Paul Tillich's insight, "and justifies itself against those who attack it, because they can attack it only in the name of another faith. It is the triumph of the dynamics of faith that any denial of faith is itself an expression of faith, of an ultimate concern" (1957, 126–27). This may be why, according to Talmudic tradition, God likes to be overcome by His children (see Bava Metzia 59b)—particularly in the light of what befalls His children—even in their refusal to believe. After listening to the screams of children being slaughtered, Kitty Hart writes, "You find it hard to believe that any faith in a benevolent God could be of value. . . . Yet I longed to produce Jewish children to make up, in however small a way, for so many who had been exterminated" (1982, 156). This is an expression of faith despite faith, for the longing to return a child to a world where children were marked for murder is steeped in the faith and ultimate concern of which Tillich speaks. God vanishes to the rear, but "there is no purpose in seeking Him in that rear," as André Neher has said, "for God is already out there in front, on the horizon-edge of a Promise which only restores what it has taken, without ever being fulfilled" (1981, 123). The child that Hart would have is the embodiment of this Promise "out there in front," revealed not in its fulfillment but in the human being's longing for what was lost, for the benevolence of the God who was lost. The Holocaust memoir is both the memory of and the longing for that God; it is God's memory of and longing for Himself, for His own deliverance from the valley of the shadow of death. Alexander Donat's citation of Chaim Nachman Bialik's *In the City of Slaughter* comes to mind: "Where the thunderbolts to avenge? / To shake the world and rend the sky?" (1978, 99). Thus, in a world turned on end, in the antiworld, God summons His witness to an affirmation that assumes the dress of refusal. If God reveals Himself through the movement of the witness, He reveals Himself perhaps most profoundly in the undoing of the witness, even in the rebellion of the witness.

An incident from the Hasidic tradition comes to mind in this connection. Rabbi Levi Yitzchak of Berditchev once knew a tailor who, after confessing his sins one Yom Kippur, cried out to God, "But You, O Lord, have taken away infants from their mothers, and mothers from their infants. Let us, on this Day of Days, be quits. If You forgive me, then I will forgive You." To which the Rabbi replied, "Oh, Yankel, Yankel, why did you let God off so lightly?" (Rabinowicz 1988, 63). As striking as this example from a tradition of conflict with God may be, however, it does not approach the undoing in Rudolf Vrba's description of a devout man named Moses Sonenschein. "It is the will of

God," he would mutter in the face of one horror after another, seeing girls freeze to death, finding the bones of children in a pile of ashes. Then one day he was overwhelmed by the unworldly, antiworldly screams of a group of women on their way to the gas chamber. "Moses Sonenschein murmured: 'There is no God. . . .' Then his voice rose to a shout: *'There is no God! And if there is, curse Him, curse Him, curse Him!'*" (1964, 160–61; emphasis in the original). Once again one collides with the terror of a God still present but who has become the enemy, not the One to whom one offers prayers but to whom one shouts refusal. If the Holocaust memoir bears the marks of prayer, it is often a prayer filled with anger, "existentially and dialectically affirmative," as Wiesel says. "For the fact that I pray means someone is there to listen, that what I am saying is not uttered to a great void. But what I do say, I say with anger" (Patterson 1991, 83). It is this anger of a believer that underlies Wiesel's refusal to accept God's silence, his refusal in *Night* to fast on Yom Kippur (1960, 75). In *One Generation After* he explains, "He who says no to God is not necessarily a renegade. Everything depends on the way he says it, and why. One can say anything as long as it is for man, not against him" (1970a, 216). This specifically Jewish tradition goes back to Abraham's argument with God over the fate of Sodom and Gomorrah; in fact, after his show of hospitality, this is Abraham's first interaction with God from the time when he entered into the Covenant. It is precisely as the People of the Covenant that the authors of the Holocaust memoirs take up their remembrance of God and this argument with God; not to thus engage God would indeed amount to a loss of the tradition altogether. "There comes a time," says Wiesel, "when only those who do believe in God will cry out in wrath and anguish" (1990b, 20). And so he cries,

> "Whether God is silent
> Or weeps,
> Ani maamin.
> Ani maamin for him,
> In spite of him.
> I believe in you,
> Even against your will.
> Even if you punish me
> For believing in you." (Wiesel 1973a, 107)

This is the song lost to the ashes but found again in the Holocaust memoir's righteously defiant memory of God. This is the memoir's memory and recovery of holy tradition despite the Holy One.

This is the song that turns memory against God in a turning of God against Himself. The Hebrew word for "question," Wiesel points out, "is *sheelah*, and the *alef lamed* of God's name are part of the fabric of that word. Therefore God is in the question" (Wiesel 1985, 3:297). It is by means of a terrible question that God turns or returns in the midst of remembrance. "The essence of man," to recall Wiesel's words, "is to be a question, and the essence of the question is to be without answer" (1964, 187). The essence of the memory of God in the Holocaust memoir, too, is to be just such a question. Although this memory cast in the mode of a question assumes a variety of forms, all assert, either directly or dialectically, an affirmation of God. "Man raises himself toward God by the questions he asks Him," Moshe teaches Eliezer in Wiesel's *Night* (1960, 16); in the Holocaust memoir this raising of oneself toward God becomes, in various ways, a turning of God toward Himself. "Did God take leave of his senses?" asks Isabella Leitner, for example (1978, 4). Pushing the question further, Eugene Heimler asks more boldly of God Himself, "Almighty God, why have you done this to us? . . . You are wicked, O Lord, as wicked as man" (1959, 30). Jewish tradition holds that God is the shadow of man; when men do nothing, God folds His arms. Therefore, as Heimler suggests, there is a parallel between the movements of God and the actions of human beings. The slumber of the one is the sleeping sickness, the sickness unto death, of the other.

Hence, Ana Vinocur cries out to awaken both humanity and the Guardian who, according to tradition, never sleeps. Both must be stirred if tradition is to be recovered. "It may be too late by the time you wake up," she cries out to the world. "And God? . . . I sometimes thought that the crying of the children was too weak to reach Him. But He had to hear them, because there was more and more crying. O God! Wake up and see what they have done to the people who have always kept faith with you!" (1976, 66). Where one reads "kept faith with you" the Spanish text has *mantener su fe y identidad para contigo* (1972, 134), "faith and identity": the Guardian of Israel is the essence of Israel, so that if the Sleepless One should sleep, then Israel would no longer be Israel (a point certainly not lost to the Nazi killers). How is God to be awakened? By addressing Him in these words of memory that address humanity, by the very memory of Him who lives in the memory of humanity. Thus, on a barracks wall filled with inscriptions that return His Name to the Nameless One, Vinocur inscribes her own outcry, one that might serve as the epigram—or epitaph—on every Holocaust memoir: "I ask God to take into account all that is written here" (1976, 71). Once again it proves useful to look at the original text where the word translated as "God" is *Todopoderoso*

(Vinocur 1972, 145), the "Almighty" or "He who can do all," and who, therefore, must do *this*. Yet the *Todopoderoso* is in need of human help: it is they who must take into account all that is written here if He is to awaken from His slumber and they from theirs. And so one recalls an insight from Nikos Kazantzakis: "Within the province of our ephemeral flesh all of God is imperiled. He cannot be saved unless we save him with our own struggle; nor can we be saved unless he is saved. . . . It is not God who will save us— it is we who will save God, by battling, by creating, and by transmuting matter into spirit" (1963, 105–6). And this transmutation is effected by memory, as one gathers when Kazantzakis writes, "I tremble. Are *you* my God? Your body is steeped in memory" (1963, 90). Although these words do not appear in a Holocaust memoir, they characterize the essence of the memoir.

"God was weeping for Auschwitz," writes Ka-tzetnik, "and his tears were running down the eyes of a man, his handiwork" (1989, 51). As much as any word on any page of the Holocaust memoir, these tears are the signifiers of the memory of God in the Holocaust memoir, the signs declaring that He may be refused or affirmed but not ignored. Through such tears comes the teaching that Gregor's father offers his son in Wiesel's *The Gates of the Forest*: "God's final victory, my son, lies in man's inability to reject Him. You think . . . you're crying out your hatred and rebellion, but all you're doing is telling Him how much you need His support" (1966a, 33). And, in the light of what has been said, it may be that through this outcry God is telling people how much *He* needs *their* support. The human and the divine work together, a Jewish notion expressed by Thomas Geve in his memoir when he writes, "We fellow prisoners respected the devotees of the Bible mainly because they helped us. . . . 'Only our conduct can be our saviour,' they acknowledged bravely and stubbornly. 'Through it He reveals Himself'" (1981, 143–44). Revealing Himself through our conduct, as well as through our outcry, God assumes a human aspect, and the human being takes on a divine image. The recovery of tradition is a recovery of this image and aspect of the human and the divine. And the one in whom the two are most closely associated, according to Jewish tradition, is the child. Remember the lines from Wiesel's *Ani Maamin*: "These children / Have taken your countenance, / O God" (1973a, 57). Hence, the memory of God, refused or affirmed but not ignored, is the memory of the child. But in the Holocaust memoir, to borrow from Edmond Jabès's *Return to the Book*, "a Jewish child has death as a cradle and the curse of death as a cradlesong" (1977, 195). I consider, then, the memoir's cradlesong in its memory of God.

The Death of the Child

Emil Fackenheim observes that "once Moses offered his life in behalf of the children and succeeded. Adam Czerniakow [head of the Jewish Council in the Warsaw Ghetto] did not merely offer but gave his life for the children. However, unlike Moses he failed. The enemy was more sleepless and slumberless than the God of Israel" (1990, 47). The children were among those who were first targeted for extermination not only to annihilate the Jewish future that they represented but to destroy the Jewish tradition that they sustained. Says Wiesel, "It was as thought the Nazi killers knew precisely what children represent to us. According to our tradition, the entire world subsists thanks to them" (1978, 178–79). To be sure, many texts from the tradition attest to the importance of the child both to the life of the tradition and to the Holy One whose presence is revealed through the tradition. In the *Midrash Rabbah*, for example, it is written, "R. Judah said: Come and see how beloved are the children by the Holy One, blessed be He. The Sanhedrin were exiled but the *Shechinah* did not go into exile with them. When, however, the children were exiled, the *Shechinah* went into exile with them" (1961, 7:106; emphasis in the original). The Rabbi Judah cited here is Rabbi Yehudah ha-Nasi, the redactor of the Mishnah; early on in rabbinic tradition, then, one sees a tight association between the presence of children and the presence of God or the *Shekhinah* in the world. A slightly different expression of this idea may be found in the *En Jacob* where once again Rabbi Judah is invoked: "Resh Lakish in the name of R. Juda the Nasi said: 'The world would not be sustained if it were not for the breath of [praise coming forth from] the school children" (1916, 1:196). And in the *Zohar* one reads, "Who is it that upholds the world and causes the patriarchs to appear? It is the voice of tender children studying the Torah; and for their sake the world is saved" (1984, 1:4). In the Jewish tradition, therefore, the memory of the child is central to the memory of God. And in the death of the child one sees Him in the throes of death.

If the Holocaust memoir is distinguished not by the memory of one's life but by the memory of one's death, the death of the self is linked to the death of this sacred other. Hence, when her little brother dies Ana Vinocur writes, "Nothing could compensate for this eternal emptiness; my soul, my mind, my thoughts, my heart had been torn to pieces by the loss of such an innocent, pure, and beloved creature" (1976, 40). It must not be forgotten that this death comes not by disease or mishap but as the calculated murder not only of this sacred other but of the Other with a capital O, the Holy One

Himself, from whom all sanctity derives. Elie Wiesel drives home this point with devastating pathos in *Night* where one encounters one of the most dreadful of all the memories in all these memoirs—the hanging of a child. In the assembly of prisoners forced to witness the hanging the young Eliezer hears a Jew next to him asking, "Where is God? Where is He now?" And from within his soul comes the terrifying reply: "Where is He? Here He is— He is hanging here on these gallows" (1960, 71). Eliezer is himself a child who sees his own soul die with the little one on the gallows. The God beseeched to heed the cries of the children is Himself reduced to their outcry. In the words of Issahar's wife, the woman in Wiesel's *A Jew Today* who sees dead children everywhere, "They are God's memory" (1978, 81). It is the memory of the One who hangs on the gallows that speaks through the memory of the memoir.

As with the death of the mother and father, then, the death of the child is the death of all the child signifies. As Wiesel states it, "The death of a child is the death of innocence, the death of God in the heart of man. And he who does not drink deeply of this truth, who does not shout it from the rooftops, is a man devoid of heart, of God, he has not seen the misty eyes of a child expiring without a whimper" (1970b, 99). The death of the child begins with the death of the child as a *sign*, that is, with the death of the image of the child: like the mother and the father, the child dies before he dies. The child is the vessel of the yet-to-be and of all meaning harbored by a living future; with the death of the child the future is made dead, absent, turned back on the child himself. Here the child is no longer the flower of youth but the broken shoot of old age, forced into a category robbed of all meaning. "For them days were months," Wiesenthal remembers. "When I saw them with toys in their hands, they looked unfamiliar, uncanny, like old men playing with childish things" (1976, 47). The Eternal One whose trace is seen along the horizon of a future time is erased in this erasure of time. In the child the Promise from a past goes out to meet the future. But when the child collapses into old age, time and eternity collapse with him, and the Word of the Promise is lost. Another symptom of the mutilation of the child's image, then, is the loss of the child's word. "Little Bina," Leon Wells says of his younger sister, "whom I remembered as a lively child, had completely altered. She went about sad and unhappy, and hardly spoke. . . . She would neither talk nor laugh nor play" (1978, 107). In the play of the child lies the play, the movement, of life, a celebration of the life and meaning signified by the child. If, as Levinas argues, "man is . . . the irruption of God within Being" (1989d, 202), the first form of that irruption is the play of the child.

When that play ceases, being loses its significance. With this in mind one recalls a passage from Alexander Donat's memoir where he says of his three-year-old son, "The lively child whose nature had been movement and play-fulness now sat for hours at a time without moving. Whenever I seemed to be leaving him, his only reaction was to tighten his grip on me, uttering only the single word: '*Daddy*' " (1978, 94). This single word not only undoes the father it announces the ontological undoing of being, for it is a word that both demands a response and makes all response impossible.

The evil of the pain that Levinas describes as "the explosion and most profound articulation of absurdity" (1988b, 157) lies not so much in the pain experienced by a father in a moment like the one Donat relates but in the suffering of the child himself. If the profound absurdity is proclaimed in the word to which it is impossible to respond, it explodes in the child whom it is impossible to save. The child *as such* is precisely the one whom one must save; this claim of the child upon one is what links the essence of the child to one's own. But in the antiworld the child is condemned even in the midst of rescue. Who can forget in this regard the haunting figure of a man trying to save a child in Wiesel's *Ani Maamin*:

> I run,
> And while I run,
> I am thinking:
> This is insane
> This Jewish child
> Will not be spared.
> I run and run
> And cry. (1973a, 89)

What Wiesel expresses so poetically invades the dream — or the nightmare — about a ghetto child named Eli, as related by Wiesenthal: "His father brought him to me in his arms. As he approached he covered his eyes with his hands. Behind the two figures raged a sea of flames from which they were fleeing. I wanted to take Eli, but all that existed was a bloody mess" (1976, 71). This is what is left of the image of the child—a bloody mess, to which all of Creation is reduced. Similarly, Nathan Shapell summons from his memory a child whom he had "rescued" from a roundup of children in the ghetto, "In the moment I looked down at her tiny, pinched face and heard my voice telling her, an infant still, that she was on her own, the insanity and depravity of the monsters who had made this moment happen engraved her small face indelibly in my heart" (1974, 75–76). "Lay this Word upon your hearts," one is told in the *Shema*. But here, where the Word of God was once engraved there is now engraved the face that bespeaks the obliteration of that Word and of the Creation it sustains. The memory of God is steeped in this face that Shapell invokes, in this face that no longer speaks but with a whimper calls upon one to answer the ontological "Why?" that overshadows the memory. What does Sim Kessel, to take another example, remember of Drancy? "The children. Some nights I still dream of the children at Drancy, clutching at their mothers' skirts and crying incessantly" (1972, 46); and on the train to Auschwitz, he recalls, "Our silence was disturbed only by the whimpering of frightened children" (1972, 50). These dreams that invade the nights of Wiesenthal and Kessel are the stuff of which the antireality of the Kingdom of Night is made. In the Holocaust memoir they are the stuff of memory.

"To dream," Elie Wiesel writes, "is to invite a future, if not to justify it, and to deny death, which denies dreams" (1973b, 64). But when the dream is of the death of the child, nothing can be justified. "The ego is the very crisis of the being of a being," says Levinas, "because I begin to ask myself if my being is justified" (1989a, 85). The death of the child precludes all but one response, or rather it precludes all response because even a "No" would imply the intelligibility of a "Yes." Recalling a child who was found alive among the bodies in a gas chamber at Birkenau, Miklos Nyiszli writes, "Everyone wanted to help, as if she were his own child" (1960, 89). But the order of being in Birkenau, the reversal of being, makes it impossible to help the very one most in need of help. There the stranger, the widow, and above all the orphan—who, according to Jewish tradition, are those nearest to God—are precisely the ones most distant from God. Yet in its attempt to recover that tradition the Holocaust memoir establishes the child as the one nearest to memory, as the one who takes over memory, involuntarily, like the horrible scream that reverberates throughout Sara Nomberg-Przytyk's memory of the slaughter of children burned alive: "Suddenly, the stillness was broken by the screaming of children, . . . a scream repeated a thousand times in a single word, 'Mama,' a scream that increased in intensity every second, enveloping the whole camp. Our lips parted without our being conscious of what we were doing, and a scream of despair tore out of our throats. . . . At the end everything was enveloped in death and silence" (1985, 81). In the Polish text the phrase rendered as "death and silence" is *milczenie śmierci* (n.d., 56), which, more exactly, means "the silence of death." In the Nazis' ontological perversion of the image or sign of the child, this silence is what the child aflame comes to signify. One gets a hint of why Wiesel comments on Abraham's argument with God by saying, "God, knowing the future of the Jews, wished to teach them the need of arguing, even against Himself" (1991, 378). But if the argument against God is an argument for life, then how can it be sustained when the child who had symbolized life is transformed into a symbol of death?

It is in a reversal of just such a transformation that Gerda Klein remembers, "I had learned to associate children with death" (1957, 227). She remembers this association in order to insist on a dissociation between the child's coming into being and a crime against being, which, as Fackenheim has argued, is a *novum* in history (1990, 87). The memory of the *novum* instills it with a history so that the process of remembrance opens a prospect for tearing asunder what should never have been joined together; it opens a path toward a recovery or a rebirth over against the linkage between birth and capital crime. Thus, memory introduces a dialectic to such observations as this one by Germaine Tillion in her memoir *Ravensbrück*, "If children were born they were drowned immediately" (1975, 73). No child, of course, is born by itself; the babe has a mother who, along with the infant, brings into the world a renewal of the world, a participation in the work of the Creator. Born to die, however, the child is no longer a child, the mother no longer a mother, Creation no longer Creation. And so in Isabella Leitner's memoir one reads, "You, dear darling, . . . belong to the gas chamber. Your mother has no rights. She only brought forth fodder for the gas chamber. She is not a mother" (1978, 31–32). This task of making the child into fodder for the gas chamber, it is noted, falls to women who must take the infant from the mother and see to its death—women who might themselves be mothers. It is they who, in Leitner's words, experienced the "smell of real life" before the infant was delivered over to death "so the SS wouldn't discover who the mother was" (1978, 49). But who could hide the mother from herself? A world in which a mother may die to save her child is a world that retains its ontological order, one upon which God may still pronounce, "It is very good." The reversal of this order is the mark of the antiworld ruled by the SS antigod. "Childbirth," writes Gisella Perl, "was still to me the most beautiful, the greatest miracle of nature. I loved those newborn babies not as a doctor but as a mother and it was again and again my own child whom I killed to save the life of a woman" (1948, 82). Her friend Olga Lengyel sees the terrible significance of this situation: "The Germans succeeded in making murderers of even us. To this day the picture of those murdered babies haunts me. Our own children had perished in the gas chambers and were cremated in the Birkenau ovens, and we dispatched the lives of others before their first voices had left their tiny lungs" (1972, 111). Again, the word smothered in the smothering of these voices is the Word of the One from whose hand they come. But, like His Word, His hand is withdrawn even as it is extended. Hands that should cradle the child turn her over to the cradle of death.

"Is it true, my dear God?" Livia Jackson puts a question to the One grown deaf. "Is it true that little children are trampled underfoot in the gas chamber? . . . They told us. And I heard and screamed" (1980, 105). Perhaps God hears after all. Perhaps He hears and screams in the screams of Livia Jackson. But a scream is no response. If the child and the God he is tied to are to be recovered, then this recovery can happen only in an act of response and responsibility. The movement of remembrance in the Holocaust memoir is itself just such an act; couched in the memory of God and in the memory of the death of the child as well is the summons to a responsibility for the child. To be sure, that summons is what links the former with the latter. It arises not from the head or the heart of the individual but from beyond the human being, from the tradition that insists on the association between the Holy One and the holiness of the little one. The memory of this responsibility that recovers a remnant of the child assumes a variety of forms in the Holocaust memoir. Eugene Heimler, for example, recalls a scene from Buchenwald, when a Russian boy asked him if he was responsible for the children. "I answered 'yes,' " he relates. "I was indeed responsible" (1959, 165). That such a responsibility is linked to a recovery of Jewish tradition is made clear in Paul Trepman's *Among Men and Beasts*. There he remembers a remark made by Mira Jakubowicz in the Warsaw Ghetto: "For many years I was far away from Jewish tradition, from the Jewish way of life that is so full of trials and sorrows. But the suffering which has come to our people now has only strengthened me in my resolve never to abandon our Jewish children" (1978, 194). Thus, one has a reply to Vladka Meed's question: "How could one go on teaching children so close to the deportation center?" (1973, 149). This teaching of children even in the Warsaw Ghetto is precisely what retains their image and their essence as children. And those who teach are as much in need of the teaching as the children are, for if one's children are not children, then one is not a human being.

No reply to Meed's question, however, can dispel it. Hidden in the question is the face of a child who silently addresses one but whose word eludes one. The sole access to that word lies in the Holocaust memoir. Primo Levi illustrates this point in his memory of a three-year-old boy called

"Hurbinek" (they did not know his real name), whom he met in Auschwitz after the Russians liberated the camp on 27 January 1945. Born in Auschwitz, the child, uttered only one, indecipherable word. "Hurbinek, the nameless," Levi describes him, "died in the first days of March 1945, free but not redeemed. Nothing remains of him: he bears witness through these words of mine" (1965, 22–23). One recalls that the Italian word for "word," *parola*, also means "promise," and once again one is reminded of the Promise that recedes into unintelligibility yet returns through the words, through the *parola*, of memory. For the word for "through" in Levi's phrase "through these words" is *attraverso* (1989, 166), which means "across," rather than "by means of." Memory places the lost child on another shore, over *there*, as though fetched from oblivion. Thus, the movement of memory and recovery in the Holocaust memoir situates the child in all the "theres," which calls to mind the Hebrew word for "heaven," *shamayim*, the abode of the Holy One whom tradition associates with the child. The means of reaching across the distance that separates one from Him is prayer. And so the memoir prays.

Prayer in the Midst of Memory

In *One Generation After* Elie Wiesel provides the link that joins together the memory of God, the death of the child, and prayer in the midst of memory. He writes, that is, he prays, "God of Abraham, Isaac and Jacob, enable me to forgive You and enable the child I once was to forgive me too. I no longer ask You for the life of that child, nor even for his faith. I only beg You to listen to him and act in such a way that You and I can listen to him together" (1970a, 242). To transmit the word of the child is to listen to the child. And to listen to the child, in this instance, is to pray, or perhaps better: it is to entrust to the child who is over *there* the prayer that one would offer to God. A tale from the Jewish tradition, in fact, suggests that only through the child does prayer penetrate the gates of heaven. It is a parable told by the Maggid of Dubno about a father who took his little boy on a long, treacherous journey to a wondrous city. Whenever they came to a narrow crossing, a dangerous river, or a high mountain, the father would lift his little boy onto his shoulders, carry him over, and set him safely on the other side. Finally, they arrived one day at their destination, the wondrous city. It was dusk, however, and the gates of the great wall that surrounded the city had already been locked for the night; the only openings in the wall were a few small windows. Realizing that he had only one possible hope of gaining entrance to the city, the father raised up his little boy so he could climb through a window and unlock the gates from within. And so it is when one longs for one's prayers to have access to heaven. Since the day when the Sanctuary was destroyed, explained the Maggid, the gates of prayer have been locked. Only through the child, who is lighter than an eagle, can one be redeemed. "For the outcry of children," he said, "is formed by the breath of mouths unblemished by sin, and is therefore capable of piercing the windows of Heaven" (Kitov 1973, 1:75–76). There is, of course, an important difference between the passage from Wiesel and the Maggid's parable. In the Holocaust memoir the child's outcry is buried in the words that convey the remembrance of the child. Because that outcry assails the windows of heaven, memory in the Holocaust assumes the aspect of prayer.

Before taking this discussion any further, however, a word must be said about the nature of prayer according to the Jewish tradition. Within that tradition, as Levinas points out, "prayer never asks anything for oneself; strictly speaking, it makes no demands at all, but is an elevation of the soul. This describes true prayer, at least, or the prayer of the just man, prayer which conforms—if we are to believe *Nefesh ha'Hayyim*—to Jewish piety" (1989c, 232). But a prayer of supplication does have its place, Levinas notes, "in circumstances where Israel as a whole is in danger. . . . It is for the sake of this sacred history, the glory of its message, that an act of supplication is permitted" (1989c, 233). Since the destruction of the Holy Temple, prayer not only takes the place of sacrifice but is more dear than sacrifice. Even before the Temple's destruction, one is told in the *Midrash Rabbah*, God said to King David, "The one prayer which you stand and pray before me is more precious in my sight than the thousand burnt-offerings which Solomon your son is destined to offer up before me" (1961, 8:43). Viewed as the elevation of the soul, or as the soul's drawing nigh unto the Holy One, prayer has much the same purpose as sacrifice. For "sacrifice" in Hebrew is *karbon*, a cognate of the word *karov*, meaning "near": like sacrifice, prayer is a drawing near to the Infinite One who at times seems to be infinitely distant. "Our devotion in prayer," says the eleventh-century rabbi Bachya ibn Paquda, "is nothing but the soul's longing for God" (1970, 2:211). As the breath or *neshiymah* of God breathed into the human being, the soul or *neshamah* is like a part of God Himself, and the longing of the soul is God's longing for Himself. "Your recital of prayer," Bachya states, "is (a mark of) the Creator's faith (in you), for He has put it into your hands and placed it under your control while none beside Him contemplates it" (1971, 2:213). And He contemplates it not from the outside but from the inside.

Prayer is a form of God's self-presence, or the *Shekhinah*, in His Creation. "As the Shofar cannot emit any sound except when blown by man," the Hasidic Koretzer Rebbe teaches, "no man can raise his voice in prayer except when the Shekinah prays through it" (Newman 1963, 335-36). Hence, "prayer," notes Harry Rabinowicz, "is part of the *Shekhinah*, which may be why the *Shekhinah* itself is called prayer" (1988, 35). According to the Jewish view, then, as soon as the memoir addresses God and, thus, takes on an element of prayer, at least a trace of the Divine is there, even if it is prayer concerning the absence or silence of God. From a Jewish standpoint prayer is above all a dialogue, a hearing in the midst of response and a response that is a hearing. Drawing an absent God into the dialogue of prayer, the memoir draws God's absence into a dialectic by which He is made present in the soul's longing for Him. A striking example of such longing, transmitted by the dead and borne by the living, is found in Alexander Donat's *The Holocaust Kingdom*, wherein he prays, "For Thou hast not granted us Thy mercy, / And Thou knowest not what Thou hast done" (1978, 119). Such a prayer transforms the silence of divine muteness into the response that can come only in the form of silence. Thus, God is, as it were, forced into a dialogue in which even His silence is a response. "Thanks to prayer," Wiesel explains, "the Supreme Judge, here the Father of humanity, leaves His celestial throne to live and move among His human creatures. And, in turn, here the soul transported by its prayer leaves its abode and rises to heaven. The substance of language, and the language of silence—that is what prayer is" (1982a, 171–72). And that is what the Holocaust memoir struggles to become in its struggle to recover the light of tradition and, thus, draw the sun out of its darkness. Like prayer, the movement of remembrance is a movement of response that creates an opening for the ascent of the human and the descent of the Divine.

In the Holocaust memoir this movement of prayer toward another place often takes the form of a movement of memory toward another person. Thus, the man robbed of his humanity arrives at the memory of himself as a human being by way of the other who affirms what is essential to the human image. For Filip Müller this other is a man named Fischl, a fellow inmate at Auschwitz-Birkenau who was known for his prayers. "Man differs from animals in that he believes in God," Müller recalls Fischl's words on one occasion. "It's prayer which makes you a human being" (1979a, 28). Humanity derives from sanctity, and sanctity derives from prayer. It is not a question of belief; prayer precedes belief and overtakes nonbelief. Because Fischl had no *tefillin*, Müller relates, he would mime the ritual of wrapping the phylacteries around his arm and head. "It seemed sheer madness to pray in Auschwitz," Müller asserts. "But here on the border-line between life and death, we obediently followed his example, possibly because . . . we felt strengthened by his faith" (1979a, 29). The men pray despite themselves. They pray because the prayer, steeped with the One to whom it is offered, has a life of its own. They pray because, just as they behold Fischl's invisible *tefillin*, so do they hear a silent summons arising from the prayer itself. The prayer that comes to lips that refuse it appears in other memoirs as well. In Wiesel's *Night*, for example, Eliezer recalls the group of men who stood to recite the Kaddish—for themselves—upon their arrival at Auschwitz. "Why should I bless His name?" Eliezer asks. But, he says, "in spite of myself, the words formed themselves and issued in a whisper from my lips: *Yitgadal veyitkadash shme raba...*" (1960, 43). The men do not choose the prayer; the prayer chooses the men. Similarly, where prayer is in the midst of the memory, memory does not choose the prayer, rather, the prayer calls forth the memory.

Memory summoned by prayer: this is the key to the endurance of Jewish tradition, for in that tradition memory is a form of prayer and prayer is a form of memory. This point is eloquently made by Eugene Heimler in his memory of the Hasidic Jews herded into a Polish ghetto. "I understood then how we have managed to withstand the persecution of the centuries," he writes. "It was because of these long-bearded men, ... who believed every word of the Torah, the Old Testament" (1959, 17–18). Once again it is the other that returns the man to himself as a Jew, even—or especially—in the gullet of the monster that is devouring the Jews. So Müller recalls the Orthodox Jews who prayed in Birkenau even as they combed out the hair shorn from their dead: "They devoted their entire free time to prayers for the dead and to the study of Jewish religious writings. Their books once belonged to fellow Jews who, like themselves, had believed in the justice of God before they were herded into the gas chambers" (1979a, 66). Reading these lines, one might get the impression that Müller invokes these faithful in order to denounce them. But he does not denounce them. He does not denounce them because, like Heimler, he knows that any recovery of Jewish life and tradition rests on the memory of Jews who prayed and who, like Fischl, demand the prayer in the midst of memory. It is neither by chance nor by sentiment that the memory of the Shoah has become part of the Jewish liturgy. The liturgy's *Siddur*, or prayerbook, itself draws forth this memory, as it happens with Vladka Meed when, at the end of the war, she surveys the rubble of the Warsaw Ghetto. "My eyes fell upon the remains of a torn, soiled *Siddur*," she recalls, "and I see again my home—my father and mother" (1973, 334). With the Word in the mezuzah affixed to its doorposts the Jewish home—mother and father— is the seat of Jewish memory and the center of Jewish life. The image of the

Siddur in ruins is precisely an image of the Jewish people, the Jewish God, and the Jewish tradition in ruins. For the torn Siddur is the torn Word that brings about the ascent of the human and the descent of the Divine. It is the book that draws the People of the Book nigh unto the Giver of the Book. And when this book of blessings emerges from the pages of the book of memory, it struggles, like Jacob wrestling with the Angel, to recover the blessing of life.

The recovery of tradition is the recovery of life, and the Holocaust memoir's memory of prayer is often a memory of life's recovery. Moshe Sandberg, for instance, summons the memory of a Jew in Dachau who was constantly immersed in his prayerbook, "until he collapsed and was taken to the hospital"; the man, in fact, survived when by every rational measure he should have died, "according to himself thanks to his prayers" (1968, 89). In another memoir Paul Trepman relates that while he and his comrades hid in the tight confines of a dark cellar, they recited the *Shema*; "it was an upsurge of religious feeling, and it kept us sane after a fashion" (1978, 65)— "sane" in a place where prayer itself might appear to be insanity. Here, of course, *sane* does not mean *rational* so much as maintaining the hale and whole relation to God that sanctifies the relation to other human beings; here, remaining "sane" means remaining human. If this may be said of those in hiding, how much more might it apply to those in the death camp who, according to Samuel Pisar, said their prayers during the High Holy Days under the direct threat of death? "In the darkness," he writes, "with prison caps for yarmulkes, every man stood in front of his bunk, facing Jerusalem. Without the chants of a cantor to guide him, every man mumbled softly, lest we be heard by the roaming guards and their vicious dogs, whatever prayers he could remember" (1979, 61). Why these prayers despite the death that breathes down their necks? Because without these prayers these Jews are dead as Jews, dead, therefore, as human beings. "There are men who are dead and do not know it," declares Moshe in Wiesel's *The Oath* (1973b, 196). Such are men who do not know how to pray.

Pisar's image of prison caps turned into yarmulkes—a mark of death made into a sign of life—exemplifies the dialectical nature of prayer in the midst of memory. You have turned us over to death? No matter: our memory will return us to life. You would reduce our tradition to ashes? Then we shall fetch from those ashes the fire that ignites our prayers. We shall dance, like souls on fire, in remembrance of the flames that consumed our souls, in remembrance of Rebbe Leib, son of the great Maggid of Mezeritch, who cried out to his fellow Jews, "Your dancing counts for more than my prayers"

(Wiesel 1973c, 46). After all, was it not Moshe Leib of Sassov who said, "When somebody asks something impossible of me, I know what I must do: I must dance" (Wiesel 1982b, 110)? Thus, in prayers transformed into dance, praying the *Kol Nidre* of Yom Kippur as they danced, a group of one hundred rabbis danced at Birkenau in the shadow and by the terrible light of the crematoria. The Angel of Death, Mengele himself, had ordered them to dance. But then, Sara Nomberg-Przytyk remembers, they began chanting the *Kol Nidre:* "Now they were no longer singing in obedience to Mengele's orders" (1985, 106). Once again one sees the capacity of prayer to turn mockery into devotion, just as it turned prison caps into yarmulkes. In the midst of memory prayer turns death into life and, thus, recovers the tradition of life that was consigned to death. In the midst of memory the prayer left unsaid finds its voice as in Gerda Klein's memory of the prayer that would not come during her evacuation march: "Through all the years I had prayed to God ardently and with hope. Now I prayed no more. I did not consciously know why, for I was closer to my Maker than ever. One short shot away . . . , but I could not pray" (1957, 185). She could not pray, and so she remembers. And in the memory of the prayer unuttered a prayer finds its utterance.

Insofar as memory in the Holocaust memoir entails a recovery of Jewish tradition, the memory of God and of the prayer that seeks God is a definitive feature of the memoir. Jewish tradition is a tradition of prayer, and it is through the prayers of tradition that God manifests Himself within the tradition. Because the memoir bears the aspect of prayer, it harbors a double reflection: it is, in a sense, a prayer about prayer, a prayer that forever seeks God through the memory of prayer. The memory itself, therefore, has a double reflection: the Holocaust memoir, unlike other memoirs, is a memory of memory. Seeking the recovery of tradition, the memoir seeks a recovery of memory, which is the substance of tradition. In the Holocaust memoir, then, the memory of God often assumes the form of the memory of memory.

The Memory of Memory

Jewish tradition teaches in the words of the *Zohar* that "the Supreme King is hinted at in the word *Zakhor* (remember)" (1984, 1:23). This passage alone is enough to establish a link between the memory of God and the memory of memory if, indeed, that connection has not already been firmly established. But, one asks, only *hinted* at? Yes, for the Holy One is the Invisible One, and the invisible can only be hinted at. The invisibility of God, Levinas explains, "is not to be understood as God invisible to the

senses, but as God nonthematizable in thought" (1985, 106); God eludes the
eye of every category that might situate Him within the horizons of being.
The One who forever recedes to the rear, He is the Good, as He is called
in the *Amidah*, who precedes all time that might be designated as "past."
Says Levinas, "The invisible in the Bible is the idea of the Good beyond
being. To be obliged to responsibility overflowing freedom, that is responsibility for the others. It is the perpetuity, or a perpetuity that would claim to
be eternity. . . . It is the trace of a past which declines the present and representation, the trace of an immemorial past" (1987a, 136). As the memory
of God, the memory of memory is the memory of the immemorial, of what
both underlies and encompasses all *possibility* of memory. As the memory of
the Good, the memory of memory is the memory of what chooses one before
all remembrance that might belong to an act of choosing; unlike others who
may nostalgically pen their memoirs in their twilight years, the Jew has no
choice in *this* memory. Recall Levinas's argument that one's connection to
the Good is before any choosing of the Good. "The Good," he maintains,
"is good precisely because it chooses you and grips you before you have had
the time to raise your eyes to it" (1990, 135). In its Jewish form the Good
is the tradition that consists of memory and summons all memory in such
a way that the memory of tradition is itself the memory of memory. Like the
Good, the tradition chooses one before one can contemplate any other choice;
one engages in one's contemplation *because* the tradition has chosen one. To
be sure, that is what makes the past a *tradition*: the past becomes tradition
not through the repetition of customs or habits but through the insertion of
an immemorial past into the remembrance of the past. This insertion is
precisely the memory of memory.

Elie Wiesel remarked that the Churban "was essentially a war against
memory" (1990a, 155), which is to say, it was a war against God and tradition, a war against the Word itself. Jewish memory is housed not just in the
brains of the chosen but in the holy texts of the sacred tradition so that the
memory of memory seeking to recover the lost tradition often becomes remembrance of the loss of those texts. In some cases this loss of the texts of
tradition takes the form of a diabolical turning of tradition against itself. For,
according to Jewish tradition, when a text containing the Holy Name is no
longer suitable for use, it is not destroyed or thrown away but is given a
ritualistic burial as one might bury an entity that was once alive. Under the
Nazis, however, these texts were buried while they were yet alive, as Thomas
Geve recalls: "We buried the scrolls of the Torah. Religious rules not allowing holy writings to be burned, the synagogues from all over Germany had

sent them to a central store at the Berlin cemetery. . . . Hundreds of them were carried to a mass grave to be given a suitably impressive burial" (1981, 30). There is no greater evidence for the fact that the war against the Jews exceeded all national, political, social, economic, and even racial bounds, that it was an ontological war against a metaphysical opponent. For this destruction of ink and paper is aimed at the destruction of what invisibly transcends the text. "The Germans had a special sense for the value of Jewish books," notes Zivia Lubetkin, "and carefully collected Torah scrolls, Bibles, and other sacred books" (1981, 113). Why the interest in the Jewish texts, if all they wanted to do was destroy the Jewish people? Because that is not all they wanted to do. Far beyond the destruction of all Jewry, the Nazis wanted to obliterate Jewish essence, Jewish tradition, Jewish memory.

"The scornful laughter of the SS myrmidons," writes Filip Müller, "was always heard when prisoners from the *Sonderkommando* had to burn prayerbooks and religious works" (1979a, 66). It is not for nothing that the members of the *Sonderkommando*—the very ones forced to gas and burn the Jewish people—were forced to burn Jewish memory. Made of the ashes of those books, of that memory, the Holocaust memoir strives to recover those texts through its own text of remembrance; the memoir that seeks to recover tradition thus finds its own place within the tradition. This, too, is an essential, definitive aspect of the Holocaust memoir, that its memory belongs to a tradition of memory. Livia Jackson makes clear the significance of the attack on memory and the nature of the recovery sought in the memoir when she describes a bonfire built in the middle of a Hungarian ghetto: "Volumes of the Bible, leather-bound Psalms, phylacteries turn and twist and burst into myriad fragments of agony. Pictures and documents. . . . Our soul. Weightless speckles of ash rising, fleeing the flames into nothingness" (1980, 38). Into nothingness: as though being itself were consumed in those flames. As the texts containing the Holy Name go up in flames, the name and the essence, the very life, of the Jew also ascend on the column of smoke and ash: photographs—the images of the Jew and of his memory—are burned with his books. Just as the Nazis set out to murder the memory housed in the Book, moreover, so did they attack the memory housed in the body.

Here, too, the memory of memory assumes a dialectical form, as the memory of memory's loss. "The lack of Vitamin B," says Miklos Nyiszli, for example, "caused perpetual drowsiness and partial amnesia: often they could no longer remember the names of the streets where they had once lived, or their house numbers" (1960, 114). Other examples of this dialectic at work in the remembrance of memory's loss abound in the memoirs. Germaine

Tillion, for example, remarks that, despite the terrible hardships of Ravensbrück, she "did not experience any perceptible diminution of mental activity except perhaps in the area of memory" (1975, 16). In Auschwitz, Olga Lengyel notes, "the inmates revealed signs of mental deterioration. They lost their memory and the ability to concentrate" (1972, 96). The removal of the Jew from the world entails the removal of memory from the Jew. For the Jew this loss has profound consequences. In the Jewish tradition memory is the link not just to a sense of self but, above all, to that responsibility for the other which signifies the higher relation to the Good. As one of the Chosen, the Jew is chosen for this responsibility; to lose his memory is to lose his chosenness *while yet being accountable* for all he confronts in the light of having been chosen. This is why Donat writes, "The weakening of my memory tormented me. I despised myself, considered it a betrayal of my own child" (1978, 239). It is the father who must impart the tradition to his child, and the means of that transmission is memory. The life of the child as a Jewish child lies in this memory of tradition; thus, when memory is threatened, Jewish life itself is threatened. To be sure, Fania Fénelon cites the loss of memory as the most telling sign of the death that approaches her and her comrades. "When the girls asked me to tell them a story," she relates along these lines, "the words came less easily. . . . They themselves were becoming less and less capable of noticing my loss of memory" (1977, 250). Memory is the substance not only of personal identity but of interhuman relation: with the loss of memory she is less able to relate, and her friends are less able to respond. So the return to life demands a return of memory, demands the memoir itself.

The return of life, then, manifests itself as a return of the relation—both to the human and to the divine—engendered by memory. And in that relation, once again, one sees very clearly the connection between the memory of memory and the memory of God, between memory and recovery in the Holocaust memoir. And this connection, it must be noted, is established in the memoir precisely because it was established even then and there, in the depths of the destruction of memory. George Topas, for instance, writes, "The scene of our family sitting together around the table, enjoying the Sabbath meal, singing, hearing my father read portions of the Bible to us about our great heritage had always been a moving one; now, lost, it was more precious than ever" (1990, 104). To grasp the profound significance of these lines, one may recall Fackenheim's insightful comments on Kurt Huber, a philosophy professor in Nazi Germany whose resistance to the Reich cost him his life. Having based his actions on a "dead idea," Huber undertook "a

Tikkun," says Fackenheim. "In obeying the unwritten law he restored that law—it must be written *somewhere—by writing it into his own heart*. In acting in behalf of Kant's Idea of Humanity, he *mended* that Idea" (1989, 276). Fackenheim goes on to show that, whereas post-Holocaust Christian thought might find a *tikkun* in the likes of Huber, the Nazi world was arranged so as to make a Jewish Huber impossible (1989, 298). Yet both within and after the Event one finds not only the mending of an idea but the mending of memory. It arises in Vladka Meed's remembrance of "the echo of the silent procession" on its way to the *Umschlagplatz* in the Warsaw Ghetto; that echo "reverberated dismally, its cadence pounding a final warning: 'Remember! Remember! Remember!'" (1973, 81). That this memory of memory is tied to the memory of God—and humanity—Meed demonstrates in the first line of her dedication, calling her memoir "a Memorial Candle" (1973, 5). The Holocaust memoir is a light fetched from the Great Darkness, a memory of God for the sake of humanity, summoned by humanity for the sake of God.

In the Jewish tradition, of course, each is tied to the other. "I rise from among you, my silent martyrs," Frida Michelson begins her memoir. "I hear your cries and screams, the thousands-strong thunder of your feet running to the grave, your last word: 'Remember!' " (1979, 11). *Bezmolvnye mucheniki* is the original Russian phrase translated as "silent martyrs" (Michelson 1973, 10); it means "mute" or "speechless tortured ones." The words of memory that comprise the memoir are words that had been murdered in the mouths of the dead, now offered to God and to humanity. Yet Michelson repeatedly indicates that it was not only the dead who summoned her to this memory but God as well. "The idea that somehow God had chosen me to be His witness," she says, "sustained me throughout the whole ordeal and was instrumental in my fight for existence when submission and death would have been so much easier" (1979, 42). And, recalling her thoughts when she lay hidden beneath a pile of clothing at the edge of a mass grave, she writes, "I was still alive! God has chosen me to be His witness. This thought had come to me over and over again" (Michelson 1979, 92). The memoir's *Yizkor*—its memorial or remembrance—is a memory of humanity for the sake of God, summoned by God for the sake of humanity. Again, memory in the Holocaust memoir lies within the relation that binds the two. And the recovery of the divine relation in the midst of human relation is the first step toward the recovery of tradition.

Thus, the memory of God initiates a movement toward the other human being, one that forms the basis of one's responsibility for the other human being. In the movement toward the other, memory rediscovers the trace of God eclipsed during those days of destruction when the sun turned to darkness. Levinas helps one to understand the ramifications of this notion, pointing out that God "shows himself only by his trace, as is said in Exodus 33. To go toward him is not to follow this trace which is not a sign; it is to go toward the others" (1987a, 106–7). Just as Moses perceived God's back in a passing of the Divine (Exod. 33), so does one perceive this unrepresentable past in the passing of the memory that rises up from the pages of the Holocaust memoir. Tradition *as tradition* harbors the trace of the immemorial past, a trace made visible by the movement of memory and recovered in the movement toward the other, in the responsibility to and for the other, which is the opposite of indifference. The recovery of tradition, therefore, entails a recovery from the illness of indifference.

PART TWO

The Recovery from the Illness of Indifference

Context

In *God's Presence in History* Fackenheim writes, "The Voice of Auschwitz manifests a divine Presence which, as a whole, is shorn of all except commanding Power. *This* Power, however, is inescapable" (1970, 88). If the pursuit of memory in the Holocaust memoir belongs to the observance of a 614th Commandment, then it must be asked: What is one commanded to do? It has already been noted that one is commanded to refuse the Nazis a postwar victory by refusing to allow Jewish life and tradition to die. But how, exactly, is memory to accomplish this? Recalling all that has been explored in part 1, one soon realizes that the commanding voice of Auschwitz summons one to a restoration of the divine image to the human being and, thus, to draw some trace of the transcendent back into the immanent. That the divine image not only can be destroyed but was indeed destroyed Fackenheim reminds one when he declares, "In manufacturing *Muselmänner*—walking corpses—the Auschwitz criminals destroyed the divine image in their victims; and in doing what they did they destroyed it in themselves as well. In consequence a new necessity has arisen for the ethics of Judaism in our time. What has been broken must be mended. Even for a Jew who cannot believe in God it is necessary to act as though man were made in His image" (Fackenheim 1987, 180). From a Jewish standpoint, the image inheres in action so that this *as though* is eclipsed by the deed. What is the action by which I act as though I were created in the image of the divine? It is the embrace of the other through *gemilut chasidim*, deeds of loving-kindness, that affirm the dearness of the other as one who is created in the image of the Divine.

As though *created*, be it noted, in this phrase the recovery of tradition entails not only the remembrance of a time past but the recovery of an immemorial past that proclaims my responsibility to and for the other human being before any stepping before the face of that human being. To be *created* in the divine image is to be imprinted with the trace of this immemorial past that both precedes and permeates sacred tradition. Creation, then, is just the opposite of chance occurrence, "natural" selection, or even the Aristotelian First Cause. As Fackenheim points out, the God of the *Tenakh* creates heaven "fully as much as earth. And yet, though infinitely above the world and the humanity that is part of it, He creates man—him alone—in His very own image! The God of Aristotle does no such thing" (Fackenheim 1987, 108–9). The recovery of sacred tradition sought in the Holocaust memoir is a recovery of this condition of having been created in such a way that the Creator is returned to the midst of His creation where He may "walk in the garden." And the avenue of that return of the Divine is the return of the one created in His image *as* one created in His image; it is the return of the human being to a responsibility to and for his neighbor. Thus, the indifference toward the neighbor that ruled the antiworld of Auschwitz might be overcome in the movements of memory that summons one to an embrace of fellow human beings. Here lies the connection between the recovery of tradition and the recovery from the illness of indifference. Because, in the words of Levinas, the face "forbids us to kill" (1985, 86), I begin the examination of the memoir's recovery from an illness with the face of the other.

4

The Face of the Other

In his commentary on the teaching in the Torah that "it is not good for man to be alone" (Gen. 2:18) Sforno (ca. 1470–1550) writes, "The (goal and) purpose intended in his being in the likeness and image (of God) will not be realized if (man) will have to occupy himself alone, to supply the needs of life" (1987, 1:25). God is He by whose Word all that is comes into being, and the human being bears the image of God inasmuch as the human being also gives utterance to the word; Adam is Adam inasmuch as he names the creatures of the world. Because the face is the origin of discourse, as Levinas has noted (1985, 87–88), human beings are created in the image of God because they are created with *faces*. And they have faces to the extent that they are able to step before the face of another human being in an act of response. This is where the recovery of the divine image and the recovery from the illness of indifference both merge and begin—in the recovery of the face. If, as Wiesel argues, it is my duty to ask every day, "Where am I in relation to God and others?" (1990b, 136), it is because this question brings me before the face of the other who, in the very humanity of his face, bears the image of the divine. There can be no recovery from the illness of indifference in isolation; my isolation from the other is invariably the isolation of a tomb. And the recovery from the illness of indifference is a recovery from death, from the very death manufactured in the Nazi death factories. For I arrive at myself—that is to say, I return to life—by way of my response to and for the other. In this relation of nonindifference to the face of the other, I assume a face of my own, a face that signifies the dearness of the other. Failing, thus, to answer the question of where I stand in relation to the other, I become faceless.

A primary function of memory in the Holocaust memoir is to once again assume a face through the memory of the face of the other. In the

Holocaust memoir every word corresponds to a face, and every face harbors its word. Although the memory of the Event has its context, moreover, the memory of the face is a memory of what transcends the confines of all contexts. It is this memory that makes the reader contemporary with all that the memoir calls forth; it is this memory that calls *everyone* forth, through the face of the other, to the recovery from an illness *at hand*. When Paltiel Kossover in Wiesel's novel *The Testament* writes, "The hungry child, / The thirsty stranger, / The frightened old man, / All ask for me" (1981, 38), one does not have to ask, "Which child, which stranger, which old man?" to make sense of what one reads. The implication of oneself does not rest on contextual implication. Levinas helps one to see this when he explains, "The face is signification, and signification without context. I mean that the Other, in the rectitude of his face, is not a character within a context. . . . All signification in the usual sense of the term is relative to such a context. . . . Here, to the contrary, the face is meaning all by itself" (1985, 86). The Nazi assault on the divine image is an assault on the face; the death that belongs to the illness of indifference is engendered by rendering the face meaningless. Is that not the "meaning" of indifference, that nothing means anything, that nothing matters? This meaninglessness, this nothingness, finds its breeding ground in the obliteration of the face of the other human being. Yet that obliteration is remembered precisely because the face is the seat of meaning.

Thus, in the Holocaust memoir one repeatedly encounters memories like the one Lily Lerner invokes when she writes, "They never really looked at our faces. They only counted bodies" (1980, 96). Hence, the name that belongs to the face is eclipsed by the number that marks the body, as one might mark an object for inventory. (Indeed, according to the language of the Nazis, in the camps people were not murdered—units were processed.) Why not look upon the face? In his memoir Sim Kessel explains, "A person's face no longer had any meaning and could no longer serve as a means of identification. Gaunt, hairless, wearing the same grisly mask of pain and terror, each skeletal head resembled another" (1972, 150). The mark of pain and terror, the skeletal mask, is a death mask that not only veils the face but erases the imprint of the sacred that instills the face with meaning. These are not faces of the ill but faces of the illness itself, non-faces muted by the wordless malediction of other faces that refuse every word of human relation. "They said nothing to us except to shout," Moshe Sandberg recalls of his days in Dachau. "They did not exchange a word with us. To questions that we ventured to ask they gave us no answer except blows" (1968, 50–51).

Here the blow is not something resorted to when all words fail; in Dachau the blow is directed at the word itself, at its very source—at the face. This annihilation of the word, again, is at the root of the destruction of the divine image, which is the image of life that memory posits over against the image of mortal illness. Upon further reflection, then, a dialectical aspect of memory emerges from the examples cited from the memoirs above. With respect both to the perpetrators and to the victims, the memory that would recover the face is a memory of facelessness. I examine, then, the memory of faces and facelessness both on the edges and at the core of the antiworld of the death camp. Upon completing this investigation, I move finally to the third term in this memory's dialectic—the image of madness.

The World Void of Face: The Spectator

Maimonides relates that a person "who shows indifference and laxity of behaviour . . . is also guilty of profaning the Name" (1967, 2:62). Conversely, one who assumes a position of nonindifference before the face of the other person sanctifies the Holy Name. At the very heart of the face-to-face relation, the One who is beyond the world finds entry into the world through that very relation. Wherever two human beings meet, therefore, a third party abides, waiting to enter. "We are always a threesome," Levinas insists. "I and you and the third who is in our midst. And only as Third does He reveal Himself" (1989b, 247). The face of the human being whom one encounters in the world brings one before this hidden face of the Third, who is the witness and judge of every encounter. Hence, in the words of Mikhail Bakhtin, "what I must be for the other, God is for me" (1991, 56). Each time I come into contact with another human being, the Name of the Holy One is placed in my care. Therefore, the father of all the prophets—both before and after him, the one who stood face to face with *ha-Shem* Himself and to whom the Name was first revealed—was called Moshe, which, says Sforno, means "he who rescues and draws forth others from trouble" (1987, 1:255). God reveals Himself to Moses by name not so that Moses may deliver others from trouble but *because* he delivers others from trouble. It is in the light of this human relation to the other that the divine descends upon Mount Sinai.

Thus, says Sforno, "a righteous man objects to a wrong being done even to a stranger" (1987, 1:140)—not just a moral man, be it noted, but a *righteous* man, that is, one who attests to the sanctity of the divine through his relation to the children of Adam, who are created in the image of the divine. The righteous man's objection is precisely the Word of non-indifference that is the one remedy for the illness of indifference. One symptom of the illness as it appears in the world is the *silence* of indifference, the silence that profanes the Name robs the world of its face. "Silence," says Sforno, "on the part of one who has the power to protest is tantamount to admission (consent), for regarding he who is silent (it is as though) he agrees with the action" (1987, 2:709). Like the word of objection uttered by the righteous man, this silence of the indifferent one has its ontological dimension. For in the void of this silence one hears the sound of the silence that André Neher describes when he asserts, "Silence—the 'inert' silence, great and solemn— comes forward not as a temporary suspension of the Word but as a spokesman for the invincible Nothingness. Thus Silence replaces the Word because Nothingness takes the place of Being" (1981, 63). The illness that drains the human face of its humanity also displaces the face of being; it is not just that this particular person turns away, but the world itself is rendered faceless, transformed into a mute and indifferent blank. Yet only from a face that might affirm the sacred humanity of the other can this dehumanizing silence find utterance. When memory calls forth this silence, it does so to set in motion a dialectic by which the silence is exposed *as* an illness. So time after time the silence that Sforno declares to be a consent to evil finds its way into the memoir that would overcome evil. Filip Müller, for example, writes, "The whole world knew [of Hitler's intention to exterminate the Jews], and knowing it remained silent" (1979a, 36). And in Vladka Meed's memoir one reads, "The world has turned a deaf ear to what's going on here. We must do everything ourselves" (1973, 136). The deaf ear is the mute mouth that refuses a reply to the supplications of the face; thus refusing a reply, the world loses every trace of its own face.

Rendered faceless, the spectator takes on the status of an object. "He is no longer he, you, or I," writes Wiesel. "He is 'it' " (1964, 171). This remark from *The Town beyond the Wall* is an important part of a tale about a man who returns to his home town to confront the spectator who from behind his curtains looked on as children crying out for water were herded into trains. In the Holocaust memoir, as in Wiesel's novel, the point of this confrontation— or the longing for it—cannot be dismissed as a longing for revenge or a desire to make the other "feel guilty." Beyond that, it is an insistence that this other assume a face through some kind of response to the face of the Jewish victim; it is an insistence that the other assume his own humanity through the recognition of the humanity of another. Only in that response can the humanity of both be recovered; if the humanity of one is to be recovered, it must be the humanity of both. In this connection one may recall Primo Levi's statement in *The Periodic Table*, "To find myself, man to man, having a reckoning with one of the 'others' had been my keenest and most constant desire since I left the concentration camp" (1985, 215). *Man to man, da uomo a uomo* (Levi 1975, 219), not human to animal or even victim to criminal, but an encounter between human and human, between word and word—if not to heal a wound then at least to acknowledge it. This memory flows like blood from a wound that refuses closure. It flows from a wound that disfigures the faces not only of this group or those individuals but of an entire world. For when one stands before the face of the other, one is not an object in the world, but rather the world is gathered into oneself. "He is You and fills the firmament," Martin Buber states it. "Not as if there were nothing but he; but everything lives in *his* light" (1970, 59). This is the light swallowed up by the Kingdom of Night, the light that the memoir struggles to retrieve.

One must bear in mind, moreover, that the encounter with the world void of face, as it appears in the Holocaust memoir, is not so often between Jew and Nazi as it is between Jew and neighbor or fellow citizens, those decent people with whom the survivor had perhaps enjoyed a face-to-face human relation before the onset of the illness of indifference, which is the illness of facelessness. "Acquaintances, friends, neighbors," says Frida Michelson, for instance, "quit talking to us. When we met on the street, heads turned away. It was as if we already did not exist" (1979, 38). Death was indeed near, the death brought on by an indifference that is deadly not only to the indifferent one but far more so to all *others*. Yet the turning away that Michelson describes is just what she would turn about through the movements of memory. Isabella Leitner, to cite another example, writes, "You, my former neighbors, I cannot live with you again. You could have thrown a morsel of sadness our way while we were dragging ourselves down Main Street" (1978, 16). Leitner does not seek any heroic action but just a *facial* expression—a look of sadness. Nathan Shapell offers a more detained account of the situation when he remembers how people he and his family had known all their lives were transformed into strangers who treated the Jews as if they had some disease. "They withdrew from us, and some made a special point of insulting and betraying us," he relates. "Yet each Sunday found them at their places of worship, and I wondered what they said to their God when they lifted their voices in prayer" (1974, 50–51). Here, too, the memory of the illness is invoked in the interest of a recovery from the illness; offered to God, it is a memory that might displace the empty prayers mouthed by the faceless ones. If Leitner says that she can no longer live with her neighbors, it is not because of her deportation but because of their indifference.

To live *with* another is to live face to face in a stepping before the face of the Holy One. Because *His* face is the face that summons one through the plight of one's neighbor, one *has* a face and may be rendered faceless by the illness of indifference. In the silence of the neighbor the primary symptom of facelessness is the muteness of the face that turns away. "When Speech is not in exile," Rabbi Nachman of Breslov once said, "then the Table is turned toward us in an aspect of Face" (1973, 205). He who prepares a table before me draws me into the face-to-face relation with the other and with Himself. In the Holocaust memoir, then, memory is far more than mere accusation: it is a stepping before the Countenance to draw speech out of exile. That is why the language of facelessness—and not just the language of cruelty—so often inserts itself into the memory that distinguishes the Holocaust memoir. It is a language calculated to make heard the silence of speech gone into exile. Commenting on the people of the town of Auschwitz, for example, Charlotte Delbo recalls, "None of the inhabitants of this city / had a face" (1968, 98), which is to say, none of the inhabitants of the town from which the camp takes its name had a tongue. Fania Fénelon relates a similar experience of the same town; emphasizing the silence of facelessness, she writes, "As we passed, no one turned around. . . . There was neither curiosity nor hostility; we didn't exist. When would we cease to be nothing?" (1977, 74–75). This absence of the other who turns away imposes an absence on the self; the world void of face renders the self void. So one function of memory in the Holocaust memoir is to speak this facelessness and thereby recover a face.

The world is made of people. The world void of face is made of people rendered faceless, beginning with "good Christians." Delbo issues this indictment when she cries out,

> You who wept for two thousand years
> for one who suffered three days and three nights
> what tears will you have
> for those who suffered
> many more than three hundred nights and many more
>   than three hundred days? (1968, 13)

It was in Poland, in the heart of Catholic Christendom, that the death factories most relentlessly manufactured the death of indifference—not only at such infamous sites as Chelmno, Treblinka, and Maidanek but throughout the nation, in city and town. Vladka Meed, for example, relates that after the *szmalcownicy*, the blackmailers of Warsaw, would leave a Jewish victim in the street, passersby would look on for a moment and then resume "their Sunday stroll. Why did the Poles remain silent?" (1973, 113). I have already noted Nathan Shapell's comment on good Christians who turned their backs on their neighbors as they headed off to church (1974, 50–51). Recalling those Polish faces void of humanity, those eyes that met his during an evacuation march, he writes, "I . . . searched their faces for—for what? Horror? Sympathy? Would I never learn? I saw instead smiles and even laughter. On the few serious faces no sign of emotion was displayed" (1974, 111). Primo Levi recalls that even after the "liberation," when it was safe to shown a sign of humanity, the facelessness of the Polish peasants continued to be unremitting. They "looked at us with closed faces," he writes (1965, 36). These and other examples demonstrate that the facelessness that arose within the Third Reich infects and feeds on the face of an entire world. The term *Nazi*, therefore, does not apply merely to a political group; no, it designates an ontological disease, a contagion to which anyone who has a face is susceptible.

In the Holocaust memoir the void that invades a world void of face takes on a spatial dimension, a stance that is a dis-stance. It is a gulf that situates the victim on one shore and a world that refuses a stance on another. The function of memory in the memoir is not just to bridge a gap in time but to transcend this distance between self and other by voicing it to and for another, that is, for a reader. In his memoir titled *The Abyss*, for example, Elie Cohen remembers a moment that captures the abyss between self and other. As he and his fellow prisoners were walking from the train station to the concentration camp at Amersfoort, they looked into the lighted windows of the homes they were passing. "You could see mothers sitting round the table with their children," he remembers. "Doesn't the world care what is going on here? . . . What a strange thing that everyone should live so much for himself alone, and that you no longer care what's happening to someone else" (1973, 45). The verb translated from the Dutch as "care" is *aantrekken* (Cohen, 1971, 28), which also has connotations of attraction or being drawn toward another. The attitude of not caring, then, is an attitude of remaining at a distance, feeling no pull or hearing no summons that might close the distance between self and other. To be sure, many memories of the refusal of the face are memories not only of a failure to move *toward* but of a graphic movement *away*. Gerda Klein recalls the day when she and other prisoners were marched through the town of Bolkenhain: "People looked at us as though they had not expected us to be human. Children were called into houses" (1957, 114). Gisella Perl relates a similar experience, saying,

"People looked at me with horror in their eyes, and I looked back at them, as if to say: All this is *your* fault!" (1948, 149). The declaration of "this is your fault" is a way of declaring, "This face that repels you is the result of your facelessness!" Issuing from the face of one who was abandoned, the words of the Holocaust memoir expose the absence of any human face on the part of those who turned away. Thus, the memoir is a refusal of the facelessness that refused the face.

Void of any reason that would impart to it a face, the world remains in an elsewhere that, from the standpoint of the victim, is nowhere. Therefore, "nothing heard these cries from the edge of terror," says Charlotte Delbo. "Only our ears heard and we were no longer alive" (1968, 57). Why no longer alive? Because the world void of face has rendered their faces void. The world void of face stops short of . . . where? The memory that would penetrate this *where* tries to reach across the void by reaching for a face. There, too, the memoir struggles to impart a voice to the face of the person rendered faceless. But there is a difference, an incommensurable difference, between one sphere and the other. For in the antiworld the victims of facelessness come face to face with the executioners and with themselves.

The Face of the Other in the Antiworld

From the depths of the face one encounters in the world the voice of life summons one. In the antiworld of the SS, by contrast, the appearance of the "face" of the executioner is an encounter with the death's head that epitomizes the one who dons it. As Fackenheim has correctly pointed out, the murder camp was not incidental to the Nazi project. "It was its pure essence" (1978, 246). And the thing targeted for murder in the murder camp was not only the body but the soul. Whereas Torquemada burned and tortured bodies in order to save souls, Fackenheim reminds us, Eichmann set out "to destroy souls before he destroyed bodies" (1970, 74). The destruction of the soul begins with the destruction of the face as a *visitation*, that is, as the very thing that forbids one to murder As soon as the face is obliterated, the principle of life is made into a principle of death; "thou shalt not murder" becomes "thou shalt murder" and renders the murderer himself faceless.

Alexander Donat relates a story that illustrates this point. A woman in the Warsaw Ghetto begged an SS officer to spare the lives of her two children. He paused for a moment and then told her that if she could guess which of his eyes was an artificial eye, she could save one of her children. Without hesitating she declared, "The right eye is the artificial one."

"Why, yes," the officer replied. "How could you tell?"

She answered, "It looks more human than the other one" (1978, 102–3).

The memory of the inhumanity of the visage of the murderers haunts the Holocaust memoir. "They treated us like the animals they had become," Nathan Shapell comments on the SS who inhabited Planet Auschwitz (1974, 115). A similar memory of the SS is found in Livia Jackson's memoir: "Their faces do not look like faces. . . . And their voices sound like angry barks" (1980, 45). In these lines once again is the linkage between the face and the soul, between the face and the voice. Confronted with the mutilation of the voice and the degradation of the soul, those who write these memoirs seek a voice by which they may breathe life into the soul. "Beginning with any text," Bakhtin insists, "we always arrive . . . at the human voice, which is to say we come up against the human being" (1981, 252–53). Coming up against the human being, I encounter the face in the midst of the text before me. The face is alive, as Levinas says; the human being is alive, hale and whole, to the extent that his or her face lives and, thus, becomes a visage or a vista that opens up the soul upon the utterance of the word. The illness of facelessness, then, is an illness of the soul, a sickness unto death that breeds death—not only through murder but through an insistence that everyone around the grim death mask assume the features of the mask itself. Thus, Rudolf Vrba summons the image of his former friend Vrbicky, whom the SS had made into a Kapo, recast in their own image: "I looked in horror into the face of my old lackadaisical, lecherous, hard-drinking friend. The lazy eyes were like little stones now. The mouth that used to smile so easily was tight. Vrbicky had been remoulded" (1964, 55–56). Looking at another example, one recalls that before murdering the prisoners on the Sonderkommando, the SS in charge of the crematoria at Birkenau forced them to play soccer with them. "You too," Levi mimics the murderers, "like us and like Cain, have killed the brother. Come, we can play together" (1988, 55). When Cain was branded as a murderer, it was his face that bore the mark.

The contagion embodied by the murderers spread throughout their victims in other ways as well. It manifested itself in the form of a self-imposed silence or an agonizing turning away from the suffering that disfigured the face of the other. Sim Kessel, for example, recalls his reaction to a murder one day at roll call, saying, "I witnessed this murder in the same manner that I had witnessed many others—with an expressionless face" (1972, 76). In the saying of this memory Kessel struggles to recover the expression and the face that the illness ate away from him. Recalling that event—calling it back to a presence or to the trace of a presence on the page—he now calls forth a trace of the face that harbors his own soul. Once again, in the creation of a text is a struggle to recreate a face. The element of confession in such a memory is more pronounced in Vladka Meed's recollection of an *Aktion* or roundup of deportees in the Warsaw Ghetto. With the faces of the victims imprinted on her mind, she writes, "What grief was in their eyes! What mute reproach! . . . Why didn't someone—why didn't I—plead for them? Flinching, I tried to silence these questions" (1973, 39–40). But in the Holocaust memoir memory is made of such questions that will not be silenced. Indeed, these questions constitute memory's quest for recovery. It is always the I that is implicated, always the I that is singled out, always the I that must remember, invaded by the other who seeks a voice in the memories of the I. "The soul is the other in me," says Levinas (1981, 193). And the other in me manifests himself through memories—through voices and questions—that will not be silenced. They are "buried within me," Ka-tzetnik declares. "Over their ashes I vow to be a voice to them" (1989, 18). Vowing to be a voice to the other, he seeks the face of the other in the recovery of his own face.

This function of memory in the Holocaust memoir comes out even more clearly when Charlotte Delbo remembers a woman on a work detail in Auschwitz. Delbo looked on as the woman risked her life to quench her thirst with a clump of snow lying on the other side of a ditch. "Why does she stare at us?" she writes, as though gazing upon the woman even as she writes. "Am I not the one she is singling out? . . . I turn my head. To look elsewhere" (1968, 30). This flight to an elsewhere is a flight to a presence that memory would retrace, if not recapture. *Nest-ca pas moi qu'elle désigne?* Reads the French line translated as "Am I not the one she is singling out?" (Delbo 1965, 31). Here the verb *désigner*, meaning "to designate" or "to appoint," conveys more than the English "singling out." It suggests that the other makes the self into a *sign* of the other so that this memory laid out in signs on a page signifies the face—that is, the holy image—of that other from whom the self turned away. The torsion experienced in the soul of the one who remembers is experienced precisely because this *is* a memory of the holy—or of the desecration of the holy. As such, the memory of this moment comes in a moment of revelation, and it is an instance of the revelation and face-to-face relation that Levinas links to the Torah itself. "The Torah," he maintains, "is given in the Light of a face" (1990, 47). When asked if they would live by the Torah, the Israelites answered, "We will do and we will hear" (Exod. 24:7); Levinas points out that this response "does not express the purity of a trusting soul but the structure of a subjectivity clinging to the absolute" (1990, 48). As a form of recovery, memory here is a form of return:

it returns a face to the other, so that the soul may return to the self through this clinging to the absolute. It is a mending of the absolute that is necessary to a healing of the soul.

The I *is* its movement toward the other; the I arrives at itself by way of the other. The voice of the other, therefore, leads me to where I am, and in the Holocaust memoir the memory by which the self may recover from its illness is rooted in the voice of the other. Very often, then, memory reveals its own structure through the content of what is remembered. A good example is found in Samuel Pisar's memoir, "In this world without mirrors . . . we were psychologically vulnerable to others' estimation of our physical state, and in our camp there was a terrible sentence that one inmate could pronounce on another: 'You are a Musulman' " (1979, 75). Just as one prisoner seeks a saving word of response from another, so does the memoir author seek a response from the reader. Thus, the reader becomes a participant on the recovery from an illness; failing to respond to this memory that is itself an act of response, the reader becomes part of the illness. If one bears in mind this parallel between the inmate-to-inmate relation and the author-to-reader relation, a passage from Moshe Sandberg's memoir is devastating indeed. Recalling his encounter in Dachau with a man from his hometown, he writes: "He only wept. This weeping, so characteristic of the broken and half-broken camp inmates, inhibited any real talk. He held me in his arms, cried, and mumbled in broken sentences: 'Can you recognize me as I am now?' " (1968, 66). The "real talk" inhibited now seeks its voice on the page before one; the face obscured by tears and broken sentences struggles to make itself heard and, therefore, recognized in the movement of remembrance. The recovery *from* the illness, then, is a recovery *of* recognition.

It maybe helpful to recall in this connection an insight from Jacques Lacan: "What I seek in the Word is the response of the other. What constitutes me as subject is my question. In order to be recognized by the other, I utter what was in view of what will be. In order to find him, I call him by a name which he must assume or refuse in order to reply to me" (1968, 63). When confronting the face of the other in the antiworld, the difficulty lies in the fact that the self must be able to recognize this other to utter the name that would generate a response. The capacity to summon the other by name is critical to recovering the name and the presence of oneself. It is not surprising, then, to discover that in the Holocaust memoir the problem of recognizing the face of the other in the antiworld is so prevalent. Elie Cohen, for example, writes, "You just didn't recognize people anymore. I shouldn't even be able to act as a witness in a trial of SS men" (1973, 97). This failure to recognize the face of the other applies not only to Nazis or new acquaintances but also to people one has known for a long time as Eugene Heimler indicates when he says of a friend, "That single night had changed him so much I hardly recognized him" (1959, 26). And when Gisella Perl meets an old friend named Ibi in a "sick block," she remembers, "When I came face to face with her I didn't recognize her. The flower-like young girl was no more. In her place I saw a shriveled, yellow-skinned little old woman" (1948, 138). What is to be understood from these examples is that the horror lies not only in the disfiguring of the face of the other but beyond that is the horror of the loss of one's own face in the confrontation with the lost face of the other. Here the face of the other is encountered as an absence, and it announces the absence of the self that is the essence of the illness.

Just as the human being is threatened by the failure of recognition, so may he be saved when recognized as a human being. Here it must be noted that even in the midst of this antiworld void of face, in the realm where the face had no place, the saving grace borne in the face did, nonetheless, appear. And because it appeared then, it peers out from the pages of the memoir now. Gisella Perl, for example, remembers that Olga Singer's "patience, her understanding, her never-waning concern for others" enable her (Gisella) to go on living (1948, 156). Similarly, Donat writes that "the warmth, compassion, and kind words" of a family he was with immediately after the war brought him back to life (1978, 237). And in *Moments of Reprieve* Levi comments on a note that a friend named Lorenzo delivered to him from what was left of the human world, saying, "That piece of paper in my hands . . . represented a breach, a small gap in the black universe that closed tightly around us" (1986b, 54). In the universe of the antiworld there are no black holes that swallow up light but rather these white holes, through the light of a human face might be glimpsed. In *Survival in Auschwitz* Levi tells us what this intrusion of a face into the realm of facelessness meant to him. "The personages on these pages are not men," he writes. "But Lorenzo was a man. . . . Thanks to Lorenzo, I managed not to forget that I myself was a man" (1961, 111). Which is to say: I managed to remember that I have a face. And to retain my face I remember Lorenzo's face.

Whether it is the SS who emerges in the world or the human being who rises up in the antiworld, both constitute the manifestation of the absolutely alien within the context of their appearance. The alien nature of each thus imparts to both an image of madness. In the Holocaust memoir, then, the face of the other as the face of the alien is linked to the image of madness.

Images of Madness in the Face of the Other

So far I have encountered the face of the other in the Holocaust memoir as it appears along the edges of the world and in the gullet of the antiworld. At the point where these two meet I encounter the images of madness. When the face of the other summoned in the memoir is steeped in madness, it is ridden with all the ambiguity of madness. If explanation entails the elimination of ambiguity, then it cannot be explained. But it can be examined. And no examination of the face of the other in the Holocaust memoir is complete without looking into these blinding images of madness. Fackenheim articulates the ambiguity at work here when he notes that if sanity entails maintaining some contact with the world, then "such sanity is destroyed when the world is Auschwitz"; in contrast, whereas insanity entails a flight from the world, such a flight is necessary when the world is the Nazi Holocaust, "if even a shred of sanity is to remain" (1970, 68–69). If, as Michel Foucault argues, "madness begins where the relation of man to truth is disturbed and darkened" (1965, 104), that relation is cast in darkness and turmoil when the human being is trapped between the flight from one world and the contact with the other. In *The Town beyond the Wall* Wiesel's character Moishe the Madman expresses this tension when he declares, "These days honest men can do only one thing: go mad! . . . That's the way to stay human" (1964, 20). Elsewhere Wiesel writes, " 'It came to pass in those days,' said Rabbi Michael Dov Weismandel, 'that normal beings had to lose their reason, and those who did not lose it—were not normal" (1988, 48). To remain human and, thus, retain a semblance of normalcy is to retain a face by which a person may come into a relation with another human being. While madness "normally" signifies an infinite distance from the other, with the antiworld's undoing of the categories of reason and reality it may now become an insistence on a proximity with the other. But when every trace of the *human* other is removed upon the obliteration of the face, madness is a flight that throws the self back on the emptiness of itself.

Such is the ambiguity, the paradox, that characterizes the images of madness in the Holocaust memoir. They are not fetched from any cloister to which the insane have been consigned but are rather drawn from the midst of the intersection of world and antiworld where flight *from* and contact *with* become absolutely confused. One the one hand, for instance, Donat writes, "Only those who were madmen did not fear the Germans and dared to behave aggressively" (1978, 45). Here those who acted against the Nazis acted for humanity; in this case, then, is a memory of a refusal to be *effaced* so that the image of madness in these faces is an image of humanity. This memory is to be contrasted, on the other hand, with Paul Trepman's recollection of Dr. Schipper, a professor sent to Majdanek who went about the camp laughing and weeping, "mumbling incoherent phrases. He had become the camp madman" (1978, 88). Trepman's description of Dr. Schipper seems to fit Foucault's description of madness as "the existence, under the body's alterations, under the oddity of conduct and conversation, of *a delirious discourse*" (1965, 99; emphasis in original). Hence, the incoherent phrases punctuated now by laughter, now by tears. Nevertheless, Trepman's is the memory not just of a madman but of the *camp madman*, suggesting that such madness is a necessary feature of the concentrationary universe, just as it is an essential element of the memory of that antiworld. Olga Lengyel recalls that "the mad rulers of the camp dictated that, while normal people were sent to death, lunatics were kept alive" (1972, 198). Why? Because the inmates' ineluctable contact—or collision—with the antiworld cannot be sustained without this repeated presence of those who take flight from it— not into another world, it must be noted, but into the void of madness. If the memoir, however, is to recover from the illness of that world and its madness, then the one who remembers must draw the delirious discourse of the lunatic into the discourse of remembrance. Once the madman's phrases are *said* to be incomprehensible, they assume a place in a text that struggles to recover the comprehensible by tracing the face of the other within the image of madness. For this saying is an act of response that takes the author to the other side of madness.

"Why do I write?" one recalls Wiesel's question, which is to ask, Why do I remember? His reply is: "Perhaps in order not to go mad. Or, on the contrary, to touch the bottom of madness" (1990b, 13). The ambiguity of madness is thus transferred—or transformed—into the dialectic of memory. There is no memory of the face of the other in the Holocaust memoir without a memory of the images of madness. And, like the self who sees the image of itself in the face of the other, memory in this memoir is itself threatened with madness. Eugene Heimler describes very well the existential condition facing the one engaged with this memory when he says, "I was perched on a ledge which overlooked the dizzy chasm of insanity, down in whose depths my memories were revolving like so many hungry whirlpools" (1959, 62). Yet, like Dante, who could find his way to a renewed life only by penetrating the bottom of hell, the authors of the memoirs can seek a recovery from the illness marked by madness only by plunging beyond the very depths that threaten them. The memory of madness, then, is a saying of "No" in such a way that it is transformed into a "Yes." And it imparts an element of madness to the memoir itself. Like Moshe the Beadle in Wiesel's *Legends of Our Time* (1968, 112–13), the author of the memoir crawls out of a mass grave to become a messenger of what only madness can convey. Suddenly the madness of the survivor becomes a means of affirming what the murderers attempted to negate through their own madness. Thus, a character like Wiesel's Zalman cries out, his voice echoing throughout the memoirs, "One has to be mad to believe in God and in man" (1974, 79). And one has to believe in God and in man in order to undertake *this* movement of remembrance.

In the Holocaust memoir the one who outlines the images of madness in the face of the other is a messenger: these authors do not simply reminisce—they transmit. What is the image they offer, the image whose message transforms one and brings one to the edge of madness? Commenting on a child suffocated to save Jews in hiding, Abraham relates in Wiesel's *Ani Maamin*

> The death of the child
> Fails to save the others....
> But I saw the mother.
> I saw her gaze fill with madness.
> I offer you that madness (1973a, 39, 41)

The gaze of a mother illuminated by flames and darkened by madness is the gaze that gazes from the pages of the Holocaust memoir. It is the gaze of Auschwitz itself, a place often mistaken—or rightly taken—for a madhouse by those who first arrived there. For they see these mothers, and they have no other way of "understanding" what they see. "Was this the courtyard of a madhouse?" Olga Lengyel remembers her first thoughts at her first glimpse of the women beyond the electrified fence at Auschwitz. " 'Evidently,' I told myself, 'these women are abnormals, and that is why they are isolated" (1972, 28). Sara Zyskind has the same memory and offers the same: " 'It must be a lunatic asylum we've been brought to,' I said to myself" (1981, 185). Soon the image she encounters in the faces of these others, however, is imposed upon herself. After being shaved and disinfected, outfitted and humiliated, she recalls, "We would ourselves be taken for lunatics by those arriving after us. Perhaps we *were* all lunatics and Auschwitz an asylum from which we would never escape" (Zyskind 1981, 192). And where does she perceive the image of madness that threatens her? In the face of the other, of her friend Surtcha. Staring at each other, they broke into laughter, but, she remembers, "our laughter lasted barely a few seconds, coming to an abrupt end as we looked at one another with eyes filled with horror. Was it possible that we had both gone mad?" (Zyskind 1981, 185). Perhaps this question alone saves her from the oblivion that closes in on her. Perhaps this question alone makes it possible for her to summon this memory of the face that brought the question to her lips.

In her memoir Sara Nomberg-Przytyk writes, "It was important to wash, even if it meant rubbing your face with a fistful of snow. The effort to wash your face is an expression of life" (1985, 19). In the Polish manuscript washing the face is an expression of the *walki o życie* (Nomberg-Przytyk n.d., 13), or the "struggle for life." Cleansing one's face with a fistful of snow in a place where such an effort is futile may itself be viewed as an act of madness. It is a *mad struggle* for life in a realm where all such struggle is rendered pointless by the predetermined outcome of madness and death. Yet this cleansing is a purification of the face that keeps madness at bay, for it is not just dirt the woman washes from her visage but the image of madness. Recalling the gaze of the mother invoked by Wiesel in *Ani Maamin* (1973a, 39, 41), however, one asks, How is a human being to wash from her face all she has seen? Leon Wells notes that it is forbidden for "anybody to see the faces of inmates who have seen the 'sands'" (1978, 143), those pits where bodies retrieved from mass graves were stacked and burned. Why forbidden? Because these are faces ravaged by the illness from which the memoir seeks a recovery. Forbidden to be seen, they are the faces that the memoir would have one see, the faces that silently bring face to face with the words of the memoir — and with the silence breached by the memoir. Ultimately, the delirious discourse of madness falls into the silence of delirium. Out of that silence *this* memory speaks.

Language, argues Foucault, is the "constituent form" of madness: "that the essence of madness can be ultimately defined in the simple structure of a discourse does not reduce it to a purely psychological nature, but gives it hold over the totality of soul and body" (1965, 100). But when the language that makes madness manifest is drawn into the literary text of the memoir, something other than language is revealed, as Foucault goes on to explain, "By the madness which interrupts it, a work of art opens up a void, a moment of silence, a question without answer, provokes a breach without reconciliation where the world is forced to question itself" (1965, 288). One sees, then, where the face of the other in the Holocaust memoir leads: proceeding from world to antiworld to madness, one arrives at a moment and a memory of silence—not just the silence of a face but an ontological silence, the silence of an imposed absence in search of presence, of a universe in need of recovery from the illness of ontological indifference. Thus, one arrives at the next dimension of the recovery from an illness in the Holocaust memoir.

5

The Memory of Silence

In the Talmud Rabbi Papa maintains that "the merit of attending a house of mourning lies in the silence observed" (Berakhot 6b). Perhaps this observance is also where the merit of attending to the Holocaust memoir lies. For here, too, as one enters this memory, one enters a house of mourning that is made of the memory of silence. Unlike the silence Rabbi Papa would have one observe, however, this silence is made of an indifferent darkness, of the ontological illness Emmanuel Levinas refers to as the "there is." It is made of the collapse of time into antitime in the pit of the antiworld; it is made of words torn from their meaning sent into exile on the reverberations of a scream. George Topas, for instance, cannot forget that when he took his first steps in Majdanek, "a mournful, eerie silence pervaded the descending darkness" (1990, 114). Wieslaw Kielar remembers the silence with which he wrestled through nights emptied of time as he was forced to stand in the narrow confines of the *Stehbunker*, or the "standing bunker," at Auschwitz. He writes, "This silence stirs me up. . . . I began to sing, I stamped my wooden clogs; in a word, I began making a lot of noise if only to chase away this damned silence which fills me—I don't know why—with fear" (1980, 158). Nathan Shapell recalls the "deathly silence, screaming silence" that permeated the ghetto after a final roundup of the Jews for deportation: "Their screams were stifled," he writes, "except in my head, where, sometimes, they still go on and on" (1974, 81–82) and on, into the words and between the lines of the memoir. In these examples one discovers the dimensions of the silence remembered in the memoir; it is a silence that issues from the absence of the other, from the vault of the universe, and from the depths of the soul. Fear and darkness are the very stuff of the silence with which memory does battle. It is the fear of a voicelessness that drains the human being of his soul; it is the darkness of an anticreation pitted against the light created upon the first utterance in the creation of the world.

How does the author of the memoir engage this silence? Through the creation of a text that would reconstitute a life and a world swallowed up by silence. Unlike memoirs that recount the words and deed that have gone into a life, the Holocaust memoir is distinguished by the memory of si- lence—the silence of a soul turned to ashes, of a world that turned its back, and of a God who turned His face. The authors of these memoirs pursue the memory of silence not to recapture it, as one might retrieve a shred of the past, but to counter it or to recover from it; silence here is a symptom of a deadly illness. As much as these words are offered to a reader, they are spoken to breach a silence that suffocates life. It is the silence that Elie Wiesel's character Paltiel Kossover describes in *The Testament* when he says, "I did not know that it was possible to die of silence, as one dies of pain, of sorrow, of hunger. . . . I understood why God created heaven and earth, why He fashioned man in His image by conferring on him the right and the ability to speak his joy, to express his anguish. God too, God Himself was afraid of silence" (1981, 209–10). The author's efforts to recover from the illness of indifference is an effort to recover the image of the divine within the human image. Here the recovery of the image entails a recovery of the word that brings life over against the silence that kills. Like the memory of mother and father, then, the memory of silence is the memory of a loss, and because the word is the vehicle of memory, the act of remembrance is itself, at least in part, a recovery of what was lost. Breaking the silence that threat- ens the human being, the memory of silence is an overcoming of silence.

To the extent that the memory of silence comes upon the recovery of the word it is linked to what Jewish tradition regards as the very essence of the human being. God creates the human in His image inasmuch as He imparts to the human being the power of speech. Maimonides, for example, declares, "The words 'speaking animal' include the true essence of man, and there is no third element besides life and speech in the definition of man; when he, therefore, is described by the attributes of life and speech, these are nothing but an explanation of the name 'man,' that is to say, that the thing which is called man consists of life and speech" (1956, 68). In the Holocaust memoir life and speech consist of memory, and memory consists of life and speech; each nurtures the other to impart a voice to the voiceless silence. Here a kind of *tikkun* or mending transpires. Although in the Jewish tradition there are various forms of *tikkun*, Aryeh Kaplan notes that they all entail "removing or rectifying the barriers that prevent us from hearing" a voice (1990, 170). Memory rejoins life and speech in a *tikkun* of the word, by which meaning is returned to the word in the act of remembrance, which is an act of *hearing*. Once this *tikkun* comes about, silence itself may speak so that the memory of silence transforms silence into voice. "The silent voice," says the *Zohar*, "is the supernal voice from which all other voices proceed" (1984, 2:294). But if the "supernal voice" falls silent in the silence that is Auschwitz, the human voice of memory must seek its recovery. This is one implication of André Neher's insight when he writes, "The first step after Auschwitz . . . is the moment of Silence, of that Silence which once, at the beginning of the world, held back the Word while also being its womb" (1981, 143). In the Holocaust memoir memory becomes just such a womb. Hence, the recovery from an illness points up the rebirth of a humanity and a divinity that have fallen prey to silence. It is the recovery of a beginning and, therefore, of time itself, in the remembrance of a past for the sake of a future.

Once again one has the fundamental elements that characterize the memory of silence in the Holocaust memoir. They are the memory of the dumb, ontological indifference of the "there is"; the memory of time collapsed so as to leave no moment, no room, for the word that might join together time and place; and the memory of the word itself muted in a severance from its meaning. These are the key elements to be examined in the Holocaust memoir's memory of silence.

Ontological Indifference: The "There Is"

"The world around us," Primo Levi says of his emergence from Auschwitz, "seemed to have returned to primeval Chaos, and was swarming with scalene, defective, abnormal human specimens" (1965, 33). These are the creatures who reflect the image not of the Creator but of the Chaos opposed by the Creator; these are the inhabitants of a new land such as the one that the Germans made out of Russia. There, says Levi, "it was more than a sack: it was the genius of destruction, of anti-creation, here as at Auschwitz; it was the mystique of barrenness" (1965, 128). The Italian word translated as "barrenness" is *vuoto* (1989, 250), which means "empty space" or "void." The anticreation is the creation of nothing out of something, a return to the void of what strives to overcome the void. This imposition of Chaos on Creation, of the emptiness of indifference on the fullness of life, is just what Levinas describes as the "there is." With the appearance of the "there is," he explains, "the absence of everything returns to us as a presence, as the place where the bottom has dropped out of everything, an atmospheric density, a plenitude of the void, or the murmur of silence" (1987b, 46). The *murmur* of silence? Perhaps better, the shriek of silence. For in the realm of the

Shoah the absence of everything is the absence of anything of significance or the absence of all that is able to signify. The face of the Holy One that imparts meaning to His Creation is eclipsed by the facelessness of indifferent being. Hence, the voice that would speak and, thus, breach the silence is rendered mute by the mute "plenitude of the void." Unable to speak, the soul is unable to signify anything. When the bottom drops out the human being descends into what Levinas refers to as the *without-self* (1987b, 49), a *non-self*, where the *non-* derives from the *in-* of the ontological *in*difference of the "there is."

"It is a noise returning after every negation of this noise," Levinas elaborates on the "there is." "I sometimes use the expression: the excluded middle. One cannot say of this 'there is' which persists that it is an event of being. One can neither say that it is nothingness, even though there is nothing" (1985, 48–49). One may think of the excluded middle as the supernal voice previously invoked in the citation from the *Zohar*, the silent voice of the voice of silence from which the dialogical voices of the face-to-face encounter derive their sense and sensibility. The exclusion of the middle is the effacement of the face in a muting of the supernal voice, which brings about the horror and the panic that Levinas ascribes to the "there is" in *Existence and Existents*. The "there is," he argues, is a presence in which "anything can count for anything else" and from which "it is impossible to take shelter in oneself, to withdraw into one's shell. One is exposed" (Levinas 1978a, 59). Here one moves to another level in understanding Wiesel's remark that "children were old, and old men were as helpless as children" (Patterson 1991, 21). The counting of anything for anything else is precisely what distinguishes the "there is" as an ontological indifference. With no place to turn, no dawn to await, the human being thrown into the pit of indifferent being is overcome with horror. It is not a horror that inhabits the self, however, but a horror that occludes the self, as Levinas is quick to note. Horror, he says, strips consciousness of its subjectivity "not in lulling it into unconsciousness, but in throwing it into an *impersonal vigilance*" (1978a, 60; emphasis in original). The *impersonal* is there as the "there is," and the impersonal is the nocturnal, the dark, . . . the *silent*.

These insights from Levinas enable one to read with deeper insight memories such as those of Charlotte Delbo, who recalls, "We feel ourselves teetering over the pit of shadow . . . of night or of another nightmare, or our real death, and we struggle furiously, endlessly. We must go back, go back home" (1968, 63). But there is no retreat from the exposure to the "there is" except, perhaps, in memory's movement of return, which goes back to the murder camp to leave it behind. Here it is worth noting that the phrase "over the pit of shadow" is a translation of *dans un trou d'ombre* (1965, 64), which may also be read, "in a hole of darkness," suggesting that they are not just *over* the pit but already inside it. Indeed, the "there is" is always encountered as something that has *already* engulfed one; that is why it is not an event in being but appears in a time that is already too late. The human being reduced to a "without-self" and stripped of her subjectivity, moreover, is not just in the pit, but the pit is in the human being; that is why the "there is" is not nothingness but acts upon the human being like an illness. "The bottom of the pit: it exists," Wiesel's words come to mind. "It's within us" (1964, 82–83). The darkness of the pit fills the man, fills his mouth, robbing him of the word, like the darkness that engulfs Ka-tzetnik's mouth during the first LSD therapy session he underwent to rid himself of thirty years of nightmares. "I sense darkness on my palate," he writes, "as if it were a thing I put in my mouth" (1989, 4). So the man swallows the thing that would swallow him, from the inside; he imbibes the emptiness turned tangible in a eucharistic merging not with his redeemer but with the very thing that damns him. This confluence with the silence arises not from any "being-with" or *Mitsein* but from the aloneness that Sara Zyskind remembers when she says, "I felt frightfully alone, a kind of aloneness I had never experienced in all my life" (1981, 186). "There is" means *there is* no other, *there is* no voice, *there is* no appeal. The child is abandoned, even though *there is* no one who has abandoned her. For the child is abandoned by a being turned indifferent, where this *there is* is all there is.

"The feeling of being abandoned," Saul Friedländer writes, "can pass through the protective wall of sleep. . . . I awaken in a panic. Everything is the room is new, odd, even terrifying, and my parents are gone" (1980, 37–38). One is reminded of the horror and the panic that Levinas ascribes to the "there is." Everything is new and odd because everything has been muted by indifference; "my parents are gone" means the loving voice is gone, the caring face has turned away, despite the fact that this memory is of a time before the departure of his parents. What makes this memory a recollection of the "there is" is precisely the groundlessness of the anxiety remembered. To be sure, later in his memoir Friedländer observes, "You feel it slowly come over you . . . fear in its pure state" (1980, 130–31). If one looks at the French text, where one finds that that "come over" is a translation of *envahir*, "to invade" (1978, 123), then one has a stronger suggestion of a penetration of the ontological illness into the very core of one's being. Yet from that core comes the memory that has as its object the fear without an object, thus displacing the fear in a movement toward recovery. When memory comes, something other than the fear matters; something other than the anxiety speaks in a movement toward overcoming the silence that eclipses the voice. Thus, something may be saved in the very memory of being drowned, such as the memory in Levi's *The Drowned and the Saved*. Describing the constant anguish that every inmate felt, he says it was "the 'tohu-bohu' of a deserted and empty universe crushed under the spirit of God but from which the spirit of man is absent: not yet born or already extinguished" (1988, 85). This remembrance of what was not yet born or already extinguished is the stirring of a spirit that seeks a presence through a refusal to desert a deserted universe, its refusal to be extinguished, although it may have yet to be born.

The memory of the deserted universe is the memory of the silence of the universe. And where does memory locate the universe? In the heavens above. Hence, in one memoir after another the memory of the ontological illness of the "there is" lies in the memory of a silent, indifferent sky. Children are being thrown into the vans headed for the gas chambers, yet, Katzetnik recalls, "silent are the heavens" (1971b, 53). Loving mothers and good fathers are rounded up for deportation to Treblinka, yet, writes Alexander Donat, "the heavens were silent" (1978, 100). One feels ashamed when one hears Bertha Ferderber-Salz say that she hates the rays of the sun "because in those dark days they dared to shine so shamelessly" (1980, 101). Yes, ashamed: not just ashamed of oneself but ashamed for a sun and a sky whose indifference did not allow them to withhold their light. "Why are the stars still shining?" asks Lily Lerner. "Who hears the cries of the sick and disturbed? . . . Who tends to the chosen people now? There were no answers, only the intense silence that was tearing me apart" (1980, 108–09). Once more the pit below reveals itself in the sky and tears apart the witness from within. "Blessed is the day," Ralph Waldo Emerson wrote in his journal on 21 December 1834, "when the youth discovers that Within and Above are synonyms" (1965, 53). But Emerson had no inkling of the silence that extinguishes the voice arising from within and from beyond. It is a principle of the Jewish faith that what transpires below has an impact in what happens above. "An arousal from above," says Rabbi Schneur Zalman, for example, "comes only in response to an arousal from below" (1981, 405). But when the arousal from below meets with indifferent emptiness, what is within collapses into silence, not the "silence of all tongues," as Buber calls it (1970, 89), but the silence of the absence of all tongues. The function of memory in the Holocaust memoir, then, is not so much to arouse what is above as to regenerate a presence that might be aroused. Thus, Lily Lerner insists that the cries of the sick and disturbed be at least remembered below, if not heard above. The presence that might be aroused is made of memory.

Once again one recalls an insight from Levinas, "Because being is ordained to height the human body is placed in a space in which the high and the low are distinguished and the sky is discovered" (1987a, 100). The sky above imparts significance to the space between two human beings; *height* means something very dear is at stake in human relation, which in turn means that the time to answer is ever at hand. Hence, it is not just the cycle of light and darkness in the sky that constitutes time but the demand for a response that arises between two people. "Responsibility for the Other," as Levinas expresses it, "signifies an original and concrete temporality" (1987b, 104). When the ontological indifference of the "there is" inserts itself into human life and thus isolates the human being in silence, however, that life suffers a collapse of time. Thus, to reconstitute time the author seeks the memory of a time past when time was lost.

The Remembrance of Time Collapsed

The Jewish community targeted for extermination is based, among other things, on common blood and not on any nationalistic, political, or economic distinction. "Only a community based on common blood, Franz Rosenzweig argues, "feels the warrant of eternity in its veins even now" (1972, 299). And a community based on common blood is based on time: it is the time of tradition, ancient and enduring, that makes the blood common from one generation to the next. When the tradition is lost, so is the blood. Thus, the warrant of eternity, Rosenzweig explains, manifests itself in time not just through the orbits of the two luminaries but in "the service of the earth, constantly repeated day in day out and year in year out" (1972, 291), repeated in the community's unabated observance of the feasts and holy days. "We must be able to *live* in our eternity," as he states it (1955, 90), and to live in our eternity is to draw it into time through the observance of the holy days. Through this communal observance the responsibility for the other affirmed here below is linked to the cycles of light and darkness traced above; time becomes *life* time—that is, time *lived* in relation to the living and to the origin of life—through this connection between the heavens and the earth.

One begins to understand, then, why the Nazis' attack on life included an attack on the observance in time that links the Eternal People to the Eternal One, why, in other words, they would plan their most cruel actions to coincide with the Jewish holy days. The project of anticreation that Levi refers to above (1965, 128), for instance, shows up in the violation and undoing of that time when the Creation is remembered and observed: it was on the Sabbath, Elie Wiesel relates, that the Germans announced the deportation of the Jews of Sighet (1960, 23). In another example Bertha Ferderber-Salz remembers an exhumation and burning of bodies that was calculated to correspond with the High Holy Days from Rosh Hashanah to Yom Kippur, the days of judgment and atonement. "Instead of festive candles," she writes, "we kindled human bodies, our own flesh and blood" (1980, 102), which is to say: we consigned to the flames our own time and eternity. Indeed, at Maidanek, Donat relates an inmate's observation, "Life is one long Jewish holiday. We live in tents as during the Feast of Tabernacles; we are dressed for a Purim carnival; we eat as on Yom Kippur [a day of fasting]; and our mood is always that of Tisha B'Av [the day of mourning the destruction of the Temple]" (1978, 212). In Maidanek, of course, the continual observance is continually out of season, out of sync, out of time; precisely because it is continual, it is removed from the cycle of time in a collapse of time.

Jewish tradition teaches that when the world was destroyed the first time and the waters of the heavens covered the earth below, all was reduced not only to silence but to timelessness; the destruction of life defined by a relation between heaven earth is the destruction of time. "Day and night ceased during the period of the Flood," says Rashi, "for the planetary system did not function, so that there was no distinction between day and night" (1972, 1:36). So it happened upon the second destruction of the world, when, in the words of Zivia Lubetkin, "darkness reigned within and without" (1981, 236); like the indifferent "there is," this is a darkness made of silence and a silence made of broken time. Removed from its orbital cycle, this darkness is one that bespeaks nothing; word and time are abrogated. This connection between the remembrance of time collapsed and the memory of silence is quite explicit in Charlotte Delbo's memoir where she writes, "Fifteen thousand women stamp their feet and it makes no noise. The silence is solidified into cold. . . . We are in a setting in which time is abolished. We do not know if we exist" (1968, 37). *Nous ne savons pas si nous sommes* reads the French version of the last sentence (1965, 37): "we do not know if we *are*" where the verb that conveys a tense and the predicate that situates a time are both undermined. "What is nearer to eternity than a day?" Delbo asks. "How can one know that it is passing?" (1968, 54). Stripped of one's predicates, one cannot know. From what has been said about the illness of indifference and the ontological imposition of the "there is" one realizes that there is more than suffering underlying Delbo's question. Time passes according to the moments that mark what matters, and what matters is revealed in a response to the other human being steeped in a nonindifference and opposed to the "there is." When the "there is" rules, the human being simply "is," without predicate or importance, without time; the planetary system no longer functions, and the day comes to a halt. During a march east of Buchenwald, Eugene Heimler remembers, "I stepped out of time, and years and hours and minutes became in my mind something created by man" (1959, 181). Thus, time itself—if it can be called "time"—shifts to an alien sphere.

Time "on planet Auschwitz," says Ka-tzetnik, "revolved around the cogwheels of a different time-sphere" (1989, xi). That sphere belongs to none of the circles of heaven or hell; like the "there is," it cannot be located within the framework of being, nor can it be said that this different time-sphere is nothing. The wheels turn, or rather twist, but not according to the measure of time that belongs to creation. Thus, says Heimler, "Time in Auschwitz was not divided into minutes, hours, and days" (1959, 36). There is no sun "like the one that shines upon Maidanek," as the Maidanek Anthem goes (Trepman 1978, 137), because the Maidanek sun does not trace the twenty-four-hour orbit of the sun that God placed in the heavens to rule the day; the week at Auschwitz does not equal seven days because all that belongs to the Seventh Day, to the Sabbath, has been obliterated. Yes, physicists continued to do their work on space-time, but the prayers that measure the cycles of the days and weeks of *life* time have been silenced. "Prayer is not in time but time in prayer," Martin Buber has said (1970, 59), and so it is, for prayer draws the eternal into time, and from the eternal time derives its measure. But in the concentrationary universe the eternal is turned over to the tohu-bohu that Levi invokes (1988, 85) and time collapses, void of all measure because it overflows with the void. This collapse of time lies behind Kitty Hart's assertion that "keeping track of time was impossible" (1982, 96) and Lily Lerner's remark that "time passed. Hours? Yes. How many? I don't know" (1980, 82). Life is threatened as much by this loss of time as by physical hardship. So the memory that would seek a return to life seeks a return of time.

One finds that the memory of the end of a life is often articulated through symbols that signify the end of time, such as the watch or clock that comes to a halt. Upon seeing a broken clock on a building near Buchenwald, for example, Heimler notes, "It was as if the paralysed hands were telling me: 'This is the end of you. Time died at half past twelve'" (1959, 164). The frozen hands on the clock tell the man that there is nothing more to be told, no life to be narrated; the remembrance of time collapsed is a remembrance of this silence. When the Nazis marched into the Polish town of Bielitz, Gerda Klein records in the opening lines of her memoir, there, too, time was paralyzed. "The hands [of the watch] seem to stand motionless at 9:10," she recalls a watch lying on the floor. "There would be a past only, . . . time had stopped" (1957, 3). Lying on the floor, the watch is out of place; it belongs on a wrist that moves a hand that traces a past and reaches toward a future. There can be no past without the movement of time that characterizes the present, as Livia Jackson suggests when she writes, "The rapid succession of events this morning [upon arriving at Auschwitz] is an evolution of eons. Our parents and families belong to the prehistoric past" (1980, 61–62). Here, too, one discerns a link between the remembrance of time collapsed and the memory of silence. The prehistoric past is the silent past, a realm without the words that constitute a history, a tradition, and an ancestry. Parents and families are lost to this silence when they lose their significance; and when they lose their significance, they lose their time. The time of tradition, as seen in part 1, is made of the mother's love and the father's word; when these are turned over to the silence of the void, time is rendered void and tradition—which is precisely the historic—collapses into the prehistoric or, in this case, into the antihistoric.

At this point one may add depth to one's understanding of a passage from Primo Levi's *Survival in Auschwitz*: "For living men, the units of time always have a value. . . . But for us, . . . the future stood in front of us, grey and inarticulate, like an invincible barrier. For us, history had stopped" (1961, 107). Noting the linkage that Levi establishes between the halt of history and the fading of the future, one returns once more to Wiesel's observation that the opposite of the past is not the future but the absence of a future (1990b, 239). In the Holocaust memoir, then, the freezing of time and the loss of the past are often expressed as a collapse of the future. At first this breakdown may present itself in the deceptively simplistic terms of taking each day one at a time as when Rudolf Vrba says, "It was a question of surviving today without thinking too much about tomorrow" (1964, 103). Such is the condition of a man reduced to a mere body or, as Wiesel states it, "perhaps less than that even: a starved stomach" (1960, 59). The stomach does not speak— it growls. The stomach knows no relation to the other human being but is preoccupied only with its own emptiness. Yet the other, as one recalls from Levinas, is the future (1987b, 77). The truth of this insight becomes clear in Leon Wells's memoir, "Never, during the time of hiding, or for the two years before, had I any dreams or thoughts about the future . . . For whom and for what?" (1978, 236). Wells's question is just what leaves aghast the adults that Thomas Geve refers to when he relates, "The tragedy of having lost their families was an all-pervading shadow. . . . When I dared to mention the future they would be aghast" (1981, 185–86). Without the "for whom"—without the being-for-the-other, for family and loved ones, that constitutes the "for whom"—there is no future, no time.

Having established this connection, one can connect the collapse of time with the illness of indifference from which the Holocaust memoir seeks recovery through a recovery of time. For in the Holocaust memoir memory is in time and of time, even—or especially—when it is the memory of time collapsed. And the memory of time passed, of time collapsed in the past, is a remembrance of the future, in a recovery of the relation to the other. Addressed to another, the memory of silence breaks a silence for the sake of a healing of the illness that had destroyed human relation. With this in mind André Neher writes, "The final letter of the Hebrew alphabet is *tav*, which indicates the second person of the future tense and thus a direction of the man who is summoned toward an infinitely open future" (1981, 228). The silence broken by the memory of silence for the sake of a healing is broken by the second person of the future tense. In the process of summoning the memory of the past the author of the memoir addresses the second person, the You, who signifies not only the future but the summons that calls one forth, into the movement of response that opens up the future. Thus, restoring the movement and the moment of response, the memoir restores the bond between word and meaning that is the necessary basis for an act of response. Yet, although it seeks to recover this linkage, the memoir must do so dialectically in a memory of the word severed from its meaning.

The Word Severed from Meaning

What is the silence of the word severed from meaning? To answer this question one might be tempted to invoke the distinction that Bakhtin draws between quietude (*tishina*) and silence (*molchanie*). "The disturbance of quietude by sound is mechanical," he explains. "The disturbance of silence by the word is personalistic and intelligible. . . . In quietude nothing makes a sound; in silence nobody *speaks*. Silence is possible only in the human world" (1986, 133–34; emphasis in original). But the silence of the word severed from meaning belongs to neither of these categories. Certainly there were sounds on Planet Auschwitz: trains screeching to a halt, doors on cattle cars sliding open, iron gates embossed with *Arbeit Macht Frei* clanging shut. And if Bakhtin's "silence" is possible only in the human realm, there was no such silence in this antihuman world. Nor may the silence of the word severed from meaning be compared to the silence of the infinite spaces that terrified Pascal (1966, 95), because even in his terror Pascal could still speak and be understood if only to declare that he was terrified. When the word is severed from meaning, one should note further, it does not necessarily follow that words are not uttered; it indicates, rather, that words are not connected, that human relation has collapsed, and that the *Shekhinah*, the Indwelling Presence of the Holy One, has vanished.

Commenting on the notion of the *Shekhinah* in exile, Wiesel explains that it is as though God has abandoned Himself, or as though the *Shekhinah* had abandoned God to be with humanity (1990a, 93–94). With this exile of the *Shekhinah*, this abandonment of God by Himself, comes the exile of the word; when the *Shekhinah* is in place, word is tied to meaning. In the condition of exile, then, a living presence is out of place, and in her place arises a silence denoting an absence or nothingness that eclipses God and humanity. According to Jewish tradition, as Adin Steinsaltz points out, "the words that made the world are constantly being spoken anew, and nothing can exist unless it is sustained by them" (1988, 134). With the appearance of the concentrationary antiworld it is not so much that the words by which the world is made fall silent or that nothing exists; rather, these words are torn from their meaning, for it is not just the words that make a world but the conjunction of word and meaning. In the *Zohar* one finds a metaphor for this joining of word and meaning: "The supernal Mother is found in the company of the male only at the time when the house is prepared, and the male and female are joined" (1984, 1:159–60). The prepared house is the home that is opposed to exile; it is the dwelling where a door is opened to the Indwelling Presence. And just as life is created in the joining of husband and wife, so is the world created anew in the joining of word and meaning. But in the divorce of word from meaning the haleness of creation is overtaken by the illness of destruction. If the memory of silence is linked to a recovery from an illness, it is because that memory entails a recovery of the marriage of word and meaning through a remembrance of their divorce.

Not only a world in which the soul may dwell is at stake in the return of the word to its meaning; the very life of the soul inheres in the word as well. Edmond Jabès insists on this point, declaring, "We become the word that gives reality to the object, to the being" (1990, 90). The word is not a sign pointing to an object; rather, when tied to meaning, it takes on a life into which is gathered the polarity of subject and object, by which both world and human being become present. "Everything that is Being for us," Karl Jaspers makes this point, "can be grasped only in the subject-object polarity. Being must assume a mode of being-an-object and at the same time a mode of subjectivity for which this is an object" (1959, 19). Thus, the breakdown of reality and the annihilation of the human image are not separate but concurrent events distinguishing the concentrationary universe. And these concurrent events transpire upon the severance of word from meaning. Levi conveys this idea when he writes, "The world into which one was precipitated was terrible, yes, but also indecipherable. . . . One could not discern a single frontier" (1988, 38). It is the word's tie with meaning that establishes the frontiers between good and evil, holy and profane, human and animal. When the word is severed from meaning there is no *havdalah*, no distinction, that would delineate the name and the face of the human image. So Levi remembers that the first days in Auschwitz were filled with a "sound and fury signifying nothing: a hubbub of people without names or faces drowned in a continuous, deafening background noise from which, however, the human word did not surface" (1988, 93–94). Here one discovers that the memory of silence is not a memory of noiselessness but of the violence done to the word. Indeed, the Italian version of this passage conveys more of this violence than does the English translation. "Sound," for example, is a translation of *fracasso*, from *fracassare*, meaning "to smash, chatter, crash"; and "signifying nothing" is *privo di significato*, or "destitute of meaning" (1986a, 72). In the remembrance of word severed from meaning the memory of silence is the memory of violence.

In *Survival in Auschwitz* Levi describes the confusion of tongues as a "fundamental component" of the camp. "One is surrounded by a perpetual Babel," he says (1961, 33). The Tower of Babel, in fact, is an image that Levi returns to in his description of the Carbide Tower at Buna, a tower made of bricks called *Ziegel, briques, tegula, cegli, kamenny, mattoni, téglak*, "cemented by hate" (1961, 66). The holiness of the divine being and the haleness of the human being retain their integrity only as long as the word retains its contact with meaning. In the image of Babel one sees the collapse of that contact in the contempt that Levi points out. To be sure, Jewish tradition also sees this contempt in the Tower. One is told in the *Midrash Rabbah*, for instance, that on top of the Tower there was to have been an idol wielding a sword, ready to do battle with God (1961, 1:305). And in the *Pirke de Rabbi Eliezer* it is written, "If a man fell [from the Tower] and died they paid no heed to him, but if a brick fell they sat down and wept, and said: Woe is us!

When will another come in its stead?" (1970, 176). At the heart of the confusion of tongues noted by Levi is this confusion surrounding the words *God* and *man*. Once the word is severed from meaning in the confusion of those words, the language of the antiworld inserts itself into creation in an undoing of creation. The language of memory in the Holocaust memoir, then, arises in opposition to this new language of meaninglessness.

"In the Camp," as Levi says, "the terms eating, food, hunger, had meanings totally different from their usual ones" (1986b, 93). Elsewhere he explains that in the camp words such as *fear, pain,* and *winter* were not the words used by free men. "If the Lagers had lasted longer," he maintains, "a new, harsh language would have been born" (1961, 112–13). Such an undoing of words silences the word; the memory of silence is the memory of words thus silenced. These words undone belong to the antilanguage of the antiworld and cannot find their way out. No sooner are they uttered than their meanings are left behind. The illness from which the memoir would recover is this illness of language where a "special dialect" arises like a virus to attack the word. Thus, says Sim Kessel, a combination of German, Russian, Polish, and Yiddish "became the special dialect of Auschwitz" (1972, 102). The planet unto itself acquires a language unto itself. Yet it is not a language in any normal sense, not a language formed from the interanimation of these various languages. Rather, it arises through the kind of corruption of language that Elie Cohen describes when he writes, "The Germans always had such fine names for things like that. In this case it was 'SB'—*Sonderbehandlung*—special treatment. And special treatment meant gas" (1973, 91). Hence, the severance of word from meaning is not just a matter of trying to convey the fact that "hungry" means "*very, very* hungry"; it is not the extremity of conditions that tears word from meaning. On the contrary, it is the tearing of word from meaning that breeds such conditions.

Sara Nomberg-Przytyk makes this point clearly and eloquently when she asserts, "The new set of meanings [of words] provided the best evidence of the devastation that Auschwitz created. . . . All of us were drawn into a bizarre transformation of reality" (1985, 72). In the Polish text the "devastation" that Auschwitz represents is *spustozeń* (n.d., 50), the root of which is *pusty*, meaning "empty" or "void," which suggests an emptying of the word of its meaning—or perhaps a filling of the world with the void. As Nomberg-Przytyk indicates, draining the word of meaning transforms reality in a mutilation of God, man, and world. It is not that words such as *gas* and *selection* signify nothing; rather they signify nothing that belongs to the language and, therefore, to the world of humanity. They signify the nothingness of antiworld and antihumanity, of antiword and antimeaning. "Words are no more," Ka-tzetnik cries out (1971b, 69), or, as the Hebrew texts reads, *chadalah sfat-adam*, "human language has ceased" (1971a, 69). And when human language ceases, the human being is no more. The language ceases upon the rending of word from meaning, which is a tearing of the human being from the human form and is thus a silencing of the human and of the Divine in whose image he is created. That is why, upon the final *Aktion* in his ghetto, Nathan Shapell relates, "I couldn't speak anymore" (1974, 111); that is why Ana Vinocur can write *A Book Without a Title*, declaring in the end, "Those who read this book will realize that it is impossible to give it a title. All words that exist grow pale at this reality" (1976, 137); all *nombres* or "names" fade (Vinocur 1972, 278). For a title or a name would convey a theme, a meaning, from that world to this, but the breaking of all connection between word and meaning breaks one's connection with that world.

"Words failed me then and they fail me now," says Fania Fénelon (1977, 181). In place of the word is the bleeding wound that remains after the word has been torn from its meaning, like the bleeding word *Jude* branded into the forehead of Shlamek's father in Ka-tzetnik's *House of Dolls*, "as though it were quite natural that the word *Jude* should give blood" (1958, 125). The failed words of memory that cover the pages of the Holocaust memoir are inscribed with the blood of this broken word. And a broken word cannot but fail in its effort to make heard the shriek and the silence that haunt its author. Thus, like Charlotte Delbo, who recalls the shriek of silence that emanated from Block 25 at Auschwitz, one comes before these memoirs and strains to connect a word with a face, which is precisely the place where word joins with meaning. "Each woman is a materialized cry," she lays bare her memory, "a scream that is not heard" (1968, 39). If, as Elie Wiesel has said, each word of memory is tied to "a face, a prayer, the one needing the other so as not to sink into oblivion" (1968, 25), then in each word one seeks a meaning, for at the heart of memory, in the very appearance of memory, there is meaning. Yet, like the cries of the women in Block 25, the meaning does not reach anyone, for it has been severed from the word. If, however, any recovery from this wound is to be realized, then, as Wiesel says, one needs these words; one needs this memory of that silence if one is ever to return meaning to the word. And because the memory of the word severed from meaning is the memory of such a silence, the wounded word becomes much like the letter that Saul Friedländer forever awaits: "As the presence of my parents began to become more blurred in my mind, their letter . . . corresponded to a more immediate need than my parents' return" (1980,

119). In a similar manner the memory of silence is all that is left of those who were silenced. And this memory is the hope for a recovery from the illness of silence.

"Where there is world," writes Franz Rosenzweig, "there is speech also. The world is never without the word. Indeed it only exists in the word, and without the word there would be no world" (1972, 295). There is no better evidence—no more dreadful evidence—for the truth of this statement than the rise of the antiworld upon the veiling of the world by the "there is." The "there is" emerges with the muting of the word severed from meaning; once the word is thus silenced, time collapses, for the word is not in time, but time is in the word as long as word is tied to meaning. The Holocaust memoir struggles to return that tie and, thus, restore a time in which a life of human relation might overcome the "there is." "Those who abuse language," taught Rabbi Nachman of Breslov, "fall into 'forgetfulness,' which is 'death to the heart' " (1983, 77). Such is the death manufactured in the death factories at Chelmno, Treblinka, Belzec, Maidanek, Sobibór, and Auschwitz-Birkenau. And the survivors carry that death, that sickness unto death, with them. "All words have wilted long ago," Delbo laments. "My memory has lost all its blood" (1968, 126). Yet few have summoned their memory more eloquently or more powerfully than she. In the poetry of that memory's language Delbo instills ordinary words with extraordinary meaning, meaning that overflows into the souls of all who encounter her memory. Does that mean she has transmitted the silent scream that poured out of Block 25? No. But it does mean that she has transmitted the memory of that silence, despite the residual death that curls around her heart like a serpent. In her response to those shrieks of silence one hears the silence. And the silence summons one's own response.

Hence, to use a term from Levinas, one is deposed as one must be to escape the deadly indifference of the "there is." This deposition of the authority and complacency of the self lies in one's relationship to one's fellow human beings. Only "responsibility for the Other, being-for-the-other," Levinas states it, can stop "the anonymous and senseless rumbling of being" (1985, 52). As one delves into the recesses of the Holocaust memoir, one is confronted with the project of responsibility not because one appropriates this past as one's own but precisely because it does not lend itself to representation, thus calling into question any present—any presence—one might generate. Says Levinas, "A

past that does not gather into representation is at the bottom of the concrete-
ness of the time that is the time of my responsibility for the Other" (1987b,
112). Only in the time of my responsibility is time returned to the present and
presence to time in a halting of the silent and indifferent rumbling of the
"there is." One sees therefore, where the memory of silence in the Holocaust
memoir takes one: it takes one into response and responsibility. Here, too, in
the memoir's memory of the past, one encounters what awaits at the threshold
of the yet-to-be.

6

Response and Responsibility

By now one can see an important distinction between reminiscence and remembrance. Whereas the former is a nostalgic musing over days gone by, the latter arises from within and from beyond the human being in response to a calling and a need. The need announces itself through the illness of indifference; the calling arises in the light of the invisible and ineffable condition that makes such a need an illness and that makes it *matter*. The author of the memoir does not choose to remember; rather, the movement of remembrance chooses the author in such a way that the appearance of the other human being within memory reveals a responsibility that the author must meet. Beyond all choosing and, thus, making every choice meaningful, to borrow from Levinas, "responsibility for the neighbor comes to me from what is prior to my freedom, from a non-present, an immemorial" (1987a, 166). Karl Jaspers has said that in thinking, "something which is not this thought awakens" (1959, 47); so it is with memory in the Holocaust memoir. In the remembrance born of responsibility for the other awakens what is immemorial and unable to appear in the said, awakens the silent summons to which the response is made, a summons made "audible" in the midst of response. The recovery from illness sought through the memoir is a recovery of this response and responsibility to and for an origin that precedes every beginning. The memoir itself, then, is evidence (if one may use that term) both of the immemorial origin and of a recovery from the illness that occludes the origin. The Holy One reveals Himself through the disturbance of His witness; the disturbance of the one who remembers arises not only from the past but from the One who precedes the past and thereby announces the responsibility.

In the last chapter I found that one way in which the illness of ontological indifference manifests itself is through the reduction of the self to a "without-self" or a nonself. Here, I find that the response and responsibility underlying memory in the Holocaust memoir approach a recovery from that illness through a recovery of self or subjectivity. Indeed, Levinas describes the proximity that comes with one's responsibility for the other person as one's very "humanity, or subjectivity, or self" (1981, 46). When the other is dead (or otherwise buried under the debris of time), this humanity is called memory. Indeed, only *others* lie in the cemeteries or abide in a sky trans-formed into a cemetery; the I or the self is a survivor to whom the other lays claim and who is rendered vulnerable and, in a sense, guilty. That is what constitutes both the singularity and the subjectivity of the human being. Thus, Levinas describes the I as the "non-interchangeable par excellence," as "what in a permanent sacrifice substitutes itself for others and transcends the world. But this is the source of speaking, for it is the essence of commu-nication" (1987a, 124). And it belongs to the essence of the Holocaust memoir, inasmuch as the one who remembers would speak. This being-for-the-other, with its vulnerability and guilt, lies at the core of memory. If, as Rabbi Hillel teaches in the Mishnah, "in a place where there are no men" one must "try to act like a man" (Avot 2:5), acting like a man lies in a response to the holy within the other grounded in a responsibility for a Third who is higher than both self and other. In the age after the Shoah this acting like a human being begins with an act of remembrance. And the consequences of such actions are immense. Before proceeding one must note this point that is so central to the Jewish tradition targeted for annihilation and to the memoirs that are now part of that tradition.

Addressing the depths of response and responsibility, Jiří Langer writes, "Everybody has a special light burning for him in the higher world, totally different from the light of every other person. When two friends meet in this world, their lights up above unite for a moment, and out of the union of two lights an angel is born" (1976, 218). To say an angel is born from human relation is to say that every deed within such relation—every capacity for response and remembrance—sends a message and a messenger, a *malakh* (meaning "messenger" as well as "angel"), into the world for good or for ill. Rabbi Kalonymous Kalman Shapira, the Rebbe of the Warsaw Ghetto, ex-presses this idea by saying, "Within you, *Sefirot* [points of divine emanation] and spiritual light are to be found. Because of this, everything depends on you: to damage your character and your self is to cause damage in all the palaces on high, whereas when you mend your attributes, you heal and repair those palaces as well" (1991, 87). Thus, memory and recovery in the Holocaust memoir—the *tikkun* or mending sought in the memoir—may have its connections with the life of the Holy One Himself. The fact that memory in the Holocaust memoir entails a response for the sake of a recovery is demonstrated by what one has seen in the recovery of tradition and in the recovery from illness. Emerging in the light of such a responsibility, this memory bears the significance that Adin Steinsaltz describes when he asserts, "The fact that man is only a very small detail, a dot and less than a dot as against the Infinite, is balanced by the fact that it is precisely he in his smallness who gives each of the parts its significance. . . . Not only is man free to act on the system, each of his deeds has—in all the worlds, in terms of space and time and of the Supreme or Ultimate Reality—immeasurable significance" (1980, 45). At Sinai God descended and man ascended. The implication of the Revelation? That, having entered into the Covenant with the Creator of heaven and earth, humans become responsible for heaven and earth, for the infinite and the finite.

Says Nachman of Breslov, "Each man is destined from on high to be in a particular place at a given time. At that time and place there is something that he must correct" (1973, 196). In the Holocaust memoir memory is not only memory of a time and a place but of a summons to *mend*. My responsibility in this begins with the human being who now stands before me. I am cut to the quick in my finitude and infinitely implicated in my being-for-the-other. To be sure, the vulnerability of my being-for-the-other manifests itself in the confessional element that runs throughout the Holocaust memoir. Very often the words of memory here convey the need for the word on the part of another human being as when Eugene Heimler recalls a moment of falling silent only to have his friend Louis beg him, "For God's sake, say something—or I shall go mad" (1959, 154). Or the words of memory may come in a remembrance of a word withheld as in Wieslaw Kielar's account of the day when, after an attempted escape, his comrade Edek was taken out to be hanged before the assembly of inmates: "I stood there, he almost touched me as he went past. A whisper would have been enough: 'Edek.' But at that moment I was not capable of even that" (1980, 253). So great is the fear of exposure that it stifles even this whispering of a name that might have consoled the one who bore the name; so great is the sense of responsibility that the survivor now shouts the name from the pages of his memoir. If the recovery from illness is a recovery of responsibility, then the man must rid himself of the excuses that feed on the soul like a parasite. Thus, Elie Cohen not only reports but *responds* to the occasion when he failed to provide drugs to ease the suffering of a man about to be gassed: "As I reasoned at the time: Was I to risk my life for someone who had already been condemned? . . . I *could* have gotten those narcotics. . . . But I *didn't do* it. *I didn't do* it" (1973,

95). The italicized repetition of "I *didn't do* it," with the *I* italicized the second time, bespeaks an awareness of the faces that turn toward the one who remembers, faces that must be faced in memory's struggle for recovery.

When Primo Levi, therefore, recalls passing through an infirmary after "liberation," one has not only the memory of a survivor but a metaphor of the Holocaust memoir itself. Recalling men who were calling for help in all the languages if Europe, he writes, "Bony hands ... grabbed hold of my clothes, touched me icily on the face" (1965, 72). Meaning in the Holocaust memoir consists of the trace of the touch of the other who lays claim to the one who remembers his being-for-the-other. If the survivor should feel some guilt for having survived when his fellow human beings died, it is the result of this existential responsibility and not because of some psychological quirk. And in his responsibility one sees the vulnerability of the one from whom a response is summoned.

Memory and Vulnerability

Emmanuel Levinas explains the basis of response and responsibility in images that are especially appropriate for an analysis of the memoirs from the Kingdom of Night where words such as *hunger* and *cold* meant something else. Responsibility, he argues, derives its meaning from attending to the need of the other, from "snatching the bread from one's mouth" and offering it to another; responsibility is meaningful, he says, "only among beings of flesh and blood" (1981, 74). Only among beings of flesh and blood can the icy touch of the other implicate the self in his responsibility and thereby declare his vulnerability. Vulnerability is the vulnerability of the body in its need for the bread that nourishes the soul, and the body is the vehicle of significance that the soul might assume. Indeed, Levinas describes signification as a vulnerability, as a complete exposure; signification "is the passivity of being-for-another," the most fundamental form of which is offering to the other the very bread I eat (1981, 72). This vulnerability of the self in its being-for-the-other makes bread not only the symbol of one's tie to creation but the very stuff of interhuman relation. Bread is the sign of this relation precisely because it is the sign of the vulnerability that defines human relation as a relation of responsibility. The deprivation of bread, then, is calculated not only to weaken the body but to undermine the being-for-the-other that is the essence of the relation to another human being and the relation to the divine being as well. The image of the Divine in a human, therefore, is made of bread, within and without, body and soul. Deprived of bread, that image is destroyed.

Thus, one understands the implications of Moshe Sandberg's statement that the problem of food was absolutely decisive "between one man and another"; it either "strengthened or terminated relations with one's acquaintances" (1968, 88). The Hebrew phrase rendered as "between one man and another" is *beyn bneiy ha-adam* (Sandberg 1967, 68), which literally means "between the children of man" or "between the children of Adam," suggesting a relatedness and a responsibility essentially linked to food. The responsibility from which the humanity and, therefore, the subjectivity of the human being derives is the responsibility to nourish the other *despite oneself*. This is why Levinas argues that the subjectivity of a human being is precisely his vulnerability (1981, 50). The other is in my care not just as other but as brother; we are both *bneiy ha-adam*. All that I am or might become is grounded in this relation to the other as my relative, which in turn bespeaks my relation to the origin of us both and to the One who precedes the origin, to Adam and to the creator of Adam. To Him belongs and from Him arises the bread that I snatch from my mouth and offer to my neighbor. I cannot hide from my brother any more than Adam could hide from Him who asked, "Where are you?" (Gen. 3:9) and who repeated the question by asking Cain, "Where is your brother?" (Gen. 4:0). In this way I am exposed to hunger for the sake of the other, and all that I am is determined by this vulnerability. Sara Zyskind tells us that a certain adage was heard throughout the ghetto: "Whoever saves another from illness must pay for it with his own life" (1981, 116). Yet one can never be saved from one's own illness, the illness of indifference, without this vulnerability. The Jewish fighters in the Warsaw Ghetto understood this truth quite well, for, as Zivia Lubetkin reports, they could act only from the conviction that "saving a single Jewish life is worth the risking of one's own life" (1981, 79). For the Warsaw Ghetto fighters, taking up arms was not to minimize their vulnerability but to increase it and thereby to deepen the substance of their Jewish being. It was not a question of military strategy and certainly held no hope of conquest; no, it was a matter of existential essence.

Because the essence of the self is tied to the fate of the other, one is more vulnerable to the onslaught aimed at the other than to the wounds inflicted upon oneself. Lubetkin, therefore, writes, "Our fear of the Jewish corpses was greater than the terror we felt for the German soldiers" (1981, 212). She goes on to describe the bond that united the Jewish fighters as "a bundle of memories strewn in the scorched ashes of a burnt soul" (1981, 256), and the ashes that burn the soul are the ashes of the other. For the soul is "the other in me," as Levinas has rightly said (1981, 191). It is worth noting that the Hebrew phrase translated as "a bindle of memories strewn" is *tseror zikhronot megulliyim* (1978, 177), which may also be read as "a bundle of memories rolled up," like a scroll, a *megillah*, a testament, or a prayer (one group of prayers said on Rosh Hashanah, the Day of Judgment, is the *Zikhronot*). The Holocaust memoir is made of those memories; it is written in an opening up of the soul to be scorched by the burning remains of the other, and to be a remnant is to be burned by those remains. It is not just that the survivors whose souls are thus wounded suffer bereavements; the point, rather, is that they have been *claimed* by the ashes and the ghosts of others. Memory is exposure. This alone can explain why Paul Trepman comments on the courtyard where hundreds of Jews had been killed outside his prison cell by saying, "The ghosts of the Jews who had been tortured in that courtyard left me no peace" (1978, 112). Why is he vulnerable to this torment? Because as Jews they have taken his place as a Jew. And now, like a man donning the shirt of another, he must wrap their lives around his own. In fact, after taking the shirt of a murdered Jew, Trepman relates that he felt as if his own body "had become covered with the blood of the Jews of Stanisławów" (1978, 132). If the Holocaust memoir can be said to be written in blood in any sense, it is written in the blood drawn from the shirt of the murdered other, for this is the blood that makes the soul of the survivor bleed. It is said that in the Soviet labor camps prisoners made ink by mixing blood with rust. The ink that taints the spaces between the words of the Holocaust memoir, however, is made from blood and ashes drawn from a soul invaded by the other.

With this in mind one recalls Miklos Nyiszli's comment that in the camp the saying "To take leave of a friend is to die a little" took on new meaning (1960, 81). If to *take leave* of a friend is to die a little, it is not only because he *takes* with him a piece of the man's soul; it is also because he *leaves* with the man a memory and a responsibility to transmit the memory. One must die away from oneself in order to meet that responsibility. And it is the only thing that joins the victim of the antiworld to the humanity of the world. It is, therefore, the one pathway to a recovery from the illness of indifference that would allow the antiworld its victory. Once the victims had been stripped of their mothers, their fathers, their children, their names, and every sign of their humanity, the relation to the other human being remained the only piece of Planet Earth that they could retain on Planet Auschwitz and the only possibility of sustaining life. "Help one another," Eliezer was told upon his arrival at Auschwitz in Wiesel's *Night*. "It is the only way to survive" (1960, 50). I have shown how the responsibility incumbent upon memory lays the soul bare and exposes it to wounds. Here arises another feature of vulnerability, namely, the vulnerability to debt incurred when one receives something from another. Just as words such as *hunger* and *bread* take on an extraordinary sense in the realm of the murder camps, so does this debt assume absolute proportions. In the concentrationary universe receiving a bit of food from the other meant far more than receiving a treat or having a favor done for oneself; the hand that offered a person a bit of stale bread offered him his very life, not only in the piece of bread but, just as importantly, in the human relation created through the act of giving.

Viktor Frankl makes this point in his recollection of an act of kindness when a foreman secretly gave him a piece of bread. "It was far more than the small piece of bread which moved me to tears," he relates. "It was the human 'something' which this man also gave to me—the word and the look which accompanied the gift" (1962, 86). The human image of the giver restores to the recipient the image of his own humanity, in all its vulnerability. Indeed, the subjectivity distinguishing humanity is a vulnerability before the other, a being subject to the other, even—and at times especially—when the other offers one a gift. The something more that Frankl receives is the responsibility displayed by the example of the foreman. Receiving the example of giving, one is summoned to become such an example, to assume the responsibility and the vulnerability that make giving possible and that makes one a human being. It was not just the food that gave him and his comrades new strength, one recalls Paul Trepman's memory of a man who helped. "It was Carl Jantzen himself, simply by being what he was. His human kindness . . . fired us with the will to hold out until freedom came" (1978, 217). Freedom, which comes in the form of a recovery, cannot come to a man if he is not a man. And he cannot become a man without becoming responsible and, therefore, vulnerable, subject to incurring the debt. How is the debt to be repaid? Eugene Heimler tells how in his memory of Neils, a Dutch prisoner of Auschwitz who treated him like a human being. When Heimler offered Neils his thanks, Neils replied, "If you wish to repay, give in your turn to others" (1959, 157). To receive a gift is to have a gift to give, which, in turn, is to have another person placed in one's care. And (despite the shocking nature of this statement) no human being emerges from the Kingdom of Night who has not received a gift. To the extent that memory in the Holocaust memoir contains the memory of a gift, the act of remembrance is an act of giving and an affirmation of the responsibility to give as well. Such an affirmation holds the promise of a cure from the illness of indifference.

What is affirmed, however, is not always what is realized; to be sure, it is the slipping away from responsibility that demands the affirmation and deepens the responsibility, ad infinitum. The more one meets one's responsibility, the more responsible one becomes; the debt increases in the measure that it is paid. Each act of response, every affirmation, instills the witness with a greater capacity for response and, therefore, with something more to offer to the other. In the Holocaust memoir, then, the summons to remembrance increases with every memory. This is what poses the danger of drowning "in your own memories," as Elie Wiesel expresses it in his introduction to Vladka Meed's memoir (1973, 14). And the fear of such drowning reveals itself in the memoir's confessional aspect.

The Confessional Aspect of Memory

Almost without exception, the "Why me?" that resounds throughout the Holocaust memoir is the "Why me?" not of a victim but of a survivor indebted to the victims: they, rather than I, should have lived, they were better than I, more deserving than I. This sense of guilt cannot be psychologically explained as a "vain emotion" or as a "survivor's neurosis," nor can it be morally relegated to a "natural" guilt over crimes committed under duress that may have cost others their lives. This guilt (if one may call it that) is an existential feature of the response to the other and the responsibility for the other constituting human relation. Referring to this relation as "proximity," Levinas describes it as "an impossibility to move away without the torsion of a complex" and as a certain "insomnia" (1981, 90). His point here is phenomenological, not psychological. Because the concentrationary universe is what it is by virtue of a radical movement away from human relation, one can well see why the authors of the memoirs may have suffered the "torsion of a complex"; indeed, this twisting of the soul is among the tortures they suffered. At the bottom of the wakefulness characterizing the insomnia that goes with such a relation is memory as response and responsibility. What was described above as a fear of drowning in one's own memories here becomes a fear for the other person. In the Holocaust memoir the fear for the other manifests itself as a responsibility that never ceases, even if, in the words of Levinas, it amounts to no more than "the shame of surviving, to ponder the memory of one's faults" (1987b, 110). One realizes why the Talmud counts the burial of the dead among the *gemilut chasidim*, or the deeds of loving-kindness, that one is to show toward others (Sotah 14a). But in the concentrationary universe even this kindness is denied so that the "shame of surviving" reveals itself in the confessional aspect of the Holocaust memoir. And because the memoir is undertaken in a movement of response and responsibility, there can be no memory of this Event without an element of confession.

Because the memoir is written in the world, and not in the antiworld, the one who emerges from that realm to write the memoir is faced with the condition Levinas describes when he asserts that one's being at home or having a place in the world arises as the result of "the usurpation of the places belonging to the other man already oppressed and starved by me" (1986a, 38). Turning to the memoirs, one finds Primo Levi repeating this observation, declaring, "each of us has usurped his neighbor's place and lived in his stead" (1988, 81–82). The Italian word for "neighbor" in this remark is *prossimo* (Levi 1986a, 61), which, when used as an adjective, means "near"; it is a cognate of *prossimita* or "proximity," a term that is very significant to ideas from Levinas that have been cited. It should also be noted that the neighbor's "stead," his *vece* (1986a, 61), is not to be confused with his position or location. The situation is not analogous to the one in which the local Gentiles have taken over the homes of murdered Jews. The neighbor who is no longer near is, nonetheless, nigh in the stead I have claimed and in the responsibility that claims me. It is as though the self had exceeded the proximity that can never be close enough; as though the self had appropriated the identity whose dearness it was summoned to signify; as though the self had signified too much, so much that it took over the other completely. One may better understand Ka-tzetnik's reply when he was asked about the author's name that should go on his first book, *Salamandra* (Sunrise over hell): "Those who went to the crematorium wrote this book! Go on, you write their name on it: K. Tzetnik" (1989, 15–16). They are there, in his stead; he is here, in their stead. So, through the movement of remembrance, he struggles to bring them here where they belong. Yet memory takes him there.

In the horror of this situation one encounters once more the scope of the Nazis' crime. The very ones whose innocent being they deemed a capital crime now experience a profound guilt over being alive. Thus, Alexander Donat endures a recurring nightmare in which he is condemned by the judges within his soul: "For having been sentenced to live instead of sharing the fate of the community, we banish him from our midst" (1978, 118). If this nightmare of exile were not enough to haunt his memories, Donat experiences one more terrible still. It is about a boy being dragged away by the Gestapo, crying out to him, "O Daddy, why did you go away and leave me?" (1978, 236). In a reversal that characterizes the antiworld's overturning of the world, the question cries out, Who should live in a man's stead if not his child? Yet, in the antiworld it is often the child whose place among the living has been usurped. One does, of course, find examples of responsibility for the loss of one's parents as well. Olga Lengyel, for instance, begins her memoir by saying, "I cannot acquit myself of the charge that I am, in part, responsible for the destruction of my own parents and of my two children" (1972, 13). But even with respect to the parents the antiworld's project of anticreation is in force. For in the world of humanity the child is the heir, not the usurper, of the parents' place. Along these lines one of the most devastating confessions in all the memoirs is found in Elie Wiesel's statement concerning his father's death: "His last word was my name. A summons to which I did not respond. . . . In the recesses of my weakened conscience, could I have searched it, I might perhaps have found something like—free at last!" (1960, 112–13). But he is no more free of his father than he is free of his memory. And in that memory he must answer to his name.

From the center formed by family relations the circle of human relation expands to include all the children of Adam. Thus, the confessional aspect of the memoir first arises from the core of a person's participation in creation through the family; then it widens in include a confession of the failed relation to all of God's creatures. Time after time memory in the Holocaust memoir goes back in time to be confronted with the either/or that distinguishes the illness that plagues the soul—either victim or accomplice. Elie Cohen, for example, is racked by guilt "at the thought that you are helping to select people for the gas chamber" (1973, 100). In *Playing for Time* Fania Fénelon sees that the time she purchased for her own life by playing in the Auschwitz orchestra shortened the time that others had to live. "I realized that we were there to hasten their martyrdom," she writes (1977, 47). And so she confesses that in order to survive, she had to "annihilate" her heart (1977, 53). But the heart cannot be annihilated without annihilating the soul. If the Nazis destroyed souls before they destroyed bodies, it was not just in their manufacture of the *Muselmänner* but in this imposed self-destruction. Indeed, Emil Fackenheim describes the longing for self-destruction as the thing that the Nazis most wanted to impose on the Jews before murdering them (1989, 209). Rendering all Jewish birth as illegitimate, the Nazis render necessary the self-imposed death of the Jews. This death extends beyond the death of body and soul that transpired in the camp to include the death of memory afterward, the death of all talk from those who managed to slip through the cracks in the machinery of murder. Sim Kessel, for example, notes that those survivors who refuse to discuss their past do so "less due to memories of suffering than to the recollection of their lost honor" (1972, 58). Yet, as Kessel himself demonstrates, some do speak despite the confession of losing their "honor" and annihilating their hearts. Nothing annihilates the heart like the illness of indifference. But confession is the opposite of indifference and is, therefore, a needful aspect of the memoir that seeks a recovery from such illness.

To be sure, confession in the Holocaust memoir is often a confession of indifference made in an effort to overcome indifference. This point is made clear by a remark from George Topas, who in his memoir writes, "The Nazi terror was succeeding, in some instances, in bringing our own people down to that level of indifference where one would close his eyes to his brothers' suffering" (1990, 176). Like Topas, Kitty Hart alludes to a forced descent into indifference when she relates, "The sheer numbers dulled any sense of reality. We laughed and sang with red, reeking hell all round us" (1982, 115). Here and in other passages hell is invoked not as a place of punishment for sins but to introduce a vertical dimension necessary to the confessional element of the memoir. For the confession's recovery from the illness of indifference is a recovery of height that would restore meaning to the human image, both in its corporeal and in its spiritual aspects. The two aspects intersect in the *face* through which one beholds the dimension of height and of the holy whenever one not only speaks but speaks *up*. The memoir's confession of failing to speak is a confession of failing to step before the *countenance*, for speaking is precisely nonindifference. So Sara Nomberg-Przytyk confesses her failure to speak to a woman selected for death: "I did not talk to her, though she lay no more than an arm's length from me" (1985, 27). Similarly, on an occasion when a woman was thrown from a train, she recalls, "None of us said anything. No one could be found who reacted like a human being" (1985, 133). Once again one sees how indifference transforms the human image into something monstrous. The self-destruction the Nazis would impose on the Jews culminates in the Jews' resemblance to those who lost their humanity by looking on as others were taken to be murdered.

To varying degrees and in various ways this resemblance is also the subject of confession in the Holocaust memoir. One finds it, for example, in Vladka Meed's acknowledgment of the guilt she felt over operating on the Aryan side of the Warsaw Ghetto wall because even as a member of the underground she could do her work among the Aryans only to the extent that she physically resembled them. "We were conscious," she writes, "of a sense of guilt at being outside the ghetto at so crucial a time" (1973, 184–85). What is largely a spatial distance from her fellow Jews in Meed's case is exacerbated by a spiritual distance imposed on those who struggled for survival by imitating the Christians. Saul Friedländer, for instance, recalls his hiding among French Catholics, saying, "I had become a renegade" (1980, 120). More painful still is Donna Rubinstein's memory of living among those who "spoke about Jesus Christ and his disciples, but not a word about the war and the slaughter of the Jews" (1982, 42). Imposing her memory and her words on this imposed silence, she writes, "Whenever I made the sign of the cross I imagined my grandfather and my whole family. . . . I begged them to forgive me" (1982, 59). Here one sees that the distance from one's fellow Jews created by a resemblance to the enemy is soon collapsed by the memory of those Jews. And because it collapses, confession is called for as the memory of a memory. But there is more: in these confessions of association with the enemy, the guilt and shame lie in having taken up not with other human beings but with beings who are not human. For the Jew the distance from Jewishness is a distance from the humanity and humaneness of all human beings stamped with the image of the Holy One. For the Jewish presence in the midst of humanity is expressive of the universal presence of the sacred that links each human being to his or her neighbor.

When the Jew is extinguished, then, all of humanity is desecrated and every person shamed. This shame is also a repeated part of the confessional element in the Holocaust memoir. Gisella Perl, for example, declares, "Every human being who watched them [the Nazis] felt ashamed" (1948, 12). Primo Levi asserts that he "felt guilty at being a man, because men had built Auschwitz" (1985, 151). And Olga Lengyel addresses her readers to include them, too, in the family of human beings, insisting that the spectacle of those being taken naked to the gas chambers was humiliating "for all humanity. For these destitute souls now being driven to the slaughterhouses were human beings—like you and me" (1972, 53). And those taking them there were human beings—like you and me. The confession of the survivor, therefore, becomes our confession, one that is read between the lines of books like this one I now write, just as it could be read in the faces of the soldiers who stumbled across the camps. Commenting on the Russians who first arrived at Auschwitz, Levi writes that in their faces he saw "the shame that drowned us after the selections, and every time we had to watch, or submit to, some outrage" (1965, 12). Thus, the response and responsibility characterizing the Holocaust memoir in its struggle to recover from the illness of indifference implicates one in one's own capacity for response and exposes in one one's own indifference. One is brought to the gates inscribed with *Arbeit Macht Frei* only to find the memories of the survivors invading one's own memory. Standing before the memoir, one confronts the bottom line of responsibility that might lead to a recovery from the illness of indifference: it is the being-for-the-other without which one has no being.

Being for the Other

According to Rabbi Nachman of Breslov, "the letters of the word *ATaH* have the power to suppress evil forces" (1986, 211). The word *atah* is the "You" by which one addresses God and one's fellow human beings. It is the *You* of *barukh atah*, "blessed are You." It contains the letters *alef* and *tav*, the first and last letters of the alphabet and, therefore, all the letters in between, all the words made of all the letters, all the meaning, every relation, grounded in the Word. Forming the word *atah*, we add to *alef* and *tav* the letter *hey*, the single letter signifying the Holy One, who created all things from all the letters and who makes possible all meaning and relation. That is why, according to Rabbi Nachman, the word *atah* and its letters have the power to overcome the forces of evil, nothingness, and destruction. That is why, in the midst of the memory of destruction, the Holocaust memoir summons the saying of *atah*, which is the being-for-the-other that returns one to life.

Beyond the wall of the Warsaw Ghetto, for instance, nothing could penetrate the walls of suffering and deprivation that encircled those marked for death, yet within the walls there was one portal to life. "We were able to endure life in the ghetto," says Zivia Lubetkin of the ghetto fighters, "because we were a *collective*" (1981, 277; emphasis in the original): each knew he was not alone. Knowing that one is not alone entails much more than knowing that one shares some space or even the same fate with another; it is not a case of misery loving company. This "collective," rather, is grounded in a being-for-the-other, a saying of *You* to each other so that *between* two a space is created where the sacred may manifest itself. Hence, what is remembered in the Holocaust memoir is the friendship that Pavel Florensky describes when he writes, "Friendship is not only psychological and ethical but is above all ontological and metaphysical. Thus, those with the most profound insight into life have viewed it throughout the ages. What is friendship? It is a knowledge of the Self through the Friend in God. Friendship is an awareness of the self through the eyes of the other, but before the face of a third, namely the Third" (1970, 438–39). If Jewish resistance faced the task of recreating Jewish selfhood, it was recreated through friendship; friendship

was the metaphysical response to the ontological assault against Jewish being. George Topas insists that friendship was his one link to life during his
confinement in Płaszov (1990, 217–18). Therefore, it happened—precisely
where it should *not* have happened—that even in a state of complete help-
lessness, even in Auschwitz, families of friends were formed to sustain the
sanctity of life. "We vow never to be separated," says Livia Jackson of herself
and her friends. "We decide to form a family of five" (1980, 68). What is a
family? It is a place where the life of each is nurtured through a being-for-
the-other. It is the first site, the primal opening, where the human being
generates life through friendship.

The essence of Nazism was murder, and the target of Nazi murder was
the image and essence of the human being; it was the image of the divine
that makes this being human, which is to say, it was the being-for-the-other
of human being. "Friendship made me feel more human," writes Ana Vinocur
(1976, 118). And Sara Zyskind remembers, "Our friendship and our care for
one another enabled us to preserve something of our humanity" (1981, 223).
Contrary to the logic of evil, the care that constitutes friendship and engen-
ders life is care *given*, not care received. Life is had only in its being offered
to and for the other human being. For in that offering to another the benevolence of the Third reveals itself, and suddenly life has meaning. This must
be kept in mind when one hears Moshe Sandberg relate that some of the
men in his Hungarian labor gang "began to stand out from the rest," not
because of their cleverness but "because of their honesty and their readiness
to help" (1968, 37). A look at the Hebrew text sheds more light on the nature
of being-for-the-other and its relation to a being-for-the-Third. The word
translated as "honest," for example, is *yosher* (Sandberg 1967, 27), which also
means "righteous"; it is a synonym of *tsedek*, whose cognate *tsedakah* means
"piety" and "charity." These terms in themselves convey the very point that
Florensky makes above, namely that within the human relation ruled by
yosher there lives an expression of the relation to God that the Nazis sought
to annihilate. One realizes, then, the depths that open up in the readiness
to help as when Fania Fénelon helps with the delivery of an infant. "I had
the extraordinary feeling," she relates, "that my hands knew what to do more
than I did, that they'd known these movements forever" (1977, 251). A Presence that transcends the people involved with this birth is at work in the
movement to help: there is something more than a Jewish child born in this
event that the Nazis deemed most criminal. The Holy One Himself makes
His appearance in this response made to a human being out of a responsibility for a higher being.

The Holocaust memoir's recovery from illness is just such a recovery of life. It comes in a recovery of the tradition and the truth that Rashi invokes when he declares, "All Israelites are held responsible for one another" (1972, 3:128b); the memoir, both by its presence and in its content, exemplifies Rashi's commentary. To be sure, Leon Wells cites this very passage from Rashi but without naming him (1978, 20). The important point is this: the Holocaust memoir not only reiterates the responsibility of each for all it *remembers* and is, therefore, part of the ontic reality of this being-for-the-other that instills human being with a life that, by every rational measure, should not be there. Time and again the memoir demonstrates that it is not looking out for oneself but caring for another that saves one's life when the greatest temptation is to die. Just when death would seduce Wells into giving up, for example, he has a realization, or a revelation: "Suddenly I felt life flooding back into me. My brothers needed me" (1978, 119). In *Night*, when the idea of dying tempted Eliezer, the only thing that kept him from slipping into the comfort of death was his father's need for him: "I had no right to let myself die. What would he do without me?" (Wiesel 1960, 90). Similarly, Lily Lerner's only link to life is the bond of responsibility to and for her sister. "Without me," she recalls, "she would have no reason to be strong and to hope. She needed me" (1980, 109). Thus, the loss that Kitty Hart experiences when her friend Simon dies in the camp is not a loss of help but of having someone to help: "I had persuaded myself that in some way I was helping him, and this helped me" (1982, 80). The sanctity of life that makes living meaningful can be affirmed only in the other human being. Only then, when it arises from beyond me, does the value of life become genuine, and not just some pretense that I have dreamed up for myself.

There are those who will say that this being-for-the-other actually ends up as a being-for-the-self, that ultimately there is no altruism. But this is a deadly confusion that ends in placing the man who saves himself by "merely following orders" into the same category as his victim. It is an instance of the obliteration of categories and distinctions that the Nazis attempted to engineer; it is an undermining of the response and responsibility without which there is neither life nor recovery of life. If you have no sister, Isabella Leitner insists, you do not have "the absolute responsibility to end the day alive" (1978, 35). That responsibility keeps the person alive because it is itself the vessel and force of life, the avenue through which the Creator continues His creation of life. There, where human being joins with human being, difference is transformed into nonindifference, and the anonymous rumbling of the "there is" is silenced. That is why Filip Müller writes, "The main motive for seeking the relationship with the women was not so much sexual, but simply the need to have someone to care for" (1979a, 63). In the German text this sentence is followed by a line left untranslated in the English edition: *so daß man das Gefühl völliger Verlassenheit loswerden konnte* (1979b, 99), or "so that one could get rid of the feeling of utter forlornness," *Verlassenheit*, abandonment, isolation. Isolation from the other is the isolation of a tomb. And it is overcome not simply by having someone there for oneself but, more importantly, by being there for another, by saying, "Here I am," to another. "You had to have somebody helping you," Kitty Hart describes the conditions necessary for any hope of survival, "and you had to help somebody else" (1982, 166). As Gisella Perl points out, it is just this helping the other that restores life by restoring a future to time collapsed: by "keeping the young and strong women alive" she was able to "smile and spread encouragement, faith, peace, and the will to live" (1948, 160–61). And what is thus spread is received in its offering.

Responsibility and the being-for-the-other that distinguishes it arise as a summons that singles out the individual as an individual before any choice that he or she can make. Therefore, being-for-the-other is not a survival measure, such as organizing food or clothing. Rather, it is a movement into the position of vulnerability that determines who I am and what I signify as one who *stands for* the dearness of the other; it is a saying of "Here I am" both to my neighbor and to my Creator, who abides in a third position from which He puts to me the question, "Where are you?" Levinas expresses this important point by saying, "The Infinite always remains 'third person'—'He' in spite of the 'You' (Thou, 'Tu') whose face concerns me. The Infinite affects the I without the I's being able to dominate it, . . . prior to all freedom—showing itself as a 'Responsibility-for-the-Other' which this affection gives rise to" (1978b, 188–89). If the recovery from the illness of indifference is a movement of return to life, that return is a *teshuvah* by which the relation to the Infinite One is regained through a relation to the other as the bearer of the trace of the Infinite. The fact that the other bears such a trace and that I am summoned to a responsibility for the other makes the movement a *return*, even if I have never made such a movement. No movement of return, no recovery from illness can be effected in isolation, a point made clear by an episode in Delbo's memoir. She relates that when she was left to dig a ditch by herself she fell into a terrible despair. Only the presence of others made possible any return to life: "I do not believe in return when I am alone" (1968, 115). That return is something to be *believed in* inserts the Third, or the Divine, into the relation to the other human being. It makes return into *teshuvah*, a word that, indeed, means "return" but also means "response." In the Holocaust memoir the memory of isolation in a ditch rises up from that pit in a movement of response to another, in the light of a Third. This memory is itself a mode of being-for-the-other, both dead and alive, by which the survivor might find an opening to life.

Having added these remarks on being-for-the-other to what has been said about vulnerability and confession, one sees a deeper dimension of all three unfold. The movement of response takes one into the open, where one is exposed to the other for the sake of the Third, who Himself endures a certain vulnerability. In one's illness it is He who suffers; in one's response it is He who returns. As Nikos Kazantzakis states it, "My God is not Almighty. He struggles, for he is in peril every moment; he trembles and stumbles in every living thing, and he cries out. He is defeated incessantly, but rises again, full of blood and earth, to throw himself into battle once more" (1963, 204). God needs people in order to be God as much as people need Him in order to be human. The confession of the loss of humanity, then, is a confession of the violation of God. And the human other for whom one must be in one's being-for-the-other includes the Holy One Himself. Just as the Nazis would destroy Him by annihilating His Chosen, so must they save Him—and with Him one another—through the loving embrace of all His children stemming from Adam. "It is not God who will save us," Kazantzakis declares, "it is we who will save God, by battling, by creating, by transmuting matter into spirit" (1963, 206). This, indeed, is the project undertaken by memory in the Holocaust memoir—to transform matter into spirit by making memory into an act of response and an affirmation of responsibility to and for the other. In the Holocaust memoir the significance of memory lies not so much in its meaning as in its answering. For its meaning derives from the event of its answering.

Says Viktor Frankl, "Man should not ask what the meaning of his life is, but rather he must recognize that it is *he* who is asked. In a word, each man is questioned by life; and he can only answer to life by *answering for* his own life; to life he can only respond by being responsible" (1962, 111; emphasis in the original). *Life* here includes both the life of humanity and the Creator of that life, the One who is Himself life. Hence, the voice that cries out to Him from the blood of Abel is His own Voice. And suddenly Primo Levi's statement that each man is his brother's Cain (1988, 81) assumes the staggering implications already understood by the sages who have gone before them. In a commentary on the murder of Abel one is told in the Mishnah, "It does not say, 'The *blood* of your brother,' but 'The *bloods* of your brother'—his blood and the blood of all those who were destined to be born from him. . . . Therefore, man was created alone to teach you that whoever destroys a single Israelite soul is deemed by Scripture as if he had destroyed a whole world. And whoever saves a single Israelite soul is deemed by Scripture as if he saved a whole world" (Sanhedrin 4:5). What is the essence of all the worlds? It is the holiness of the Holy One. Thus, Rabbi Kalonymus Kalman Shapira enjoins, "Remember the yoke of responsibility rests upon you. All the worlds, even the fate of God's holiness in this world, depend on you" (1991, 121). In this passage responsibility is linked to remembrance and remembrance to responsibility. Each adds depth to the other; each infinitizes the other in a sanctification of the Infinite. What Elie Wiesel has written is true: "Man changes whenever he confronts his fellow-man, who, in turn, undergoes an essential change. Thus every encounter suggests infinity. Which means: the self is linked to infinity only through the intermediary of another self" (1973b, 88), an assertion that is a paraphrase of the wisdom found in the *Mekilta* of old: "When one welcomes his fellow man, it is considered as if he had welcomed the Divine Presence" (1961, 2:178). Because the Divine Presence, or the infinity of the *En Sof*, can never be contained, the depth of response and responsibility can never be deep enough. Both the recovery of tradition and the recovery from illness sought in the Holocaust memoir, therefore, remain forever incomplete: the *Holocaust* memoir cannot contain its memory.

This brings me to the third dimension of memory and recovery in the Holocaust memoir—the open-endedness of recovery.

PART THREE

The Open-Endedness
of Recovery

Context

In the movement of response that characterizes the Holocaust memoir is an effort to overcome the illness of indifference that threatens to drain humanity of its soul. In the responsibility to which that movement attests lies the portal to a recovery of a relation to sacred tradition through human interaction. If the Holocaust memoir cannot contain its memory, it is because the proximity to the human and to the holy cannot be close enough. Through the approach to the neighbor human beings draw nigh unto the Holy One; drawing nigh unto the Holy One, they realize the greatness or the glory of God; and with that realization their eyes are opened to the infinite difference and distance between the human and the divine. Hence, the realization of the need and the demand for a never-ending drawing nigh in an eternal movement toward the Infinite, a movement that, again, consists of an approach toward the neighbor. As always, the approach is rooted in a hearing where the Voice is heard ever more deeply with every act of response. Like the Israelites gathered at Sinai who shouted, "We shall do and we shall hear" (Exod. 24:7), the survivors gather before the commanding Voice of Auschwitz and declare, "We shall remember and we shall hear!"

If one views memory as a form of hearing, then the more one remembers, the more memory is called for. The utterance of "I" in the Holocaust memoir is a declaration of "Here I am": I who saw, I who endured, I who emerged. But the I who makes this declaration becomes more than the ego can hold, for the one who emerges from the antiworld bears the voices and the silences of more than himself. Says Elie Wiesel, "When the surviving friend emerges from the desert, he is no longer alone; he will have to live two lives, his own and that of his dead friend" (1991, 240). Therefore, as Levinas shows, "responsibility for others has not been a return to oneself, but an exasperated contracting. which the limits of identity cannot retain" (1981, 114). The principle of identity is broken in the mending that draws human beings nigh unto the other, broken by the recovery of the holy in the midst of the human. The problem of identity, then, is a definitive aspect of the open-endedness of the recovery sought in the Holocaust memoir. Instead of having an I equal to itself, survivors are faced with being who they are *not yet* defined not by a fixed position but by a never-ending movement toward recovery. Recovery, therefore, is not a matter of setting right a broken past but of positing a future that is continually yet to be. Thus, the Holocaust memoir reintroduces to memory a messianic yet-to-be that is a *tikkun* or mending of time itself. Indeed, the wait for the Messiah, Levinas argues, "is the duration of time itself—waiting for God—but here the waiting no longer attests to the absence of Godot, who will never come, but rather to a relationship with that which is not able to enter the present, since the present is too small to contain the Infinite" (1989d, 203). Like the name of the Messiah, which, according to the *Midrash Rabbah,* is among the six things that preceded the Creation (1961, 1: 6), the Good sought in the witness borne is not only awaited it precedes the wait that constitutes time and confounds identity.

Recovery is open-ended and identity confounded because the Good sought in the yet-to-be has already laid claim to me. The Good is neither something that suits me nor something that pleases the other; the Good is not what feels good. Rather, it is what chooses and commands—from beyond—and one is forever contemporary with its commandment; although He may be the farthest, the Third is ever nigh in an open-ended present as an undisclosed and unenclosed Presence. Whereas the present is "a beginning in my freedom," Levinas expresses it, "the Good is not presented to freedom: it has chosen me before I have chosen it" (1981, 11). Thus, liberation from the antiworld is never consummated not only because there is no returning to a family and a home destroyed but also because the new home, the new world, is forever yet to be established. "For the man of the Exodus," André Neher points out, "encounters with the Word are inevitably 'missed appointments' " (1981, 123). If in Jewish sacred history the Shoah bears a significance comparable to that of Sinai, the memory of the Shoah represents an Exodus equally comparable. In the Holocaust memoir memory would couple with the word and, thereby, achieve a recovery of life long sought after. But no sooner does memory reach for the word from the past than the word recedes to the open-ended horizon of the future. Hence, the need to bear witness is ever upon those who remember and those who receive their memory. Neither they nor I is ever free of this responsibility. So all are faced with a problem of identity that is ever yet to be resolved.

7

The Problem of Identity

In the antiworld, remembers Seweryna Szmaglewska, "you lost the capacity of proving to yourself, in a moment of doubt, that you are still the same human being you were when you came here. That being is gone, and only a miserably wretched creature remains in her place. A naked creature deprived of everything and avidly covering her body with someone else's sweat-saturated garments in spite of keen disgust" (1947, 78). Contrary to generating a relation to the other that might engender an identity, the self here is invaded by the other, both in the form of blows received and in the form of the very skin and sweat of the other, resulting not only in disgust but in *disjuncture*. Identity is lost in a removal of the self from here to there, from first person to third person, from the same to not-the-same. Or is it from here to nowhere, from first person to non-person, from the same to nothing? The voice is there, but the body is different. The body is there, but the soul is lost. Someone speaks, but there is no saying who. For in this realm all names are confiscated. So with this chapter I ask: Who is the I who speaks in the Holocaust memoir, and who is the I of whom it speaks?

The question announces itself in the splitting of the self that one finds in the memoirs. In his, for example, Eugene Heimler comments on the memoir he would write one day, saying, "That this book might be written in the first person singular I never dared even to think" (1959, 93). The difficulty that Heimler confronts in writing this memory in the first person is exemplified more powerfully still by Ka-tzetnik. In *Shivitti* he explains that all he has written is a testimonial of "I, I, I . . . till half way through a piece I suddenly had to transform *I* to *he*. I felt the split, the ordeal, the alienation of it" (1989, 71). One sees the depth of the ordeal in the first person's struggle with itself as a third person, moreover, when one looks at Isabella Leitner's pleading with a self that haunts her *as* a third person who will not allow her to leave the antiworld even after she is "liberated": "She tells me what I was afraid she'd say: '*I will live as long as you do*' " (1978, 90). The voice of memory contains another voice, one that declares, "I am the you who you are not: you will never become who you are! You have no I! You are dead!" Thus, the I speaks, struggling to regain an identity along the edge of its own grave.

The I who undergoes the ordeal of making itself into he is an I who has lived through its own death to now encounter itself as *other*. Jean Améry insists that "no one can become what he cannot find in his memories" (1980, 84). But the memory of this other self that never leaves the self is a memory of the "senescence beyond the recuperation of memory" that Levinas describes as a "disjunction of identity where the same does not rejoin the same: there is non-synthesis" (1981, 52). In the disjuncture between the I who remembers and the he who is remembered—in this nonsynthesis—the echoing rustle of the "there is" can be heard. Here one discovers that the memory of silence discussed in chapter 5 includes a memory of the silencing of one's name and the consequent obliteration of one's identity. The loss of identity is a problem because it belongs not to the verb *to be* but, in the words of Levinas, to "a noun which has detached itself from the anonymous rustling of the *there is*" (1978a, 87). With the loss of identity the noun or the name is lost, and the "there is" manifested at the core of the antiworld first makes itself felt upon the fragmentation of that noun. "The *I* of Then and the *I* of Now," says Ka-tzetnik, "are a single identity divided by two" (1989, 100), but what splits in the tearing of the first-person pronoun is not only time but also an inner space. In the Holocaust memoir, as in many literary texts, the device for opening up this broken inner space is often a mirror. For when human beings gaze into a mirror, they see not only their outward images but the inward depths of their own gaze staring back at them from the circles of darkness in the eyes of their reflections. Not only do they look *at* the mirror; they look *into* the mirror. The inner event of contemplation is torn out of them and placed before them: they split. In this way the mirror becomes a metaphor for memory itself. The survivor summons the memory, and the memory holds up the image of a broken self.

Sara Nomberg-Przytyk remembers the rare event in Auschwitz of looking into a mirror. "I looked terrible," she says. "I was sure that there was somebody else standing behind me and that the mirror was reflecting her face" (1985, 40). Looking terrible in this case does not mean looking disheveled, thin, or dirty; it means looking *other*, bearing an image that is not the image of oneself but of someone or something else. It means bearing the image of death. Rudolf Vrba describes his encounter with a mirror by saying, "I stared into that mirror, and the face of a Moslem [a *Muselmann*] stared back. The thin death's head of a man about to collapse" (1964, 157). The question of who speaks and of whom one speaks in the Holocaust memoir is here reflected, as it were, in the question of who looks into the mirror and who looks back. But there is a difference: in the memoir stirs the voice of life, whereas from the mirrors stares the face of death. In the last line in Wiesel's *Night*, for instance, "From the depths of the mirror, a corpse gazed back at me" (1960, 116). Similarly, near the end of her memoir Ana Vinocur writes, "I looked at myself in the mirror. . . . I thought that a dead body . . . would look more beautiful compared to me" (1976, 136). The dead to whom the self is compared and whose gaze forever haunts the self is the self that died with the dead and that now becomes their tomb. Hence, the problem of identity.

Here death, says Ka-tzetnik, is "a circular mirror held up to your eyes" (1971b, 68). And when memory holds up its mirror to the mirror of death, one has the infinite progression that characterizes the open-endedness of recovery in the Holocaust memoir. The death of the self reflected in the mirror begins with the loss of the name that is the essence of the self. It proceeds to the breakdown of the body that is the image of the self. And it culminates in the decomposition of the soul that is the life of the self. Memory in the Holocaust memoir seeks a name and an image to go with it. It speaks to reconstitute a soul. Although it offers no resolution, it does make the movement of response through the offering of a word that summons response and remembrance in an infinite, open-ended progression. So one proceeds.

The Loss of the Name

In his *First-Person Essays* Aharon Appelfeld writes, "We had been taught to speak about the Holocaust in the language of big numbers, and no language distances you from contact [with the human being] more than such language" (1979, 21). In none of the Holocaust memoirs does one find the language of big numbers, of overwhelming statistics and mind-boggling figures; there is much that is overwhelming and mind-boggling, but it does not lie in the numbers. The language of numbers is antithetical to the language of memory. Numbers numb. Like a stone that seals off a tomb, they place the sign of closure and conclusion on the event, leading—or rather misleading—some to foolishly declare that the facts are in. Such "facts" are opposed to the ongoing, dialogical process of recovery and return to life. Numbers are the beginning of death in the death camp, for they signify that end of all life on the other side of the gate that clangs shut. Germain Tillion, for example, remembers being stripped of everything, even her name, upon her arrival at Ravensbrück: "All we had now were a few filthy rags which didn't belong to us—and a number" (1975, 6). The number, of course, is more alien and alienating than the rags because the rags once belonged to people who once had names. But the number is the opposite of the name. The Holocaust memoir, then, includes the memory of big numbers, inasmuch as they were used as weapons to rob the human being of his or her name and thereby remove any identity that may determine the *who* of the human being.

The substance of the name of the human being, his very *I*, derives from the One known as *ha-Shem* or the Name, from Him who alone can say, "I." Inscribing the number on the body is the first step toward draining the body of its soul, which is the divine image of the Name. So Sara Nomberg-Przytyk says much in these few words: "In Auschwitz we were just numbers, without faces or souls" (1985, 15). It is, indeed, a part of Jewish tradition that the name and the soul, the name and the person, are of a piece. In his commentary on Isaiah, for example, the twelfth-century sage Abraham ibn Ezra asserts that the word *shem* (name) is to be understood to mean "the person himself" (1943, 73). And in *Tikkun* Nachman of Breslov writes, "All a person's deeds are inscribed in his name. That is why after death a person is asked if he remembers his name. Because the name *is* the soul" (1984, 102). When the number takes over the name, it is not just the word but the *being* attached to the word that is assailed. So through the number the Nazis make the human being into an object consisting entirely of an exterior, all surface, void of any inner depth that would distinguish the individual as a *being*. Numbers, therefore, are opposed to being: they are the ciphers of nothingness and the spokesmen of indifference. They are the first weapons drawn in the ontological war to slay the human being by slaying all blessing that derives from being. Remember the teaching of the Talmud: "Blessing is not found in something weighed, nor in something measured, nor in something counted" (*Bava Metzia* 42a). And numbers are precisely the language—or the anti-language—of weight, measurement, and enumeration. Robbed of his name and marked with a number, the human being is robbed of what makes him human. "A serial number," Sim Kessel states, "dispenses you from having had a name, having had a soul, having had a life" (1972, 169). Thus, seeking the recovery of their humanity, the authors of the memoirs recover a name by remembering a number.

"I became A-7713. After that I had no other name" (Wiesel 1960, 51).

"Henceforth I would be, merely, KZ prisoner Number A 8450" (Nyiszli 1960, 26).

"Mine was 55091—my new name from now on" (Zyskind 1981, 211).

"I looked at my number: 7,115. From that moment I ceased to be a man" (Donat 1978, 168).

"That, indeed, was the last time I used my name . . . for now I was prisoner number 44070" (Vrba 1964, 78–79).

"A filthy needle . . . erased Natan Schapelski from the human race and brought into being Häftling 134138" (Shapell 1974, 116).

"I was number '25,403.' I still have it on my right arm and shall carry it with me to the grave" (Lengyel 1972, 116).

"We ceased to be human beings with family names. . . . In my metamorphosis I was No. 124753" (Sandberg 1968, 55).

Life was finished, no longer human, ceased to exist, no other name: memory clutches at these phrases of straw in an attempt to convey the death that the survivor survives but never lives through, for it follows him to the grave. Inscribed with the number, the human being does not merely experience the Shoah; rather, the Shoah becomes part of the human being. He leaves Auschwitz, but he does not leave it behind: the prisoner is not in Auschwitz—Auschwitz is in the prisoner. "This is an indelible mark," the tattoo declares, "you will never leave here" (Levi 1988, 119). In her memoir Judith Dribben explains, "Once the number was there, there was no chance to escape. It bound us more strongly than any chain. It was something that could only be removed together with a piece of flesh" (1969, 185). Through the needle Auschwitz invades the flesh and stains the image of the human being; through the flesh it enters his soul and substance. In the Holocaust memoir, then, memory seeks to recover not only the events of the past but all that a lost name might convey and with it the significance of the loss. Here the man chooses memory over the number; the number was calculated to obliterate the name because the name is full of memory—the memory of a life, the memory of a tradition in which others bore the same name, the memory of response to the name. Stealing away the name, the number murders memory.

"I find it difficult," says Primo Levi, "to reconstruct the sort of human being that corresponded, in November 1944, to my name or, better, to my number: 174517" (1985, 139). In *Survival in Auschwitz* he dwells at length on the significance of the number in the antiworld itself, describing the details of the tattooing process, and the aftermath of the process as well.

Prisoners would not be fed, for example, without first showing their numbers and repeating them in German. "For many days," he adds, "while the habits of freedom still led me to look for time on my wristwatch, my new name ironically appeared instead, its number tattooed in bluish characters under the skin" (Levi 1961, 23). In Levi's remarks about the number much is revealed about the loss of the name and the problem of identity. First, the eclipse of the name is tied to the breakdown—to the slow starvation—of the body: showing the number in exchange for food, the prisoner declares his namelessness and his nothingness as he wastes away on the meager ration. Further, not only is the number alien to the man but the German language in which the number is spoken adds to the prisoner's alienation by removing his new "name" from his native tongue. Finally, the man who seeks the time only to find the number—not *on* the skin but *under* it—continually collides with the collapse of time, with his exile from time, and with the end of his life time. "You must watch over your name and your soul," says Rabbi Nachman (1983, 301). Knowing this, the Nazis assailed Jewish being by forcing these men and women to watch over a number.

The loss of the name in the Holocaust memoir manifests itself in other ways, particularly in the exchange of one name for another and, thus, assuming a new identity. From a Jewish standpoint this exchange has far more significance than it may seem at first glance. "When a person is judged Above," Rabbi Nachman states, "he is judged by his name. It sometimes happens that the [Heavenly] messengers exchange his name with another, so that the decree of death or suffering falls upon someone else" (1986, 65). And so it happened to Alexander Donat, who was born Michael Berg. While in a camp at Vaihingen, Michael Berg met Alexander Donat, an inmate who was to be transferred out of the camp. "Let's swap places," Berg suggested, and he was shipped out. Later he found out that all those who remained in Vaihingen were sent to a labor detail in the swamps of Kochendorf, where they died (Donat 1978, 258). Thus, a name is lost and with it a life. With the new name comes a new life that must now become the bearer of a lost life: Alexander Donat in Michael Berg, Michael Berg in Alexander Donat. "A man's destiny and mission in life," says Rabbi Nachman, "are determined by the name he is given. Sometimes a man completes his mission before his destined time to die. He must then be given a new name" (1984, 103). And with the new name comes a new mission: to remember the exchange of names that brought life to one and death to another and that confounds the identity of both. For in the case of Donat/Berg the name given was a name taken, a name that took hold of the one who took it.

In other instances, however, the name is exchanged not with another person but for another name. Donna Rubinstein, for example, remembers, "The priest made the sign of the cross over me and pronounced my new name: Maria Filinuk" (1982, 42). One could escape the Nazis, but the Jew could scarcely escape the annihilation of the name by which the Nazis sought to annihilate every trace of Jewish being. For the Jewish name had to be exchanged for a Christian name, for a name that would make the Jew, if only provisionally, into one of those who for centuries had been the murderers of the Jews and were now, to a large extent, the accomplices of the Nazis. When Saul Friedländer entered a Catholic boarding school to escape the Nazis, he, too, took a Christian name and became Paul-Henri Ferland, to which the name Marie was added when he was baptized. Perhaps, he speculates, it was to invoke the protection of the Virgin, "less vulnerable than the earthly mother who at this very moment the whirlwind was already sweeping away" (1980, 79). In the world invaded by the whirlwind of the antiworld the baptism intended to save the soul threatens to destroy it. For this baptism of the soul is precisely the opposite of the circumcision inscribed upon the body. It renders the body of the Jew unrecognizable, just as the change of name renders the soul alien. Thus, even for those who escaped the death camp by such means, the body was assailed by the baptism that would break the body by breaking the sign of the Covenant with the sign of a "new" testament. Even so, this breakdown of the body did not approach the one that transpired in the death factories themselves.

The Breakdown of the Body

"The boundaries of my body," says Jean Améry, "are also the boundaries of my self" (1980, 28) where the German word rendered as "self" is not *Selbst* but *Ich* (1977, 56). The I that is central to identity is definitively attached to the body from DNA patterns to fingerprints, from gesture to posture. When the I speaks, the mouth moves; when the I embraces, the arms extend. But because the I is *attached* to the body, it is not reducible to the body. In the caress, for instance, what is sought is never touched. When the I is reduced to the body, it is lost, and with that reduction the body breaks down. It becomes, in Améry's words, the calamity of the I: "I was my body and nothing else. . . . My body, debilitated and crusted with filth, was my calamity" (1980, 91). In the identification of the I—or the soul—with the body identity is lost because the soul finds its identity through the noncoincidence of the embrace of another soul. It derives its significance from its ability to signify the dearness of another in an act of response and responsibility through which the self arrives at itself by way of the other. Signification, to recall an insight from Levinas, "is the one-for-the-other which characterizes an identity that does not coincide with itself" (1981, 70). When the soul is reduced to the body and nothing more, identity coincides with itself, and the body is drained of the soul. For this identity is the identity of $0 = 0$. Once the soul or the self is reduced to the body and is nothing more, relation is reduced to delivering and receiving blows; the metaphysical violence always has its physical manifestation and always, in its violence, tears the self from itself. Thus, the body drained of the soul is less than a body; it is just one more object with which the remnant of the soul must contend. "I could feel myself as two entities," Wiesel complains of the oppressive weight of his skeletal form, "my body and me" (1960, 89). This splitting of the self from the body points up a breach within the self or soul of the man. One function of memory in the Holocaust memoir is to heal that wound, even though it stubbornly refuses closure.

Or, perhaps, the point is to recover the wound itself, making the process of recovery as open-ended as the wound is open. For only an animate body, instilled with the *animus* of the living soul, can be wounded. Once the body is broken down into an object—a stomach and nothing more—it cannot be wounded any more than one can wound a stone. Like a stone, the body of the Jew in the antiworld was raw material for soap, fertilizer, clothing, and lamp shades. Filip Müller points out that human flesh, Jewish flesh, was used in experiments to grow bacterial cultures; the flesh of a horse would serve the same purpose, but, compared to the Jew, "it is too valuable for that sort of thing" (1979a, 47). When the flesh of the body thus becomes a mere commodity, the distinction between the quick and the dead collapses. One finds an illustration of this point in Leon Wells's memoir where he relates, "We build pyres of two thousand or more 'figures,' the name the Germans gave to the bodies. They call us 'figures,' too" (1978, 196). The human being bereft of his identity comes to resemble the number that marks his body as *no more than* a body, as one more item in an inventory of goods. "I was a shadow without identity," says Gisella Perl, "alive only by the power of suffering" (1948, 56). With the breakdown of the body, the body does not cast the shadow—it *is* the shadow. And the whole purpose of inflicting so much pain on her emaciated body is to constantly remind the Jew that she is *all* body, *all* pain, with no name, no identity, that might make her more than a body.

One thing that renders the body recognizable as a person and not as an object is the hair. Why did the Nazis shave the heads of their victims? It was not merely to control lice because there is no evidence that they were concerned whether lice ate the prisoners alive or not. Shaving the head was a means of collapsing these bodies into a sameness that deprived each of her identity, rendering each unrecognizable to another. "With shaven heads," as Kitty Hart expresses it, "everybody looked so much alike. That was part of the Nazi plan after all: to reduce all of us to impersonal, downtrodden nothingness" (1982, 76). This form of breaking down the body, with the consequent problem of identity and recognition, is a motif in the Holocaust memoir. Gisella Perl, for instance, recalls the moment when she and her comrades emerged from the shaving area unable to recognize each other. In place of the women who entered, she relates, "a ghastly carnival procession" came out, "marching toward the last festival: death" (1948, 30). And this death begins with the death of identity not only as individuals but as human beings; indeed, to be a human being is to be an individual. When she and the other women entered the first of a series of rooms, Perl elaborates, they were still "human beings, women wearing our own clothes.... We still had hair on our heads.... Above all we still had our identity" (1948, 42–43). And, after the shaving: "When we looked up again we hardly knew one another any longer" (1948, 44). Any sense of who I am derives from my ability to recognize and to be recognized by the other; this mutual recognition is the basis of responsive relation. In the Holocaust memoir memory would reconstitute reciprocal recognition through the remembrance of its collapse. For in the movement of remembrance the one who had been reduced to nothingness by being reduced to the finitude of the body now regains an identity through a memory that belongs to no one else. Yet, in many cases, the others who might recognize this memory did not survive the death that began in the shearing room. Thus, memory forever seeks something that will never come.

Livia Jackson also sheds light on the significance of shaven heads. Age and other marks of distinction fade away, she comments. In the place of facial expressions there is only "a blank, senseless stare.... There is less of a substance to our dimensions" (1980, 59). The face no longer speaks; when the hair is shorn from the head, the word is severed from the tongue. That is why she declares that there was "less of a substance to our dimensions." Eyes stare and convey emptiness. Losing its expression, the body, again, is reduced to an object to which no identity can be attached. Jackson notes that upon being shaven, the women felt the "burden of individuality" lifted from them, and with it their past (1980, 60)—and with their past, their life. This burden of individuality and history and life is what Levinas refers to as "the gravity of an animate body" (1981, 70). The difference that is the basis of relation ruled by nonindifference disappears. So these inmates are not only initiated into the antiworld they embody it in their reduction to mere bodies. Thus, Jackson cries out in horror, "The shaved, gray-cloaked group which ran to stare at us through the barbed-wire fence, they were us!" (1980, 61). These are the ones whom Jackson had taken for lunatics in an insane asylum when she first saw them (1980, 58). Lily Lerner, in fact, had a similar reaction when she came out of the shaving area. "I wasn't sure it was Margaret," she says of her sister standing next to her. "I wasn't sure it was me. We all looked like lunatics in a mental institution" (1980, 81). To have an identity is to have a capacity to *signify* what no one else can signify, insofar as no one else has my body. Here lies the reason why Jackson and Lerner associate this new, unidentifiable form with madness: madness is a disruption of the signifying activity that distinguishes the self in its flesh and blood. Everything can mean anything, and, therefore, nothing means anything. The body is merely what it is, equal to itself; in that equation it breaks. And memory tries to mend it.

But time is the enemy of memory, just as it is the enemy of the body. In this connection one finds that just as the past is lost when identity is lost, so is the future lost with the breakdown of the body and often graphically so. One sees an expression of this loss in the premature aging that many of the survivors endured. Fania Fénelon, for example, relates that when her hair began to grow back after her head was shaved, she discovered that it had turned completely white (1977, 84). In Dachau, says Agnes Sassoon, "I felt more like an old woman than a girl on the threshold of her teenage years" (1983, 23). And at the time of her liberation, Livia Jackson was mistaken for a woman of sixty-two, when in fact she was a girl of fourteen (1980, 168). What I examined in chapter 5 as an ontological and metaphysical collapse of time here assumes a physical form in the breakdown of the body, which is normally a measure of time itself. The silence of the "there is" solidifies into this broken remnant of the individual who has lost a future, for here the future is something that must be retrieved from the past and returned to the body by returning to the body its human image. How does the body thus regain an open-ended future? Through memory's recovery of an identity. But the moment will not linger, and time slips through the net of memory so that memory is continually thrown back on itself. Again and ever again the survivor searches the mirror of memory for an image that she can recognize; in this eternal return lies the open-endedness of recovery, open-ended because the body reduced to an object is reduced to something alien to itself and is, therefore, unrecognizable to itself.

Hence, the breakdown of the body is signaled by the failure of recognition. "Body! Who are you?" Ka-tzetnik cries out, unable to recognize the form to which he is attached (1971b, 116). The body broken beyond recognition is a body that has lost every trace of its humanity, of what might *identify* it as the body of a human being. Void of its human image, the body becomes a monstrosity, as Isabella Leitner suggests in her memory of passing through the delousing process. "Some naked-headed monster," she says of her sister Chicha, "is standing next to me. Some naked-headed monster is standing next to her" (1978, 26). The one "standing next to her," of course, is Leitner herself, who now is not just some*body* else but some*thing* else, made perceptible only through her perception of her sister Chicha. Similarly, Sara Zyskind recalls her return from the camp hospital and her reunion with her friends, only to be terrified at what she was able to see of herself through their eyes. "My illness," she writes, "changed me into something monstrous" (1981, 119). And when Alexander Donat encounters his old friend Izak in Maidanek, "Izak did not at first recognize me," he relates, because his appearance had severely degenerated (1978, 205). Unlike the body of an animal or an object, the body of the human being is gathered into his face; in the face lies the primary nudity or exposure of the body. The breakdown of the body, therefore, manifests itself in the breakdown of the face, and it is announced in the inability of the other to recognize the face of the self. This recognition is tied to a recollection of the self by the other, and the identity of the self depends on this recollection. In the Holocaust memoir, then, memory searches for this memory that comes from the other in a recognition of the self.

But, like the word constituted by the duality of listening and response, identity has its other side: the ability of the self to recognize the other, beginning with those who are most dear to oneself. If the I is to know who it is, it must be able not only to gain the recognition of the other but to recognize the other. Here, too, the breakdown of the body that undermines identity originates in the mutilation of the face. That is why one senses a real horror in Ana Vinocur's outcry, "I could not even recognize my own mother!" (1976, 64) which is to say, I could not recognize the one from whom I received my first recognition as a being who means something, who is someone, in short, who is loved. In chapter 1 I explored the implications of the fact that the mother lies at the origin of the family; here I add to those implications the fact that the individual is part of the body of the family. In the family mutual recognition is essential to self-recognition because the family is the wellspring of the life of the self. Thus, Livia Jackson's search for her brother Bubi in Dachau entails not only a struggle to find him but to recognize him according to his physical appearance; indeed, *finding* him means recognizing him. But when she finally encounters him she has trouble recognizing him. He looks "unlike a human being" with nothing in his "appearance to connect him with Bubi" yet, she insists, "it is he, I know it" (1980, 144–45). Something beyond the body appears in the breakdown of the body, in the breach between *him* and Bubi. It arises from memory where the remembrance of this something else derives not from the insignificance of the body but from its importance to the life of family and home. "*Recol-lection* and *representation*," Levinas points out, "are produced concretely as *habitation in a dwelling* of a Home" (1969, 150; emphasis in the original). In the Holocaust memoir memory struggles to reestablish a connection be-tween the brother recollected and his representation. Here is another link to the memory of the mother, father, and child discussed in part 1. The break-down of the body is definitively tied to the destruction of the family. Seeking to recover an identity first established in the bosom of the family, memory strives to overcome the breakdown of the body through this recollection and representation.

The body is rendered unrecognizable, moreover, not only through mutilation and emaciation but through sheer filth. When an SS doctor asks Olga Lengyel, for example, if she is the wife of the famous Dr. Lengyel, she recalls, "Here I was, covered with mud, with shaved head, in rags. . . . No, I was not the wife of a respected surgeon" (1972, 159). In the world of human beings the clothing that covers the body is an extension of the body and a sign of personal identity. In the antiworld the creature is covered with filth and rags that obliterate the body and, thus, destroy identity. There the clothes unmake the man so that it is not a matter of being dirty in any ordinary sense. The dirt of the world is accumulated on a body that dwells and labors and plays and lives and loves in the world; the dirt picked up from the world is the dirt of the earth and affirms the activity and there the identity of the individual. The filth of the antiworld, by contrast, is the excrement to which the Nazis would reduce the Jew; it is the antiworld itself. Hence, one finds in the Holocaust memoir an accent on the importance of cleansing the body of this filth as one means of sustaining some contact with life. Ceasing to wash, Alexander Donat notes, drew a man one step closer to death (1978, 173). Carl Jantzen, the man who saved Paul Trepman's life, did so in part by urging him to bathe each day (1978, 216). And Olga Lengyel brings out both the physical and the metaphysical significance of a ritualistic cleansing of the body, declaring, "That was our only way of waging war against the parasites, against our jailers, and against every force that made us its victims" (1972, 131). This act of bathing is not a mere hygienic measure; it is a rite that affirms the dearness of what does not meet the eye, the dearness of the holy, a rite of purification. It is not a matter of being unclean but of being impure, contaminated by the death that is the essence of the antiworld. The cleanliness of the body is sought for the sake of a purity of the soul that is essential to the relation to the holy, which is at the core of life itself.

In the ritual of bathing the body, then, one finds an affirmation of the life of the soul. Washing the surface of the body that comes up against the antiworld is a cleansing of the interior of the soul that is threatened by the antiworld; that interior is the core of the human being. The target of the assault on the body, then, was the very soul of the person whom the Nazis would make into a nonperson. Jewish identity cannot be broken unless the Jewish soul is broken. Thus, in the Holocaust memoir the memory that arises from the soul seeks a recovery of identity through the recovery of the soul.

The Dissolution of the Soul

One indication that the Nazis assailed the soul through the body is found in Livia Jackson's recollection that under the eyes of the SS the women "felt no nakedness without clothes" just as they "felt no clothedness" in their rags. "Our soul is naked," she writes. "Our bodies have lost dimension" (1980, 75). If the body is expressive of the soul, it is because the soul belongs to an interior that is to be expressed. One form that the onslaught against the soul assumes, then, is the reduction of the Jew to something that is all exterior, like an animal or an object, to be either manipulated or eliminated. This, indeed, is the purpose of the yellow star. When Livia Jackson was forced to wear the star in the ghetto, for example, she notes, "I was singled out at will, an object" (1980, 16). Made into an object, the Jew is leveled, brought down to the insignificance of one more thing in a landscape of things unable to signify anything higher than themselves and, therefore, unable to justify their existence. Fania Fénelon uses the term *object* to describe her status upon her arrival at the murder camp where she first caught sight of the SS. Under their eyes, she says, "I felt considerably less than human: a peculiar, grubby object upsetting the natural order" (1977, 19). If she upset the natural order, or the *ordre établi*, as the French text reads (Fénelon 1976, 35), it was because the order established was opposed to the nature in which a human being is a spiritual being and not a dead object. Such a nature is characterized by an order of good and evil, holy and profane, high and low. It is an order in which the soul appears as a You through the "epiphany of the face," as Levinas calls it. "The gaze that supplicates," he argues, "is precisely the epiphany of the face. . . . To recognize the Other is to recognize a hunger. To recognize the Other is to give . . . to him whom one approaches as 'You' ['*Vous*'] in a dimension of height" (1969, 75). In the antiworld, however, hunger is not acknowledged or alleviated it is enforced; there is no giving but a complete taking, down to the hair on the body, unto to the very name. In the antiorder of the antiworld, therefore, there is no dimension of height, for the face of the human being from which the soul emanates is veiled with a filth that reduces the person to a grubby object.

Where Jackson and Fénelon use the language of objects, others use the terminology of the animal. Frida Michelson, for instance, recalls the day in the ghetto when she was knocked to the ground by a Latvian schoolboy and complained to a policemen. He told her that the schoolboy was the boss there. "I was nothing," she writes. "I was worse than a dog, an insect that can be squashed by anyone" (1979, 68). And, recalling her deportation to Auschwitz, Ana Vinocur writes, "Wagons full of people, like us. But why was I saying this? Cattle, like us" (1976, 58). The human being endowed with a soul stands taller than a cow or a dog or an insect; to be drained of a soul is to be brought lower than those animals. Mikhail Bakhtin describes the soul as "spirit-that-has-not-actualized-itself" so that the project of the soul is to turn matter into spirit through "the loving consciousness of another (another human being, God)" (1991, 111). Central to the Nazi project of the dissolution of the soul, then, is the transformation of spirit into matter; the human being—the Jew—had to be made into an object or an animal of surfaces and nothing more, that is, into something already dead, something nonhuman. One realizes that with respect to the Jews the Nazis were not racists because they viewed the Jews as animals or objects that have no place among the races of humanity and, therefore, no place in the time of humanity. As Bakhtin has shown, the essence of the human being *as human* lies "in the categories of *not-yet-existing*, in the categories of purpose and meaning— in the meaning-governed future" (1991, 123). The soul is nourished by the truth and meaning it seeks; meaning posits a direction, and direction implies a place that I have yet to reach, a being I have yet to become. Human being is human becoming. Objects and animals have no life in this sense because they have nothing that they have yet to become; a man is faced with becoming more of a man, but a dog need not become more of a dog or a stone more of a stone. Reducing the Jew to an animal or object, then, is one more means of depriving the Jew of his *time*, of his future and, therefore, his past, of his truth and meaning. One wonders, however, whether the Nazis thought there was, in fact, something of which to deprive the Jew. For the Jews, according to the Nazis, had no souls.

Yet the Nazis must have had some sense that these were people, otherwise they would not have gone to such lengths to transform them into soulless objects or animals. The aim of memory in the Holocaust memoir is to reverse this transformation by calling forth the loving consciousness of another. Only in this way can the human image be returned to those who were made into something other than human. Memory restores the dimension of height to a humanity brought low. If it crosses a threshold from world to antiworld, it does so to undertake a movement of never-ending return. What distinguishes the threshold is the transformation itself, such as the one Eugene Heimler describes when he writes, "I had mounted the train of death wearing European clothes, a European man; I alighted at the other end a dazed creature of Auschwitz" (1959, 21). The dazed creature is a creature void of any memory that might define his presence in this place that in a nonplace; void of memory, he is dissolved of a soul, a *creature* and not a man. The sealed car in the train to Auschwitz is a chamber in which the transformation from a man with a name into a creature without identity is inaugurated. Once inside the camp, as Sim Kessel notes, it required only a few days for the prisoners to realize that they "were no longer men" (1972, 59). For Elie Wiesel and his comrades it took less than that. "Within a few seconds we had ceased to be men," he comments upon their entry into the barracks at Auschwitz. "A dark flame had entered my soul and devoured it" (1960, 46). What makes a man a man, a *ben adam*, endowed with identity and humanity, is the soul, the *neshamah*, breathed into the first man, transforming him from dust into a human being, from matter into spirit. When the dark flame of the antiworld obliterates the name and consumes the soul, spirit is reverted to matter; both identity and humanity, which are of a piece, are dissolved. The memory of the termination of humanity and of being human, then, is a central feature of the memoir that seeks to recover an identity through the renewal of the soul.

"We ceased to exist as thinking, feeling entities," says Sara Nomberg-Przytyk, commenting on her arrival at Auschwitz (1985, 14), which is to say: we ceased to exist as human beings, for thinking and feeling belong to the love of life that characterizes human life. Likewise, Sara Zyskind recalls that although they had managed to cling to a trace of their humanity while in the ghetto, in the camp "that vanished" (1981, 203). But it must not be forgotten that in the ghetto, too, the humanity—the soul—of the human being was threatened with annihilation, as Zivia Lubetkin, a Jewish fighter in the Warsaw Ghetto, reminds: "We had almost lost all semblance of humanity" (1981, 252). Jews in hiding were also subject to the dissolution of the soul, as seen in Vladka Meed's memory of a mother and child whom she discovered hiding in a hut on a Polish farm. They "looked like spectres," she relates, "they no longer seemed human" (1973, 259). Why? Because, like the shadows of Hades, they had been reduced to bare existence void of any inner space that might be called a home. There was, indeed, no place to hide from the attack on the soul; not all the victims of the Nazis were Jews but all Jews were victims, for the Nazis' prime directive was the annihilation of the Jewish soul. The soul signifies the insertion of the infinite into the finite, and the Nazis' enemy in their ontological assault on Jewish being—and thus, on human being—was the Infinite One who is manifested through the humanity of that being.

It was said above that the soul is an interiority that is to be expressed; to have a soul is to have an interior to be externalized. Here one realizes that this *within* comes from *above*; the insertion of the infinite into the finite is announced through the expression of the infinite—through the burning eyes of the soul—in the face of the human being. To recognize a human being is to recognize this expression of an interior from within the face that comes from beyond the face. In the concentrarionary universe, when the human is no longer recognizable, it is nearly always because she has been emptied of an interior, of a soul, that might be expressed. So it happened to one Mrs. Frankel, as Sara Zyskind recalls: "Before long her appearance changed beyond recognition. . . . She even stopped talking about the troubles at home and instead maintained an embittered silence" (1981, 75). This is not the silence of someone who refuses to speak but of someone who has been drained of everything to express. Thus, in the Holocaust memoir the movement of memory is a movement toward an interior that has been drained of interiority. The memory that reconstitutes the interiority of the soul is the memory of having been emptied of that interiority. To be sure, the language of the memoir in this regard delineates an interior by designating it as absent or dead. Ana Vinocur names the time of this absence "the Stone Age: everything inside us had now turned to stone" (1976, 83–84). The image of stone once again suggests the dead object, the thing without a future, removed from the process of becoming essential to the life of the soul. The dissolution of that inner life is like the disease of leprosy to which Fania Fénelon compares it: "Bits of oneself rotted and fell off without one's even knowing they'd gone" (1977, 106). The pieces of the self are pieces of the soul, of an inner substance slowly made into an inner emptiness.

This is the death of the soul that the Nazis engineered before killing the body. When prisoners stood for selection, in fact, the SS often looked not only at their bodies but into their eyes to see whether the soul was dead as it happened to Akiba Drumer in Wiesel's *Night*. Why was he taken in the selection? Because "his eyes would become blank, nothing but two open wounds, two pits of terror" (1960, 81). It happened, too, with Leon Wells just before his escape from Janowska: "He [the SS] has crossed us off the list of the living. . . . Where my heart should be there is a boundless chasm" (1978, 97). Yet being selected to "live" was little better because this meant being returned to the slow death brought on by the leprosy of the soul. Upon surviving a selection at Maidanek, Alexander Donat comments, "I felt nothing, absolutely nothing. A complete vacuum" (1978, 167). Reflecting on these example, one perhaps better understands why Wiesel declares, "The ultimate mystery of the Holocaust is that whatever happened took place in the soul" (1985, 1: 239). For what happened was annihilation, beginning and ending with the dissolution of the soul from the inside. Returning to the Kingdom of Night, memory returns to the inside, moving from the interior of memory to the interior of the Event that can never be fathomed no matter how deep the penetration. Hence, the recovery of identity is forever open-ended.

Memory and recovery are open-ended because this Event that transpires in the interior of the soul cannot be confined to historical time. "Interiority," Levinas explains, "institutes an order where everything is *pending*, where what is no longer possible historically remains always possible" (1969, 55; emphasis in the original). In the Holocaust memoir memory seeks not what was but what is pending, not a return to Auschwitz but a rebirth from the ashes of Auschwitz. This new birth, however, is ever intrauterine, for each memory, each name, summons another memory and another name: identity recedes as it is approached. The body and soul that constitute the human being are gathered into a name, which initially has its place in a native, natal language. But for the Holocaust survivor this is just what has been lost. It is no accident that many of these memoirs are written under names and in languages other than those of the authors' births. These include, for example, memoirs written by Jean Améry, Alexander Donat, Saul Friedländer, Ka-tzetnik 135633, Nathan Shapell, and Leon Wells. The change in name and language among these survivors is the result not merely of a geographical relocation but of an ontological decomposition from which memory seeks recovery. Thus, the I who speaks from these pages is like the I that Levinas describes as one whose existence "consists in identifying itself, in recovering its identity throughout all that happens to it" (1969, 36). Because all that happens to the I is gathered into the domain of memory, the primary work of identification is the work of memory. It is the work of the Holocaust memoir.

Saul Friedländer underwent a series of name changes from Paul to Shaul to Saul, transformations that he views as a source "of a real and profound confusion" (1980, 94). The confusion is not peculiar to Friedländer; or rather, in its peculiarity to him as a Jew, it expresses a universality about the problem of identity confronting not only this individual but all the world after the Shoah. Flooded with displaced persons and displaced identities, the world is itself displaced. Thus, the Holocaust memoir announces the difficulty facing all Jews, and here, as ever, what threatens the Jew also threatens humanity. "The question of identity," Adin Steinsaltz asserts, is indeed "threatening, and not only stirs a vast number of possible answers but offers a glimpse into an abyss of yet further, unanswerable questions" (1980, 140). The unanswerable question underscores the open-endedness of recovery and places it in the realm of the eternally pending. Yet for us Jews, in the words of Edmond Jabès, "we create our identity through that interrogation. . . . The affirmation 'I am Jewish' is already a regression. . . . We suffer from an absence of identity which we desperately try to fill. It is in this despair that identity really resides" (1990, 67). In this absence memory establishes its presence where it struggles to recover the identity that might set it free. But in this despair lies the failure of that liberation.

8

The Failure of Liberation

In part 1 I showed that the abysmal absence that Auschwitz imposes upon humanity is the absence of the mother, of the father, and of God. In a word, it is the absence of a home, of a dwelling place that might provide a center from which human life derives its meaning. Indeed, all the Jewish victims of the Shoah—which is to say, all the Jews of Europe—were homeless: Jewish homes and possessions, all the having that goes into having a home, were confiscated before Jewish lives were obliterated. When that center is destroyed, so is the meaning it generates. When meaning is lost, so is any direction that one might pursue. And when direction is lost, so is freedom. Liberation comes not only with the breaking down of the prison gates but with the opening up of a path to follow. If that path has been erased, then there can be no liberation. When the gates of the camps were unlocked, many did not move, for they had nowhere to go. Having lost a home and a center to which they might return, the Jews were faced with a movement of return that could never be consummated. Saul Friedländer asks, "Where did this need of a return, a return toward a decimated, humiliated, miserable group, come from?" (1980, 139). The answer is it comes from the loss of a home and a center to which memory incessantly returns—incessantly because the one who remembers has been robbed of every avenue of return. The need announces itself not only in the absence of a dwelling place but also in the impossibility of the return; thus, it bespeaks the failure of liberation. Yet what is absent assumes a kind of presence precisely in the need for it. This presence-in-the-mode-of-absence (if one may speak thusly) fuels the movement of memory and recovery in the Holocaust memoir. But because this presence is manifested as an absence—manifested, that is, in the mode of longing—the movement is ever open-ended.

Charlotte Delbo remembers that in the death camp the discourse among the inmates was itself steeped in a liberation longed-for and in a return that would not come. Among those women, then, the memory of home was oriented toward the future, so that when speaking of home they not only recollected a past but plotted a time yet to come. "The women who had stopped believing in their return," Delbo relates, "were dead" (1968, 114). Death here arises not only from the loss of belief but from the loss of all memory of a place to return to; death happens when the memory of the future dies. Near the end of her memoir Delbo makes this point by describing the living death imposed on every woman turned over to the antiworld: "Her eyes have emptied out / And we have lost our memory. / None of us will return" (1968, 126). The loss of memory is signified by the emptying of life from the eyes; they cannot return to life because the memory of life will not return to them. If the function of memory in the Holocaust memoir is to recover a trace of what was lost through the remembrance of the loss, the first thing retrieved is memory itself. The Holocaust memoir not only seeks a recovery of life and a liberation from the kingdom of death it *is* that recovery and liberation; or rather it is a movement *toward* a recovery that does not come and a liberation that cannot happen. For in one memoir after another what is remembered is the ineluctable fact that "none of us will return." To be liberated from the antiworld would mean leaving it behind, in the past, so that the past, present, and future of life's time might be regained. But Auschwitz will not be left behind, and the passing of the years yield no past. In her memoir Bertha Ferderber-Salz declares, "Pictures from the past and the images of the people I loved are always with me. It is not natural to live constantly in the past, but I cannot do otherwise" (1980, 56). One gets the impression that something other than the survivor speaks in the memoir, that in the memoir lurks a voice with which the voice of memory constantly struggles.

"It's not me who's doing the thinking," Fania Fénelon insists, " 'it' thinks *for* me. . . . I spend every night there—every night!" (1977, ix). Liberation would entail a liberation from the dominating voice of the *it* of Auschwitz. In the act of remembrance the survivor's voice engages this other voice but is never free of it, never liberated. Freedom, then, is not possible, as one sees in Ferderber-Salz's recollection of the day of her release from the camp. Although the smell of spring is in the air, she writes, "In every limb of my pain-racked body I feel that freedom is not possible for me. I am still totally immersed in the nightmare of yesterday" (1980, 15). The images of spring here are not just descriptions of the time of year or of a vernal environment; beyond that, they signify an image of life diametrically opposed to the survivor's own image as one who has lived through her own death. She who has lived through her own death cannot be free because she cannot die; for her death is not the last thing but instead lies in a past that she cannot leave behind. She is immersed in a past that cannot be left behind because every prospect for a return that would leave it behind has been wiped out with the annihilation of family and home. She cannot die because she has no future whose meaning is shaped by a death that is *not yet*; for her time has collapsed, as in chapter 5, leaving her *outside.* "You are outside," writes Ka-tzetnik in a memory of his release from Auschwitz. "You weren't buried in the pit. Somebody else was. Who now is the free one?" (1971b, 35). Perhaps the SS were right after all: the only way out of the camp was through the chimney. One may now better understand the story that Wiesel tells in A *Beggar in Jerusalem* about a survivor who threw himself on top of a mass grave and begged the dead not to reject him (1970b, 80): it was his only pathway to liberation. But he cannot crawl into that grave, for it has crawled into him. Because the Nazis set out to destroy not only the body of Israel but its very soul—because their enemy was not only the Jewish people but Jewish *being*—the soul remains a prisoner even when the body is freed.

"I remained stranger," says Livia Jackson of her so-called liberation. "Even with the Americans, our liberators. Oh, God, what is liberty?" (1980, 179). The Americans opened the gates, but they could not show the prisoners the way out. Why? Because neither they nor anyone else could offer any understanding or explanation that might place a closure on the Event. Neither they nor anyone else could return the home and its sacred center to the survivors. Neither they nor anyone else could free the survivors from the death that overtook them before their lives were over. Where indeed, then, is the liberation? The prisoner released from the prison becomes a fugitive relentlessly pursued by a place and a past. And a fugitive, it is written in the Talmud, "is like a captive" (Bava Metzia 39a). In this case he is the captive of silence, of homelessness, and of death. There is no getting the Event "off his chest" because it is curled up in his soul. He speaks, but no one listens, for no one can understand. He returns home but finds nothing. He longs for a life that has death as its closure, but that death has been killed by the premature death manufactured in the death factory. "Our motionlessness and our silence betray reality," says Jackson. "We are dead. Dead survivors of a long-lost struggle" (1980, 166). Dead survivors: in the Holocaust memoir, unlike other memoirs, this is not a contradiction of terms. It means that with his memory the survivor is turned over to an unending struggle for life and liberation; it means that liberation has failed. Why?

From Silence to Silence

"Auschwitz," writes André Neher, "is, above all, silence" (1981, 141). But when Eugene Heimler was finally freed from the concentrationary universe of silence, the silence followed him into an open field. "I became aware that the silence was within me, too," he writes, "a silence such as there must have been before the days of creation" (1959, 188). Why the silence before the days of creation? Because this is a silence imposed by an absolute, ontological destruction; it is the mute silence of an imposed absence, the silence of the word torn from its meaning and of the man torn from a life that inheres in language. "There is the silence which preceded creation," Wiesel has said, "and the one which accompanied the revelation on Mount Sinai. The first contains chaos and solitude, the second suggests presence, fervor, plenitude" (1970b, 108). The second is the silence of meaning within and beyond the word, the silence of human relation, *adam l'adam*, expressive of the relation to the divine, *adam la Makom*. The return to freedom lies in a return to these relations that constitute the substance of life; it lies in having a place, a *Makom*, to return to. Liberation from Auschwitz, then, would be liberation from the silence of chaos and isolation and a return to presence and plenitude. For the survivor this liberation means that when he speaks to a human being, he receives a human response; it means that when he speaks, someone listens. For this offering and receiving of the word is just what creates a place where presence may enter human life. "Only as the You becomes present," Martin Buber expresses it, "does presence come into being" (1970, 63). Liberation from Auschwitz, then, would be a return to the You to whom a word is offered and from whom a response is received. But this is precisely what does not happen.

The case of Moshe the Beadle in Wiesel's *Night* may be seen as a paradigm for the condition of the one who emerges from the Kingdom of Death. Like Moshe, the survivor returns from the depths of a mass grave to tell his tale, but he cannot complete his return, for no one listens. "He no longer talked to me of God or of the cabbala," Wiesel relates, "but only of what he had seen. People refused not only to believe his stories, but even to listen to them" (17-18). In *One Generation After* Wiesel remembers Moshe, saying, "He alone survived. Why? So that he could come back to his town and tell the tale. And that is why he never stopped talking. But his audiences, weary and naive, would not, could not believe. . . . Finally he understood and fell silent. Only his burning eyes revealed the impotent rage inside him. His muteness bordered on madness" (1970a, 28–29). Like Moshe many other survivors were locked into the muteness of their own silence by the silence they encountered in others. Liberated from one prison, they were delivered over to another, to the prison of refusal and disbelief erected by those who were outside the antiworld.

The victims who had been removed from the human world could be liberated only by regaining contact with that world. The most essential element of this contact lies in the word, in a language that would engender the human relation within which freedom lives. But the word lives through the response it invokes. When the response fails, so does the liberation. One realizes, then, how profound is the urgency underlying the word that comes through the Holocaust memoir. And one realizes what is placed in one's hands: shall I, too, refuse to listen and thereby refuse these witnesses their liberation? The Holocaust memoir puts this question precisely in its memory of the failure of liberation arising from disbelief and the refusal to listen. It is not a matter, moreover, of being unable to hear or incapable of belief; all too often it is a question of being unwilling to believe or afraid to listen. Kitty Hart, for example, recalls that her uncle in England told her not to speak of what she had seen. "I don't want my girls upset," he explained. "And *I* don't want to know" (1982, 12). Everyone in England was telling their war stories, but those who has emerged from the Kingdom of Night were tacitly forbidden to speak of what they had endured. Whenever she was asked about the tattoo on her arm, Hart recalls, she would at first tell the truth. But "the reaction was always an awkward silence, as if I had said something terribly ill mannered" (1982, 13). The soldiers are not the only ones faced with the task and the responsibility to liberate the Nazis' victims; those who receive their words also have a part in that liberation. To refuse them an ear is to refuse them their return to life; it is tantamount to refusing the fact of the Event itself.

Among the spokespersons for those who react in such a manner, then, are the historical revisionists, who have tried and continue to try to argue either that the Holocaust did not happen or that it was not as bad as the Jews make out. Others who aid and abet this effort to kill the victims yet again are people who would plug up their ears by putting the blame on the Jews, spouting such lies as "They went like sheep to the slaughter," "They were rich and naturally aroused the anger of their neighbors," "They could have run away," and "They cooperated with their own murderers." All of this rhetoric goes into the attitude or the wall of silence that cuts off the path of liberation for the survivors. Many do not want them to be liberated because then one would have to listen to them. One does not want to listen to them because in their testimony lie questions that implicate one in one's own responsibility, in one's own humanity. The dark side of human being that is revealed in this memory is hidden in all people. The survivor speaks, and from beyond her words comes the first question put to the first man: Where are you? And one does not want to hear it. In the Holocaust memoir, therefore, the memory of the indifference that shrouded the Kingdom of Night includes the memory of the indifference that precluded liberation from that Kingdom. Even within the death camp itself no sooner did the dream of liberation arise than it turned into the nightmare that Primo Levi describes as "varied in its detail but uniform in its substance: they had returned home and with passion and relief were describing their past sufferings, addressing themselves to a loved one, and were not believed, indeed, were not even listened to" (1988, 12). In Charlotte Delbo's memoir is confirmation of what Levi has observed, for there she describes a dream common among the inmates, one in which they return home and tell their tale only to have their loved ones turn away from them like strangers (1968, 63). The fear expressed in these dreams is a fear of the failure of liberation, the fear that once one is inside Auschwitz there is no getting out.

In the French version of Delbo's text the verb translated as "return" is not *retourner* but *rentrer* (1965, 64), that is, "to re-enter." Liberation lies not only in the exit from the camp where these nightmares occurred but in an exit from the nightmares themselves, and this can come about only upon the reentry into the home where loved ones listen, into human relation ruled by human response. The wall toward which these figures turn in Delbo's dream is a wall barring the reentry that would make liberation possible. To be sure, the dream of the encounter with the silence of refusal becomes reality as when Levi attempts to relate his story to a group of Poles in Katowice: "I felt my sense of freedom . . . ebb from me. . . . I had dreamed, we all had dreamed, of something like this in the nights at Auschwitz: of speaking and not being listened to, of finding liberty and remaining alone" (1965, 54). The silence of chaos and isolation once again comes to mind. Freedom ebbs into that chaos; in that isolation liberation fails. For liberty is not to be found when a man finds himself alone. Even after the enemy is defeated, then, he continues to do his evil and to imprison his victims as Moshe Sandberg indicates. "You spoke," he affirms, "but it was as if you were talking to yourself, and you lived through it all again, . . . so that even after his defeat the enemy continued doing his evil. Thus not a few of us were prevented from becoming adjusted to new life, from returning to normal existence" (1968, 2). And so the one who seeks a return to the world is returned to the antiworld.

Here, too, the impossible turns out to be possible, the nightmare reality. If history does not repeat itself, the suffering does. Thus memory speaks in the memoir in the hope that if the survivor cannot enter the world once more, then at least his memory might. But this hope no sooner arises than it is shattered by yet another collision with yet another wall: even if the survivor can gain a listener, he cannot be understood. And so he remains locked inside his memory faced with a never-ending process of recovery. Like the dream that forebodes the reality, the prospect of this failure of liberation arises before the gates of the camp are opened. Says Sim Kessel, "Such was our withdrawn solitude, our intrinsic loathing for all humans including ourselves, that I frequently asked myself whether we could ever return to normal life" (1972, 82). And so it came to pass for Livia Jackson when she was faced with relating her story to a Russian soldier who had befriended her but could not fathom what she had to say. She writes, "Who can understand this inconceivable futility that is Auschwitz? . . . I belong to this void" (1980, 211). Belonging to the void called Auschwitz, the survivor's search for a home, for the one place where recovery might happen, is without end. The void to which she belongs *is* this absence of a home, for home is where a person may be understood.

But she cannot be understood. Hence, she moves from silence to silence; she cannot return home.

No Return Home

Given the dreams of freedom that did not console but only troubled the inmates of the antiworld, it is not surprising to find that they were afraid of their return to the world, even if such a return should be possible. "We are afraid of freedom," Paul Trepman asserts. "Now that I'm free, all I feel is a terrible ache of loneliness" (1978, 222). Trepman's ache of loneliness is the ache of homelessness for which there is no balm; it is the ache of the wound inflicted not by hardship but by the absence of a home. The fear of freedom, then, is not a fear of release but of return. Alexander Donat says it well when he explains that his only wish for the freedom he feared was to become a watchman in a Jewish cemetery, where he could be alone with the dead. Why was he afraid of going home? He answers, "I was afraid that when I did, my last ties to life would be irrevocably broken. There would be nothing left" (1978, 292). Better the cemetery than the home because the home has been made into a cemetery: that is where Jewish mothers and fathers and children now reside. For the living, however, the ties to the dead are not enough to constitute a home. And where those ties that go into a home fail, so does freedom.

The absence of these ties is the absence that feeds Primo Levi's fear of a return. "We felt in our veins the poison of Auschwitz," he writes. "Where should we find the strength to begin our lives again?" (1965, 220). Here is an important reason for the failure of liberation: the poison of Auschwitz is not behind its victim but within him and before him. The death camp does not follow him like a shadow but rather precedes him, making him into *its* shadow and every place of return into a desert. Thus, Levi declares, "Liberty . . . had come, but it had not taken us to the Promised Land. It was around us, but in the form of a pitiless deserted plain" (1965, 37). What distinguishes the desertedness of the plain is not the absence of vegetation or of artificial signs of human life, it is the absence of a place to return to. Again, the antiworld destroys not only homes but the very notion of home; with the murder of mother, father, and child the home is obliterated *as a category*. The deserted plain, therefore, has nothing to do with the distinctions between urban and rural settings. The city itself can be transformed into a deserted plain; this is why Vladka Meed feared the liberation that approached Warsaw, saying, "We dreaded the bleak void and the isolation that would have to be faced" (1973, 321). Even though the city may be rebuilt, there is no escaping this bleak void and isolation. For the survivor's situation is neither an environmental condition nor an existential circumstance; rather, it is an ontological category that belongs to the uniqueness of the Shoah. What is annihilated in this annihilation of a people is not only the person of the Jew but the possibility of his liberation: he has no place to go, in all of being, no place to go. Why? Because every place of origin, every trace of the home, has been rendered unrecognizable.

One recalls Emil Fackenheim's assertion that "Eichmann sought to destroy souls before he destroyed bodies" (1970, 74) and his insistence that in the death camp the object of murder was the image of the divine within the human (1978, 246). And one understands more deeply the scope of these insights. For the divine image imprinted upon the soul lies not only within the human being but also within the home that sustains and is the essence of human being. The murder of the soul, therefore, entails the annihilation of the home. And, because any genuine liberation has to include the liberation of the soul, the murder of the soul entails the murder of liberation through the destruction of the home. This murder is effected by making the home into something alien, as demonstrated in many memoirs. Further, because the soul suffers the fatal blow within the death camp, the alienation from home precedes the return home, cutting off that return before it has even begun. Says Gerda Klein, for example, "Perhaps, I thought, we will survive, but what then? I will go home, of course. . . . And for the first time in all those years, the thought of going home did not ring right" (1957, 210). The thought does not ring right because the word has lost its meaning, severed from all but emptiness. It has lost its meaning because the home has lost its life, turned to the silent, broken stones that Donna Rubinstein encounters upon her arrival in her home town of Krasnostav. "And," she relates, "my past was in every brick, every stone" (1982, 90). Part of what makes a home a home is a past that goes into a tradition so that the home becomes a center in time and space from which the world derives its meaning. "The dwelling is not situated in the objective world," Levinas states, "but the objective world is situated by relation to my dwelling" (1969, 153). Thus, Rubinstein laments, "I no longer belonged to Krasnostav. I was homeless and alone" (1982, 92). That this homelessness extends from the home town into a larger realm is shown in Lily Lerner's memory of her return to Hungary. Not only did she find that in her village of Tolcsva her house "was some other house, beyond recognition" (1980, 128), but in Budapest also she asks, "Was this really home? What were we doing here? Why had we returned?" (1980, 121). And one may add another question, Can this be deemed liberation?

Home, of course, is made of far more than bricks and furniture. Its essence lies in human relation; a human being liberated is a human being returned to human relation. The breakdown of this relation is just what underlies the failure of liberation and the alienation from home. Very often this failure and alienation are revealed in the failure of the word, that is, in silence. In Tolcsva, for instance, Lerner encountered people who had known her family: "They said nothing. . . . No one saw us. No one met our eyes" (1980, 127–28). No person is free whose liberation is not accompanied by a greeting; the simple saying of hello is the portal through which the return to the world is made possible. But that is just what is withheld from Lily Lerner. This collapse of human relation essential to human being is also at the core of the failure of liberation that Rudolf Vrba experienced when he and his friend Fred Wetzler went back to Czechoslovakia: "We found ourselves relating everything to Auschwitz. . . . Just as we thought we were human beings again, a jagged edge came out of the past and scratched us" (1964, 249–50). For Vrba, the past that scratched him and rendered him other than human left a wound on his face; in the face the word finds its tie to meaning and the home its linkage with life. But when Vrba first saw his mother, who had survived the war, she did not recognize him: "I had seen 1,760,000 people die and it had left a mark on my face" (1964, 251). There is no more painful manifestation of the miscarriage of the return home than this loss of recognition from one's own mother, unless, perhaps, it is the return to a completely empty, voiceless home, as happened to Nathan Shapell. "I . . . approached the entrance to the building I had once called home," he recalls his appearance in Sosnowiec. "waiting to be greeted by someone, anyone. No one, not a voice I knew" (1974, 167). The deserted plain, the desert itself, of which Levi speaks (1965, 37) extends not only into the streets of a town but into the heart of the dwelling itself. And the definitive feature of this desert is the absence of a voice.

"In the desert," in the words of Edmond Jabès, "one becomes other: one becomes the one who knows the weight of the sky and the thirst of the earth; the one who has learned to take account of his own solitude" (1990, 16). Under this weight and plagued by this thirst, the survivor writes the memory of liberation's failure. One sees why the concentrationary universe is called a universe: it is not another universe, for there is "room" only for one. Rather, it becomes *the* universe, the desert enveloping one, so that ultimately there is no return home; once more one realizes that the recovery that memory seeks in its movement of return is ever open-ended. Memory speaks incessantly, straining to hear the voices of home, only to be thrown back on its own voice. One of the memoirs in which this point is made most powerfully is *And the Sun Kept Shining* by Bertha Ferderber-Salz. "Once again I was in Cracow," she remembers. "Emptiness emanated from every corner, every street and every house" (1980, 179). "I wandered like a ghost through the streets of the city where I had grown up and lived most of my life. The streets, the houses and the people all seemed alien" (1980, 189). The emptiness that emanates from every corner is the emptiness of her own ghostlike self; the alienation from houses and people is born of the self-alienation imposed on her in Auschwitz and Bergen-Belsen through the breakdown of the body and the collapse of the soul. In desperation she goes to her parents' village of Kolbuszowa, but there, too, Auschwitz precedes her, making that return also impossible. "Everything in my village was strange to me!" she writes. "No one came to greet me. Where were the well-loved voices that had chorused words of affection and welcome whenever I visited my parents' home?" (204). Again, one more question repeats itself, Can this be deemed liberation?

The pattern of a terrible motif continues: there was no one to greet me. Why are the Ten Utterances at Sinai, the site signifying Israel's liberation, divided into the relations of *adam la Makom* and *adam l'adam*, of man-to-the-place and man-to-man? Because the place of liberation arises where human presence arises; each requires the other in order to be present, and liberation requires both. And *place*, one is taught in the *Midrash on Psalms*, means God as the *dwelling place* of the world, for it is He who makes dwelling in the world possible (1959, 2:93). When the image of the divine within the human is destroyed, there is no return to the Place of dwelling, which is to say: there is no return of the human to the human. "The vacuum was unbearable," Livia Jackson says of her return to Hungary (1980, 201). And in this vacuum a need essential to life and to liberation is announced: "I need people who need, and I want to give. I reach out and there is nothing" (1980, 208). The reaching out in this instance is a gesture not of grabbing but of offering, and the void encountered renders the self void. "The self," as Levinas has shown, "is nonindifference to the others, a sign given to the others" (1981, 171). The significance of my being lies in my capacity to signify the dearness of the other through the act of meeting the need of the other. Unable to greet the other, the survivor is unable to engage in this process of signification; without this signification liberation is without significance. Hence, it fails. "Suddenly we became shatteringly aware that we meant exactly nothing to anyone," Sim Kessel recalls the opening of the gates of Auschwitz (1972, 185); which means: there is no one in need of us, no one *for* whom we might be in the being-for-the-other essential to the life and to the freedom of a person. "Who would be waiting for us at the station?" Fania Fénelon wonders (1977, 258). And Sara Nomberg-Przytyk remembers her first day of release from the camp, saying, "I was alone, no one was waiting for me, there was no one to return to" (1985, 154). For all of these survivors the tragedy lies not in the absence of an embrace that might have been received but in the absence of anyone to whom an embrace might be offered.

Thus, it happened that those who were freed embraced their liberators, but for their liberation to be complete they needed others who needed their embrace. When that failed, the one who was "liberated" went from one pain to another, from one exile to another, as did to Primo Levi. "In the very hour," he writes, "in which a hope of a return to life ceased to be crazy, I was overcome by . . . the pain of exile, of my distant home, of loneliness" (1965, 15). The distance from home is not so much geographical as it is metaphysical. It lies not in the miles that separate the man from Italy but in the void that isolates him from the human beings around him, both living and dead. That void has a name: it is Auschwitz. It extends beyond the barbed wire, spreading not only over the face of the earth but into the soul of the human being. The satisfaction of physical hunger, therefore, merely intensifies a metaphysical hunger. "The end of our hunger," says Levi, "laid bare and perceptible in us a much deeper hunger. Not only desire for our homes, . . . but a more immediate and urgent need for human contacts" (1965, 165). Made of human contact, the home is the place where one is *touched*, where the caress is offered and received. In the caress the physical meets with the metaphysical, with the truth and the holiness of humanity that is eternally sought but never seized. "As soon as we touch a You," Buber asserts, "we are touched by a breath of eternal life" (1970, 113), eternal because the touch opens up a realm of the ever yet-to-be that introduces the eternal into time. The caress, as Levinas expresses it, searches for "what slips away as though it *were not yet*" (1969, 257–58). What does it seek? The divine within the human. Where does it search? In the place, the *Makom*, where dwelling takes place: in the home.

The man freed from Auschwitz searches for a home, but because he searches for a *home*, he is unable to search for the very thing that would sanctify his liberation *from within* the home. Even if he should find his way home, as Levi did, the time that constitutes the home—that is, the future opened up within the home—is eclipsed by a past that inserts itself like the jagged edge that marked Vrba's face. For Levi it comes as an alien word that invades his sleep and stands in the way of his liberation, the alien command to rise to meet the Auschwitz day that will not be left behind: *Wstawàch* (1965, 5). Once again Auschwitz precedes the man who struggles to return home. When the human being is at home, abiding in his native tongue, the word is tied to meaning so that it is not in time, rather time is in the word: the man is liberated, free to offer his word and his soul to another and for another. But with the invasion of an alien antiword from the antitime, the antiworld of Auschwitz cuts him off from the world and foils his liberation.

Thus, in *The Reawakening* Levi speaks of the nightmare to which he has reawakened. It is "a dream full of horror," in which he at first takes himself to be in a familiar and comfortable setting only to have the scene shattered, "I am in the Lager once more, and nothing is true outside the Lager." The sign of his imprisonment? It is the alien command that overwhelms his consciousness again and ever again: *Wstawàch* (1965, 221–22). Upon this command to rise the man falls once again into the void, his world falling around him. Once again he dies a death that is never over, robbed even of the death that would set him free.

The Murder of Death

It has been said that these memoirs are written not by people recounting their lives but by people who have lived through their deaths. In this section I examine why this aspect of memory in the Holocaust memoir precludes a complete liberation from the death factories and turns the survivor over to a never-ending struggle for recovery.

In the world of family and home, where human relation is sanctified as an expression of the relation to the divine, death is an essential part of life. It imparts to life an urgency and opens up to life a direction, filling it to overflowing with a meaningful future. Far from robbing life of its meaning, death defines the parameters of the yet-to-be from which life derives its direction and, therefore, its meaning. In the world of humanity, to cite Levinas once more, "time is precisely the fact that the whole of existence of the mortal being—exposed to violence—is not being for death, but the 'not yet' which is a way of being against death" (1969, 224). The point of the mortal "being against death" is not to destroy death but to situate it in relation to life in such a way that it is part of, and not opposed to, life's meaning. Here death is not the thief who steals my life away but the occasion for the offering up of my life for the sake of others. Thus offering up my life, I make my death into a testimony to the dearness of life; hence, the mortal overcomes death by making it part of, and not the end of, life. According to Jewish tradition, as expressed by the eleventh-century Rabbi Bachya ibn Paquda, "Life and Death are brethren, dwelling together, clinging closely to one another, inseparable, holding fast to the two ends of a tottering bridge over which all the world's creatures pass" (1970, 2:389). Situating life and death together as brethren, the family sanctifies life upon every burial and every memory of the dead; it is one's family who brings one into the world and lays one into the earth. Thus the *Kaddish*, the Prayer for the Dead, is a regular part of Jewish ritual, intended to sanctify the Name and to affirm the dearness of life. In their attack on Jewish being and, thereby, on human being, the Nazis attacked that form of death that is part of human life and on the occasion of which the *Kaddish* is recited. In their absolute, ontological overturning of Jewish being the Nazis decreed and carried out the murder of this death.

One example of this crime that rests on the complete confusion of life and death is found in Elie Wiesel's *Night*. There, on his first day in Auschwitz, he, his father, and their comrades were manipulated into reciting the *Kaddish* not for the dead who have passed away but for themselves, for the living, who in that setting have died before their passing (1960, 42). Thus, these men find themselves in a place that is antithetical to the Place; it is a realm from which there is no liberation, any more than there can be a liberation from the tomb—except, perhaps, on the day when all the dead will be resurrected and roll their way to Jerusalem. But that day is not one of the days remembered in the Holocaust memoir. What is remembered is the mirror through which, day after day, the once-living gaze upon the dead only to have their own reflection thrown back at themselves. Thus, Wiesel remembers the dead along the death march that took him out of Auschwitz but no nearer to freedom: "In every stiffened corpse I saw myself" (1960, 92). Hence, he is robbed of his death; robbed of his death, he is deprived of the "not yet" that would give him meaning and direction, life and liberation. It is not death, therefore, that he sees in the mirror image of every stiffened corpse but the murder of death. One finds more evidence of this in one of the most haunting passages in Livia Jackson's memoir *Elli* where she writes, "The heap of dead bodies, the large pool of blood . . . is this death?" (1980, 84). Her question, of course, is rhetorical. This is not death but the murder of death, the destruction of burial rites, of the *Kaddish*, of the closure on a life that would be a testimony to the dearness of life and to the holiness of its Creator. It is the annihilation of the Lord's giving and the Lord's taking away, of words spoken over the dead for the living, of every elegy sung in the name of all that is sacred.

Part of the process of the soul's liberation from horror and oppression lies in the ability to put it all behind oneself, to die away from it. And this dying away, this burial of a terrible past, entails the burial of the dead. But such a consummation of liberation is just what the anti-world denies its victims; long after the death factories ceased operation they continue in their murder of that death which is part of life and liberation. So the horror endures. Horror, Levinas explains, is "a participation in the *there is* . . . that has 'no exit.' It is, if we may say so, the impossibility of death, the universality of existence even in its annihilation" (1978a, 60-61). The heart continues to beat when it should have come to a stop. The soul continues to live, and yet it *has* no life, for it has been stripped of the sign, of the category, that would seal the tomb of the past and open up the way to the future. What is the sign that signifies such a closure and brings about a liberation from the horror? It is the cemetery. But, as Wiesel has said, "my generation has been robbed of everything, even of our cemeteries" (1968, 25). One function of memory in the Holocaust memoir—one way in which memory seeks recovery and liberation—is to become such a sign. "For me," Wiesel asserts, "writing is a *matzeva*, an invisible tombstone, erected to the dead unburied" (1968, 25). If the signifiers that go into the writing of memory in the Holocaust memoir struggle to lay to rest the dead unburied, they also mark the life ended for one who has lived through his own death. Writing in this instance is an effort to die on the part of someone who cannot die away from the horror. For this death has been murdered in the obliteration of the grave sites of Jewish mothers, fathers, and children.

In his memoir Miklos Nyiszli describes Auschwitz as a "cemetery of millions, a cemetery without a single grave" (1960, 151). Millions were murdered. But no one was buried. Hence, their deaths were murdered with them. In the world of humanity one buries the dead, marks their graves, and leaves the cemetery; it is burying the dead and marking their graves that enables one to leave the cemetery. But there is no liberation, no leaving, from the cemetery without a grave or gravestone. The one who departs from the antiworld—from the "world" without a grave, the "world," therefore, in which death was murdered—becomes a grave himself. "Even death is too good for a Jew?" asks Isabella Leitner (1978, 23). To this question not only about death but about death as a part of human life and human being the Nazi answers, "Yes." Thus, in the process of murdering Jewish being, they murdered Jewish death; they erased the sign of Jewish being from the earth by erasing the Jewish grave and gravestone. Nor was this destruction confined to the death camp; here, too, the ontological assault on Jewish being extended far beyond the electrified fence. Vladka Meed, for example, records her memory of the Jewish cemetery destroyed in Warsaw. "Wherever I turned," she recalls, "there was nothing but overturned tombstones, desecrated graves and scattered skulls. . . . Yes, the Jews were persecuted even in their graves" (1973, 334–35). This is one reason why the Nazi assault was ontological: in the murder not only of the Jews but of Jewish *being* they targeted for death both the living and the dead, both the Jewish past and the Jewish present and, therefore, any Jewish future. Once again the Holocaust memoir not only contains the memory of the dead but becomes the epitaph inscribed over their absent graves. From this memory there is no liberation, for the dead will allow no freedom from the question that issues from their invisible eyes: Why?

It is the Nazis' murder of Jewish death that makes the survivor's relation to the dead so problematic. In this connection one realizes that the matter of forgiveness raised in Simon Wiesenthal's *The Sunflower* is, in fact, a difficulty concerning the murder of death and the failure of liberation. A dying SS soldier seeks from Wiesenthal the forgiveness that would set him free to die. Wiesenthal refuses, insisting quite rightly that he cannot offer forgiveness for the suffering and death endured by others. Yet he becomes a prisoner of his refusal; true liberation requires reconciliation, but this he cannot have. For he is the prisoner of the dead whose forgiveness he cannot grant to the soldier. Why a prisoner? Because the death of those dead has been murdered, inasmuch as their every tie with the living was obliterated through the denial of any grave site for them. Refusing to transmit the forgiveness of the dead to one of their murderers, Wiesenthal becomes the signifier of the dead: he becomes their grave and their gravestone, and they will not set him free. The very title of the book establishes this linkage between the murder of death and the failure of liberation see when Wiesenthal gazes upon an SS cemetery. Watching butterflies flitting from sunflower to sunflower on the graves of the SS, it strikes him that from those butterflies "the dead were receiving light and messages. Suddenly I envied the dead soldiers. Each had a sunflower to connect him with the living world, and butterflies to visit his grave" (1976, 20). Wiesenthal's envy is steeped in the conviction that he was doomed to an oblivion without a grave, that he was himself already a dead man, even as he continued to breathe. "Each of us," he says, "was carrying around his own death certificate" (1976, 190). So the question born of the murder of death and precluding his liberation arises, Why are you still alive?

The memory of this question is found in many of the Holocaust memoirs; indeed, it is a question that shapes the memoir and its quest for recovery. Leon Wells, for instance, returned from the concentrationary universe not to be greeted with a liberating welcome or even to be asked about his ordeal. Rather, he recalls, the only thing people wanted to know was why he was alive (1978, 244). This question posed by others is the question that the man fears to confront within himself. He knows he ought to be dead, and this knowledge taints his life and his liberation. For Alexander Donat, in fact, the question comes not from the other but from within himself: "Why was *I* permitted to live?" (1978, 293). And, whereas Donat is haunted by the question that he must answer for himself, Zivia Lubetkin wonders how she could possibly answer others: "How will I be able to explain how I survived?" (1981, 246). Writing the memoir is a way of responding to this question that comes from within and from beyond, both for the self and for the other. There is much more than mere guilt underlying the question. Deeper than guilt, what is at work here is the problem of liberation confronting a person robbed of his death and now faced with being a marker for those who have no gravestones. Plagued by the question of "Why didn't you die?" it becomes "impossible," in the words of Bertha Ferderber-Salz, to live not only in the past but "in the future by detaching oneself from the past" (1980, 18). Thus, the survivor eternally seeks her liberation by seeking the death denied her, the death that would enable her to detach herself from the past. For death denied is a living death. And the recovery from a living death is ever open-ended.

In *The Jews of Silence* Elie Wiesel tells the story of a woman who was shot but only wounded at the mass grave site known as Babi Yar. After crawling out of the mass grave, he relates, she managed to find shelter with a Ukrainian, only to be handed over to the Germans. Again she was taken to the mass grave; again she was shot and merely wounded. This time, however, she managed to escape. But, says Wiesel, "her mind had snapped. Now she rants aloud, remembering forgotten things, and people say, 'Poor woman, she lives in another world' " (1966b, 36). This woman's condition exemplifies the condition of the survivor, for whom liberation fails. Although it may be true that not every survivor's mind snapped, every survivor's soul has been wounded. And the wound refuses closure; refusing closure, it refuses liberation. "The injury," Primo Levi insists, "cannot be healed: it extends through time, . . . denying peace to the tormented" (1988, 224–35). I have examined the facets of this torment: the movement from one silence only to collide with another, the return to a home no longer home, the murder of Jewish death and of the death by which the Jew may die away from the Event. And there is no dying away from the memory; the survivor leaves the death camp, but the death camp does not leave the survivor. "Bye, Auschwitz," writes Isabella Leitner. "I will never see you again. I will always see you" (1978, 51). For she will always be seen, always summoned, by the dead who have no graves, whose cemetery is the sky that looks down upon all. "I belong here," Kitty Hart remembers her return to Auschwitz. "I have never been away" (1982, 163). She returns to the site of the antiworld seeking a liberation from it, just as memory returns in a search for recovery. But it does not come; the movement remains open-ended, unconsummated.

For the evidence of the eyes declares that there is no world outside of the antiworld, as Kitty Hart suggests, "I still see the features and the routines of Auschwitz everywhere . . . . : personal viciousness, greed for power, love of manipulation and humiliation" (1982, 159). Primo Levi makes this point in even stronger terms; remembering his passage through Austria after the war, he writes that he and his comrades experienced the "threatening sensation of an irreparable and definitive evil which was present everywhere" (1965, 215). Reflecting on these lines, one finds that the problem of liberation has a scope much larger than one may have first anticipated. What is in need of liberation is not just a group of Jews who cannot say why they survived but all of humanity; what is in need of mending is not just the antiworld's invasion of the world but the world itself, now as much as then. Says Emil Fackenheim, "Jews after Auschwitz represent all humanity when they affirm their Jewishness and deny the Nazi denial" (1970, 86). The recovery sought by memory in the Holocaust memoir, therefore, is far more than a personal matter concerning only the memoir's author. It is a world-communal issue that continually demands a never-ending process of bearing witness. Humanity's need for this memory is as great as the need of those who must remember.

9

The Summons to Bear Witness

"The greatest *mitzvah*," Lily Lerner remembers her mother taught her, "the greatest respect, one can give is to accompany a dead person to burial" (1980, 35). Late in life she continues to observe one of her first lessons in life, accompanying the dead to a burial that is never finished. Lerner's struggle to perform this *mitzvah* that can never be consummated opens up vast implications for the murder of Jewish death discussed in chapter 8. In every Jewish community a group of the faithful are assigned the task of accompanying the dead to burial, the *Chevrah Kadiysha*, in whose care the *kadosh* or the holy is placed. For the duty of the *Chevrah Kadiysha* is not only to see to the proper burial of the dead but to ensure the proper remembrance and observance of the Holy One. With the murder of Jewish death and the obliteration of Jewish burial, every survivor—indeed, every Jew—is summoned to become a member of the *Chevrah Kadiysha* eternally accompanying the dead to their burial, not within the earth, for that was denied them, but within themselves. Thus, the ontological order has been twisted: the Jewish remnant from the Kingdom of Night has become the cemetery for the Jewish dead. "Those of us left alive," declares Sara Zyskind, "were the walking tombstones of the six million who had perished" (1981, 276). Hence, the survivor becomes a sign and her memory a voice unto those swallowed up by an Imposed Silence. "They and the others are buried within me," Katzetnik states. "Over their ashes I vowed to be a voice to them, and when I left Auschwitz they walked with me, they and the soundless Auschwitz blocks, the soundless crematorium, the soundless horizons, and at the front the mountain of ash to show me the way" (1989, 18). Just as the dead are both within and beyond, the vow that comes to the lips of the survivor comes not only from within but from beyond. It comes not as an assertion of the individual's will but as a response to a summons to bear witness despite the will or the wishes of the individual.

To be sure, the temptation here is precisely to forget, for the pain and the responsibility of memory appear to be more than the individual can bear. These survivors write their memoirs not because they desire to do so but because they have been called to do so; they have been entrusted with the memory not only of a terrible event but of a great treasure whose burial site they alone know. Livia Jackson, for example, relates that when her father told her where the family's jewels were buried, she cried out, "I don't want to be the one to survive!" (1980, 15). Why such a reaction? Because in her father's revelation lies a summons to remember something far more precious than jewels. Although the memory lays claim to her alone, she is not alone; the summons to bear witness will not leave her alone. Similarly, when Germaine Tillion had the opportunity to return to Ravensbrück and recover the evidence of what took place there, she, too, had to struggle against the temptation to forget. "It took an enormous effort," she says, "to avoid trying to forget this world of horror" (1975, 16). It is worth noting that in the French text the word translated as "forget" is *détourner* (1973, 43), meaning "to turn away from." If it were only facts that had to be remembered, the issue of forgetting would not be so urgent. But, more than the facts, there are people whose memory cries out to be attested to; to forget them would be to turn one's face away from them, away from the faces that summon one's own face, one's own word. To turn away in this instance would be to lose not only one's memory but one's face as well. "I, too, want to forget," writes Olga Lengyel. "But . . . in setting down this personal record I have tried to carry out the mandate given to me by the many fellow internees at Auschwitz who perished so horribly. This is my memorial to them" (1972, 216). The notion of a mandate is very important here because it inserts into the relation between memory and the ones remembered the *significance* of all that is remembered.

The significance of memory derives neither from the one who remembers nor from those remembered. Rather, it arises from a third position, from a third presence, between the two. It is not only the dead who summon the survivor's memory but a Third whose Presence makes this memory *matter*. "If you have begun to forget," Rashi warns, "your end will be that you will forget *all*" (1972, 5:59). This *all* includes not only the dead who are remembered and the living who remember but the One who summons the testimony, the One who is All. It includes the "Great Voice," who, as it is written in the Zohar, "is at the root of all things" (1984, 4:274). From the Holy One who is at the root of sacred tradition comes the sanctity of the mandate with which the witness is entrusted and by which the Chosen continue to be chosen. In the Holocaust memoir, then, one often finds explicit reference to the Third who lays claim to the witness. Paul Trepman, for example, writes, "Perhaps Providence intended that I . . . should live to record this one event which otherwise might have been omitted from mankind's testimony against Adolf Hitler" (1978, 138). Ana Vinocur states it more firmly, more succinctly: "God chose us to be the witnesses of this story" (1976, 134). As the *witness* of the story, the survivor is more than the teller of the tale; she is the respondent to the Voice that summons the tale so that the tale of the Shoah includes the tale of the Voice Himself. This is why memory in the Holocaust memoir entails not only the recounting of events but also the recovery of a tradition, the recovery from an illness, and an ongoing, never-ending process of recovery—never-ending because the tale of the Voice who summons the witness is itself without end. The Holocaust memoir, in short, is the tale of transcendence, for transcendence, Fackenheim insists, *"is found at Auschwitz in the form of absolute Command"* (1978, 109). The command arises in the midst of the summons—bear witness. In this the Chosen have no choice.

Yet having no choice is just what opens up for the survivor, as well as for all humanity, any prospect for freedom and recovery. Freedom, says Franz Rosenzweig, "must lead to form and [therefore] to a Thou shalt!" (1955, 84). Because the "Thou shalt!" underlying memory in the Holocaust memoir has its origin in the Eternal One, the process of answering the summons is as eternal as the Eternal One Himself. Just as the Commanding Voice of Sinai never leaves off its commandment, so does the Commanding Voice of Auschwitz continue to enjoin one to continually pursue a recovery through this memory. From a Jewish standpoint, as Abraham Joshua Heschel points out, history is not "the 'gone' or the dead past, but the present in which past and future are interlocked" (1962, 1:173–74). Memory is the place where the two are interlocked, and the summons to bear witness announces the interlocking. Examining the summons to bear witness as part of the open-endedness of recovery, one finds that the summons emerges not only from the dead who dwell in the past but from the yet unborn who abide in the future. For the aim of memory's recovery of the past is the recovery of a life in an open-ended future. Memory, then, encompasses time: its movements are the movements of the eternal. Thus the three main points to be addressed in this chapter are the summons of the dead, the summons of the unborn, and the eternal movement of memory.

The Summons of the Dead

Charlotte Delbo comments on the last words of the dying by saying, "They confided nothing that could be construed as a message" (1968, 16). So she asks, "Why have I kept my memory?" (1968, 124)—*gardé* (1965, 128), Why have I "guarded," "watched over," or "preserved" my memory? Although she does not answer this question in the memoir, the writing of the memoir is itself an answer: she has kept her memory not to convey the last word or message of the dead but to uphold the summons to bear witness. Upholding that summons, she preserves the premise that the dead matter even if their last words were meaningless. It is not a last utterance or message that is entrusted to her but the sanctity of what is first and last: she guards her memory because her life is tied to those lost lives by what is sacred in all human life. From the Jewish tradition an expression of this connectedness can be found in the *Mekilta* where it is written, "The people of Israel are compared to a lamb. What is the nature of the lamb? If it is hurt in one limb, all its limbs feel the pain" (1961, 2: 205–6). The tie that binds Jew to Jew binds every human being to every human being. According to this teaching, all are created in the image of the divine. Although each individual has his own life, all life derives from the omnipresent divinity. Therefore, each is tied to all: when one is hurt, all feel the pain and are obliged to ease the pain. Similarly, when the voices of the dead are silenced, those who survive are summoned to become a voice unto the dead, summoned by the very silence of those voices. For out of that silence issues the *kol demamah dakah*, the thin voice of silence, of the Holy One Himself. At the heart of the summons of the dead, then, one hears what Fackenheim refers to as the "Commanding Voice of Auschwitz" (1978, 19–24).

Indeed, Donna Rubinstein heard this summons arising from her dead parents long before Fackenheim formulated the "614th Commandment," "An inner voice whispered, 'Don't leave our heritage. Don't forget the past. . . . You have a deep responsibility to your parents, to all of your family lying in unmarked graves. Don't contribute to Hitler's cause by helping to decimate Judaism and the Jewish people'" (1982, 87). Once again, in this summons is the connectedness, through the family, to humanity (the Jewish people) and to God (Judaism). The response to the summons, then, is made not only to the dead but to the One in whose image they were created. This point is quite explicit in Ka-tzetnik's vow to the dead, a vow that is uttered as a prayer: "I will not cease to tell of you even unto the last whisper of my breath. So help me God, amen" (1971b, 191). The root of the verb rendered as "tell" is *safar* (Ka-tzetnik 1971a, 191), which has connotations of narration or storytelling: the summons of the dead is not to report facts but to relate a tale. Why? Because it is the narrative form that imparts meaning to the facts and urgency to the summons. Levinas describes death as the "source of all myths" (1969, 179) because, in the words of Joseph Campbell, myth is conceived "in depth, but susceptible of interpretation on various levels. The shallowest minds see in it the local scenery; the deepest, the foreground of the void; and between are all the stages of the Way from the ethnic to the elementary idea, the local to the universal being, which is Everyman, as he both knows and is afraid to know" (1959, 472). Like the blood of Abel, the blood of these dead cries out to God through the voices of human beings in tales that bespeak what both God and humanity are afraid to know. The function of memory in the Holocaust memoir, therefore, is a narrative one by which authors narrate their own lives through the narration of life lost. And what speaks in those narratives speaks not in so many words but in the process of narration itself.

This realization is often found either at the outset or in the development of the memoir. Early in her memoir, for example, Gisella Perl writes, "I offer this book as a monument commemorating . . . Nazi inhumanity and the death of their six million innocent Jewish victims" (1948, 12). But as her memory takes its course, she sees that she has been called not just to commemorate events but to narrate stories. "Those six million dead are so many terrible, heartbreaking stories," she asserts. "Every one of them represents not only the second of death, however horrible that is, but an entire, colorful, exciting human life, a past, and what is more, a future" (1948, 137). Whereas Gisella Perl arrives at an understanding of what she is summoned to remember, Gerda Klein begins with that realization: "I am haunted by the thought that I might be the only one left to tell their story" (1957, vii). Two things must be noted in these passages from the memoirs of Perl and Klein. First, the tale they are summoned to tell is not only the tale of life lost in the past but of life never lived in the future; it has a double reflection, a double orientation. Second, the survivor has a sense that *I alone* am the one summoned to tell this story; and her past and future lie in this having been singled out. Hence, the summons of the dead provides an illustration of Levinas's insight that death "is *present* only in the Other, and only in him does it summon me urgently to my final essence, to my responsibility" (1969, 179; emphasis in the original). Further, Levinas explains, "I can substitute myself for everyone [even and especially for the dead], but no one can substitute himself for me" (1985, 101). The survivor cannot rid herself of her responsibility by noting that there are other survivors. No, the summons of the dead singles *me* out for this responsibility and for this substitution. The blood of Abel cries out to *me*, not only from the ashes and the earth but from the depths of my own blood. *I* must be the voice of the murdered.

This assignation comes out very forcefully in Eugene Heimler's memoir where he declares that he had to speak "on behalf of the millions who had seen it also—but could no longer speak. Of their dead, burnt bodies I would be the voice" (1959, 191). In Heimler's text is an overwhelming repetition of *I* not because of any self-centeredness but precisely because of a conscious-ness of the others who lay claim to the I: "I had to, . . . I had to, . . . I had to . . . ," he writes, until finally he asserts, "I would." This future is inter-locked with the past *in* a present overflowing with an open-ended responsi-bility; thus, the recovery that memory seeks in discharging the debt to the dead is forever open-ended. Summoning the witness, the dead summon responsibility; calling forth the responsibility, they call forth a future denied them. In the Holocaust memoir, then, memory is memory of and for the future in the sense that Bertha Ferderber-Salz conveys when she says, "I wrote down everything I could recall, vowing that at some future date I would publish what I had written. . . . Or perhaps the sighs of those who were burned and slaughtered dictated to me what I should write" (1980, 18). Recording the dictation of the dead is an instance of the substitution that Levinas mentions above. And it is a substitution of which Ferderber-Salz is very much aware: "My heart bled at the thought that I would have to take the place of mothers, aunts, sisters, relatives, and friends" (1980, 212). Heimler's "I had to" and "I would" combine to form this "I would have to." And in her "I would have to" Ferderber-Salz not only hears the summons but makes it heard. That is what response and responsibility are about: hear-ing and making heard—not only one's own voice but the voices of those for whom the survivor substitutes.

The word *substitute* derives from the Latin *sub*, meaning "in place of," and *statuere*, meaning "to cause to stand." The voice that substitutes for the voices of the dead does not stand in their place but causes them to stand in place, creating a place where those who are absent may find a certain pres-ence. Mourning both the death of her loved ones *and* their absence, Lily Lerner writes, "They have gone from the earth completely. They, and those like them, both Jew and Gentile, are why I force upon myself the torture of remembering" (1980, 13). Not only are the dead present in her memory but her memory imparts a presence to the dead by making their summons heard through her own act of response and remembrance; only one who is in some sense present can be heard. Thus, Frida Michelson affirms "I hear your . . . last word: 'Remember!' " (1979, 11). To be sure, this hearing, this assignation, this summons that transforms her into a witness resounds throughout Michelson's memoir. "I must survive as a witness," she repeats (1979, 42). For the voices speak to her, insisting, "There, before your window, before your eyes, the tragedy of your whole nation is being played out. Remember. Do not forget!" (1979, 78). The summons of the dead is powerful indeed. It enables a person to survive hardship that would otherwise be fatal; it can lead the living to chance death itself. When Miklos Nyiszli, for example, was a doctor in Auschwitz, the summons of the dead drew him into the crematorium, into the very gullet of the death factory, at the risk of his own life. "I felt it my duty," he relates, "to be able to give an accurate account of what I had seen if ever, by some miraculous whim of fate, I should escape" (1960, 75). Whence arises this duty? From the muted cries of the dead that are heard above the roaring flames of the ovens.

The summons of the dead, moreover, can make mute objects themselves into signs that cry out to the living, even from beyond the other shore of time. "It is always after the fact," says Friedländer, "that mute things manifest themselves as so many signs" (1980, 77). To be made manifest as a sign is to speak; to recognize an object as a sign is to hear. And, as Friedländer indicates, neither this speaking nor this hearing is subject to erasure by time. Thus, time does not heal but only aggravates the wound; the voices do not fade but only grow louder and more insistent. There is no end, then, to the recovery that memory seeks; in the act of remembrance recovery recedes. The dead have vanished, but the signs proliferate: memory summons memory endlessly, ad infinitum. Contrary to rendering the movement of remembrance futile or meaningless, however, this condition floods it with significance. Recall, for instance, Eugene Heimler's memory of his dead friend Dr. Ekstein. "Someone had already stolen his shoes," he writes. "As he lay there naked he seemed so small, so insignificant. But later, in my memories, he was full of significance" (1959, 132). The sign of his significance? It is the stolen shoes that had walked the ash-covered grounds of Auschwitz and that traced the path of a life made into a living death. Stolen, their absence signifies the absence of a life that should be present; it is this absence of what *ought* to be present that lends the sign its power to speak. The sign speaks and is heard in memory's response to it, heard in the realization of what there is to love: only one who loves the living can hear the summons of the dead. Thus, the body that had seemed to be an insignificant object in a landscape of indifference takes on a meaning that bears implications both for the dead and for the survivor, indeed, for all of life. "If the power of things to communicate ceases," Karl Jaspers warns, "then they sink back into the lovelessness of indifferent uniformity" (1959, 39). And when that happens, the Nazis win their victory. What I termed the "there is" in chapter 5 takes over to swallow up all signs and significance, everything that the Jews and Judaism signify and that the Nazis tried to destroy.

Thus, the observance of the 614th Commandment that enjoins one to embrace one's Jewish faith and, thereby, refuse the Nazis their victory is an observance that entails a response to the summons of the dead. Those who were not turned over to the Kingdom of Night are situated along its edges by the witnesses who transmit that summons; they, too, are subject to the 614th Commandment. They not only receive this memory they are issued this summons, entrusted with the lost lives whose outcry this memory transmits. That is why Elie Wiesel urges, "Perhaps every Jew ought to pick a dead man, woman, or child, whether known or unknown, and say: from this point on, I shall live for myself and for him or her" (1990a, 37). For these dead have already picked them through the witness of the surviving remnant borne in the Holocaust memoir. In the Holocaust memoir memory is a summons that lays claim to them before they ever receive what is transmitted; in the Holocaust memoir memory opens up a passageway that draws them into the past and that launches the dead into the present. One is reminded of the practice at the U.S. Holocaust Memorial Museum of offering the visitor a card filled out with information about a victim who, during the days of destruction, was approximately the visitor's age; it is referred to as your "ID card." The aim in this is not to generate sympathy or empathy or some sense of "how it felt" but to summon response and responsibility. Similarly, in the Auschwitz Museum one can see the mounds of hair shorn from the last groups of women sent to the gas chambers; that hair continues, in the words of Levi, "to whisper its mute accusation to the visitor" (1988, 124). Why accusation? Because the visitor arrives too late, always too late. Too late one hears the memory of the survivors and the summons of the dead. Too late one struggles to respond to what was. But one is not too late for what is yet to be, and that is just the point: answering to the summons of the dead, the Holocaust memoir listens to the summons of the unborn. And it summons one to listen.

The Summons of the Unborn

From a Jewish standpoint the summons of the dead is part of a sacred past that imparts significance and substance to our present; history is revelation so that answering to the summons of the dead entails the receiving of God's Word in the form of God's Commandment. The ultimate aim of revelation is redemption at some time that is yet to be, and one's response to the yet unborn is part of one's relation to the promise of redemption. If memory in the Holocaust memoir seeks a recovery of tradition, it seeks a recovery of revelation; in the aspect of open-endedness the recovery sought by memory is tied to redemption. Belonging to a future ever yet to be revealed, the unborn signify the full, redemptive revelation of the Face that was hidden from Moses when God passed before him (see Exod. 33:20–23). Here, too, if one allows oneself a midrashic elaboration, one sees the Commanding Voice at work. For one is told in the Talmud that when Moses stood in the cleft of the rock and looked upon God's back, he saw the knot formed by the straps of the *tefillin* on the back of God's neck (Menachot 35b). One may assume, then, that on His forehead, between His eyes, was the frontlet or the box in which His Word is hidden away, the redemptive Word withheld from Moses and yet to be revealed. In the *tefillin* are the words one offers and the words one seeks in one's *tefillah*, in one's prayer. And one's prayer is offered in response to the summons of the revealed and the yet to be revealed, of the back and the face—of the dead and the unborn. The summons of the unborn, then, is the "other side" of the summons of the dead.

As one receives the word of the dead, moreover, the fate of the unborn is placed in one's care: the children who signify the potentiality of redemption stand as surety that one will abide by the revelation. This very point, in fact, is made in the *Midrash on Psalms* (1959, 1:125). There one is told that when God was about to offer His Torah to the Israelites, He asked them what they would put up as a kind of collateral to ensure their remembrance and observance of the Torah. "The Patriarchs," they replied. "We offer them as surety for what we are about to receive, for they received the Covenant."

"No," God refused. "They are already in My debt."

"The Prophets," the Israelites offered. "They will stand as surety, for they are the most righteous of men."

"No," God repeated. "They too have debts of their own."

Finally, after a moment of hesitation and reflection, the Israelites said, "We give You our children. For they are without sin."

God then asked the sucklings at their mothers' breasts and the embryos within the womb, "Will you be sureties for your fathers and mothers, so that if I give them the Torah they will live by it, but that if they do not you will be forfeited because of them?"

And they answered, "Yes."

So one sees what is at stake in memory's struggle for recovery: answering to the dead, one answers for the unborn. The words of memory offered in behalf of family and friends no longer present are addressed to strangers yet to be present. Part of what Lily Lerner calls "the torture of remembering" (1980, 13) lies in not knowing who will receive the testimony or even whether it will be received. But the unborn stand as surety for the truth of the testimony so that the survivor speaks nevertheless in a profound movement of faith. It is a movement exemplified in Jewish tradition, for example, by Yehudah Halevi in his poem "Acquainted with Truth," "It is well if thou wake the dawn to serve Him . . . / And fear not to leave the earth to strangers" (1924, 110). Waking the dawn to serve Him, one dons the *tefillin*, the front and back of which join together past and future and knot them into the present. In this way one fashions one's tomorrow and create a place of dwelling for those one has yet to meet. One need not fear to leave even the ash-covered earth to strangers because these "strangers" are one's children. While the dead robbed of their cemeteries cry out for burial, the unborn issue a summons for birth. Once again one discovers that the 614th Commandment to preserve the Jewish faith returns one to the First Commandment to have children (Gen. 1:28). Through this relation to the as yet unborn and in the hearing of their summons the Jewish faith, the Jewish people, and the Jewish person are eternally reborn. "In the deepest part of myself," Mikhail Bakhtin has understood, "I live by eternal faith and hope in the constant possibility of the inner miracle of a new birth" (1991, 127). This "constant possibility" is a large part of what characterizes the open-endedness of recovery in the Holocaust memoir. From a Jewish perspective, however, this possibility entails not only an inner miracle but also an outward manifestation of that miracle: the new birth by which the self becomes other to itself is not simply a rebirth of the self but the birth of another, of one's child.

Levinas argues that the one way in which the self can become other to itself is through paternity. Paternity, he explains, "is a relationship with a stranger who, entirely while being Other, is myself. . . . Paternity is not a sympathy through which I can put myself in the son's place. It is through my being, not through sympathy, that I am my son" (1987b, 91). If the summons of the dead is a cry of "Remember," the summons of the unborn is a cry of "Live!" And a human being can live, that is, can generate his being, only by bringing another being into the world. In this participation in the Creation one declares with the Creator in whose image one is made and who summons one to this bearing of children, "*Kiy tov!* It is very good!" In this fecundity one affirms the eternal truth of one's subjectivity as it derives from the Eternal One. For the "truth of subjectivity" to be realized, says Levinas, "it is necessary to go back to the primary phenomenon of time in which the phenomenon of the 'not yet' is rooted. It is necessary to go back to paternity" (1969, 247). In the Holocaust memoir the "not yet" of time is manifested precisely in the summons to paternity. Indeed, the Nazis sought in calculated ways to destroy Jewish being by destroying Jewish paternity, and one way in which they carried this out was through various forms of sterilization. This measure was aimed not just at population control but at population eradication and, thereby, at the eradication of the witnesses to the Creator of life. Fania Fénelon, for example, remembers that when the women in the death camp ceased having their menstrual periods, they prayed to be free themselves from "this curse the Germans were holding over us: sterility" (1977, 89). That sterility has metaphysical significance is indicated by the metaphysical measures taken to fight it: the women prayed to the Eternal One in an effort to recover the eternal aspect of life through a recovery of their fertility. Just as the Nazis tried to murder the Jewish dead, so did they undertake a Slaughter of the Innocents in the murder of the Jewish unborn. The unborn too, therefore, are among the victims whose summons the survivor must answer.

In other memoirs the summons of the unborn, like the summons of the dead, arises both during the ordeal in the antiworld and after the return to what was left of the world. Gerda Klein, for example, writes, "The idea returned that someday I must have a baby of my own. I felt that I would endure anything so long as that hope was not extinguished" (1957, 156). Whereas Pelagia Lewinska "felt under orders to live" (1968, 150) when faced with Nazi atrocity, Gerda Klein felt summoned to bear life. And Fackenheim's comment on Lewinska's response applies equally to Klein's resolve. "*Whose* orders?" Fackenheim asks. "Once again 'will-power' and 'natural desire' are both inadequate. Once again we have touched an Ultimate" (1989, 218; emphasis in the original). Whose orders? The orders of the Ultimate, of the Holy One, who calls upon one to bear life (Gen. 1:28) and to choose life (Deut. 30:19), whose Voice does not operate according to "natural desire" and is confined neither to time nor to place. Thus, He summons one endlessly and despite ourself through those created and yet to be created in His holy image. After her release, then, after she was "safe" and "free" to do as she wished, Kitty Hart receives the injunction: "A family of my own—that is what I must build" (1982, 16). Reading the word *build* in this declaration of life, one recalls a passage from the Talmud: "R. Eleazar said in the name of R. Hanina: 'The disciples of the wise increase peace in the world, as it says,

"All thy children shall be taught of the Lord, and great shall be the peace of thy children" [Isaiah 54:13]. Read not *banayikh* (thy children) but *bonayikh* (thy builders)' " (Berakhot 64a). Kitty Hart, too, is a disciple of the wise: building a family, she builds peace by bearing children. Peace, or *shalom* in Hebrew, is tied to wholeness, or *shlemut*. Any wholeness that may be recovered in the world entails the recovery of children. For they are the builders of peace and wholeness.

Examining the survivor's resolve to bear children, reminds one also of the story of Job. After the loss of his children, Job had seven sons and three daughters (Job 42:13). Whereas Kierkegaard argues that Job received not new children but resurrected the ones who were lost (1941, 130–33), a Jewish outlook would maintain that this cannot be the case—not because God is confined to the laws of natural necessity or that He cannot raise the dead but because the summons to regenerate human life arises from the unborn, not from the once born. It is not a question of God's performance of miracles despite nature but of the human being's transformation of the natural into the miraculous. When Kitty Hart had every reason to say no to the world, she said yes in her resolve to have children. If it were just a matter of returning the dead to life, then one could simply wait until the blowing of Gabriel's horn, and there would be no need for the resolve that characterizes faith and the relation to human life expressive of the life of the divine. In short, there would be no need for this memory or for this memoir. Whence arises the need for the memory and the memoir? From the children to be born and named in memory of the children and mothers and fathers robbed of their lives and of their deaths. In these who are other endures a trace of those who were. Through these who are other we hear the summons of those who were.

Thus, bearing his witness, Samuel Pisar writes, "It is our children that I have in mind as I write this book, a book that is not about the past, but about the future" (1979, 23). Why about the future? Near the end of his memoir he explains, "When I see mankind heading once more toward some hideous collective folly, I feel that I must either lapse into total silence or broadcast to the world my urgent sense of the horrors that threaten to destroy our own and our children's future" (1979, 304). What is at stake in memory's struggle for recovery, what is to be recovered again and ever again is not the grand future of the world or of an anonymous humanity but the future of one's children, of *this single child*. The summons of the unborn is the summons of a single voice, and through that voice resounds the Voice of the God who is One. "Hear, O Israel!" one prays upon rising and upon lying down.

And, in its movement of response and remembrance, the Holocaust memoir adds, "Hear the Voice of Him who is One and who summons us through the voice of this little one, both dead and unborn!" To the words hidden away in the *tefillin* the Holocaust memoir adds these words. One recalls in this connection the words from the last pages of Isabella Leitner's memoir. There she remembers her late mother by linking her mother to her first-born child Peter and to children yet to be born; in this way she makes the summons of the dead and the summons of the unborn into a single summons to bear witness. "Mama, I'm pregnant!" she cries. "There is another heart beating within that very body that was condemned to ashes. . . . [We've] started the birth of a new six million" (1978, 96). The one who had been marked as a corpse becomes the vessel of a seed, and the seed is the vessel of generations. Her child has that much in common with Isaac. The knife was raised over him, however, before he was born, and not by his father but by the murderer of the father.

But Leitner's child may have one thing more in common with Isaac. For it was Isaac's privilege, as Wiesel has pointed out, to remain the defender of Israel by transforming suffering "into prayer and love rather than into rancor and malediction" (1976, 97). This transformation is the aim of the summons of the unborn. And it is one that can be wrought only by a faith that comes *despite all*; the summons of the unborn is a call to faith. "From the heart of 'no,' " André Neher observes, "there arises a 'yes.' Faith is a genesis; it appears ex nihilo" (1981, 207). The heart of "no" is as bottomless as the pit of the antiworld, and memory must eternally return to that nothingness if it is to transform "no" into "yes" and malediction into benediction. The open-endedness of recovery in the Holocaust memoir lies above all in this eternal movement of memory.

The Eternal Movement of Memory

The "no" is never finally turned into a "yes"; faith is a process, not a finished product. "Truth," as Edmond Jabès expresses it, "is always on the point of coming into being" (1990, 76). Or, to put it another way, recovery is what memory seeks, not what it has found; to find it would mean the obliteration of memory, which in turn would mean exile, not redemption. As that which is yet to be found, recovery posits a direction for memory; although memory may at times set out without knowing where it goes, the recovery that is yet to be summons it to set out. Because the summons to bear witness, more-over, is a summons, memory's response has a dialogical aspect—it is addressed to someone. The truth of the recovery sought through memory, then, is situated in a realm that is between the participants in the dialogue. In the words of Mikhail Bakhtin, "Truth is not born nor is it to be found inside the head of an individual person, it is born *between people* collectively searching for truth, in the process of their dialogical interaction" (1984, 110). Therefore, Bakhtin maintains, "each dialogue takes place as if against the background of the responsive understanding of an invisibly present third party who stands above all the participants in the dialogue" (Bakhtin 1986, 126). Once again the truth belongs to the Third, who eternally remains Third-Person, He; for He is Himself the Eternal One. It is His Presence, which happens when two are gathered in His Name (cf. Avot 3:2), that imparts to recovery its open-endedness and to memory its eternal movement. And it is He who summons the eternal retracing that Fackenheim invokes when he insists that a Jewish thinker is "obliged to retrace, again and again, the *via dolorosa* that led one-third of his people to the human sacrifice in the Nazi gas chambers" (1978, 44). Moment upon moment, millennium upon millennium the ground shifts each time the path is retraced; words take on new and deeper shades of meaning each time they are voiced or held back. Which means: both the witness and those who receive his testimony are summoned to retrace the path again. Which means: the movement of memory is a movement backward that continually takes one forward.

Further, this eternal movement of memory is not only incumbent upon Jewish believers but it makes Jews into believers, inasmuch as they believe that this memory *matters*. Even Primo Levi, who held that "there is Auschwitz, and so there cannot be God" (Camon 1989, 68), sees in this memory a stake of universal significance. He maintains that the survivors speak because they perceive in their imprisonment "the event that for good or for evil has marked their entire existence. They speak because they know they are witnesses in a trial of planetary and epochal dimensions" (Levi 1988, 149). In Italian, as in other languages, the word for "trial," *processo* (Levi 1986a, 121), also means "process," suggesting once more an open-endedness in the testimony of the witness. Each time he tells his tale the agony returns, not only in the form of suffering relived but in the agonizing knowledge that the tale he must tell cannot be told once and for all, rather, it can only be told *again*. Thus, in his poem "The Survivor" Levi writes, "Till my ghastly tale is told, / This heart within me burns" (1986b, 13). Levi published this poem in 1981, long after he had repeatedly told his tale. Why, then, does the heart continue to burn? Because the tale demands retelling each time it is told, eternally. "The story lives in just this way," he writes, "transmitted from mouth to mouth, with the risk . . . that it may be mistaken for a fictional invention" (1986b, 117). From mouth to mouth, be it noted: the tale, like the memory, is received in its utterance so that the line "And till my ghastly tale is told" is placed in *my* mouth. The tale lives in its transmission, and each telling demands that its path be retraced, from mouth to mouth, eternally. "What enables the soul to rise to truth is nourished with truth," writes Levinas (1969, 114). So it is with the tale, with memory and recovery in the Holocaust memoir: what summons the movement stirs within the movement itself.

The agony of survivors lies not only in being locked into their memory but in having to tell the tale *again*. Yet, as Wiesel has said, the tale "belongs as much to the listener as to the teller. You listen to a tale, and all of a sudden it is no longer the same tale" (1970b, 107). Why? Because each offering and receiving of the tale becomes part of the tale itself: thus, memory proliferates, eternally and infinitely in an opening up of the eternal and the infinite within the witness it bears. If "the Jew is in perpetual motion," as Wiesel says (1970a, 214), it is because the Jew is a teller of tales and the heir to memories that grow deeper with their every utterance. That depth, the eternal aspect of the memory and the tale, is made of a question without answer; the eternal movement of memory is made of eternal questioning. Thus, "the Jew and his questioning," Wiesel asserts, "are one" (1970a, 214), which is to say, the Jew and his memory, the Jew and his tale, the Jew and his tradition and his struggle for recovery are one. And the thing that makes the Jew a Jew is the humanity that makes the human being human. In the peculiarity of their condition Jews announce the human condition; this is what they are chosen for. Like Jews, then, Germaine Tillion can say, "All the while [during the Ravensbrück war crimes trials] the representation—re-presentation—of their crimes unfolded, and I became all too aware of the widening gap between what really happened and that imprecise representation known as 'history'" (1975, 180). History is not only an account or a description of past events; it also entails some analysis of the *significance* of those events. And this is where the account of the Shoah breaks down. The problem lies not in the inadequacy of language or in the limits of imagination, as some have supposed, but in the collapse of meaning. For, unlike other historical events, in the Shoah meaning itself was under attack. "I saw what happened at Auschwitz," Ka-tzetnik once told me. "I can say what happened. I know what took place. But what Auschwitz *was* I do not know and I cannot say." The tale of the event is not the event; the survivors are alone with the event. Yet they are not alone with the tale they are summoned to tell.

But can they tell it? "Perhaps the best way," Zivia Lubetkin writes, "is to sit down together and weep, or cry out in a single voice as the tale is told" (1981, 275). Why tears and outcry? Perhaps because this is the only way for the One who summons the testimony to hear it. "From the day on which the Temple was destroyed the gates of prayer have been closed," said the talmudic sage Rabbi Eleazar. "But the gates of weeping are not closed" (Berakhot 32b). Not everyone has seen the destruction of the Temple or the annihilation of a people. But all have shed tears. These tears can open up the gates to the soul, where words alone cannot penetrate, so that those who receive the tale can begin to understand or begin to see that there is no understanding, no final word to convey what must be and yet cannot be conveyed. "I will never be able to express what I want to say," says Saul Friedländer (1980, 134). The tale can be transmitted but not the memory, and this poses a tremendous problem for those who come before these memoirs. As the survivor is summoned to bear witness, one is summoned to receive their testimony. For the survivor's unending pursuit of recovery reveals one's own need, the world's need, for this memory and recovery. Handling these texts, one takes one's soul in hand only to confront an impenetrable wall. This memory is not my memory; nevertheless, I am summoned to remember, as a Jew and as a human being. Seeking the memory, I respond with my own text, but here, too, the lines are removed from the memory and recovery I seek. Yet, says Friedländer, "writing retraces the contours of the past" (1980, 135). By "writing" one should understand not what is written but the *process* of writing, the *saying*, and not the already said. Again, in the process lies recovery's open-endedness, and in its open-endedness lies its truth.

"It is a peculiarity of man," Viktor Frankl observes, "that he can live only by looking to the future—*sub specie aeternitatis*. And this is his salvation" (1962, 72–73). One lives only by looking to the future because only in this realm of the yet-to-be does one discover a direction that instills life with meaning or that at least opens up the prospect for the recovery of meaning. And the portal through which one gazes into the open-ended yet-to-be is the eternal movement of memory. In this book I argue that the Nazis' ontological and metaphysical assault on the Jews aimed at the destruction of meaning. Here is one more reason why such an assault is also aimed at time, that is, at the future. And, targeting the future for destruction, they attempted to destroy memory. Indeed, both Primo Levi (1988, 31) and Elie Wiesel (1990a, 155) have described the Nazi project as a war against memory. Thus, the cry of "Remember!" that one finds, for example, in Bertha Ferderber-Salz's memoir is much more than a summons or a response to a summons; it is an essential part of an open-ended struggle for the recovery of meaning, time, and memory. She writes, "Until my last breath I will pray for the world to stop the insanity of hatred. I am not yet old, but I am very tired. When my time is up I will shout with all my strength, 'Remember and don't forget! Please, don't forget!' " (1980, 232). The urgency of the mission that comes to one and that summons one in these lines is overwhelming. As much as ever memory in the Holocaust memoir has nothing to do with the nostalgic reminiscence of self-indulgence. It is, rather, a duty, and that makes it both a summons and a response.

"Because I remember, I despair," says Wiesel. "Because I remember, I have the duty to reject despair" (1990b, 248). Indeed, once one has wept, this is one's duty: to rejoice in life when one has lost every reason to rejoice. With tears of despair one listens to the tale. But one must seek to respond to it with the resolve of affirmation. "Why is the water of the eyes salty?" the *Midrash* asks, "Because if a man wept for the dead continually his eyes would soon be blinded" (1961, 7:740). And he could not see the future to which he must look and into which he must lead his children. For Jews, that future lies not in the hereafter of heaven but in the here of this earth—that is where Jews must recover their tradition and seek a recovery from the illness that threatens all of humanity. "The highest achievements of the spirit," says Rabbi Menachem Schneerson, "are won in earthly and not in heavenly realms" (1986, 282). So Rabbi Yehoshua cried out, "The Torah is not in heaven!" (Bava Metzia 59b). For the earthly realm is the realm of the Covenant and the place to which the Ark of the Covenant is entrusted. Why? Because the earth is the realm of time and memory and, therefore, of the meaning that memory eternally seeks. "The Ark of the Covenant," Rashi reminds us, "is referred to as the Great Searcher" (1972, 4:100a). The Ark of the Covenant, then, is the Ark of Memory, for there is no searching greater or more sublime than the searching found in the eternal movement of memory.

Epilogue

If the task confronting the authors of the Holocaust memoir and those who respond to them is to return some trace of light to a sun turned to darkness, then it is to return to the world and to human life what Levinas calls "the glory of the Infinite" (1985, 109). This task precisely opposes the Nazi project of the *total* destruction of Jewish being, a project that continues to threaten Jewish being long after the crematoria have ceased operation. "Infinity," says Levinas, "is produced by withstanding the invasion of a totality, in a contraction that leaves a place for the separated being. Thus, relationships that open up a way outside of being take form" (1969, 104). Surviving the invasion of a totality, the Jewish remnant retains a memory that opens up a movement outside of being to an "otherwise than being" from which human being—and with it divine being—once again may recover its sanctity. And memory is the avenue of that recovery.

In the attempted annihilation of Jewish being the Nazis attempted the obliteration of divine being. What is at stake in the memory and recovery of Jewish being, therefore, is the recovery of the divine being that sanctifies all human being. Coming before this memory, we become the ones charged with this recovery: it is we who must return the light to the sun turned to darkness by struggling to be a light unto the nations. Only in this way can we be the Jews and preserve the Jewish being targeted for annihilation. This "we" applies not only to the Jews but to all of humanity. "There comes a time," as Wiesel has said, "when one cannot be a man without assuming the Jewish condition" (1970b, 77). And that time is now.

The lives of humanity's children are in our hands, and with their lives the life of the Holy One Himself. "With Israel's distress," Heschel writes, "came the affliction of God, His displacement, His homelessness in the land, in the world. And the prophet's prayer, 'O save us,' involved not only the fate of a people. It involved the fate of God in relation to the people" (1962, 1:112). This prayer echoes throughout the texts of the memoirs examined here. In the texts of the tradition that memory would recover in its effort to recover from an illness the prayer is confirmed: "Salvation is the salvation of God" is taught in the *Midrash Rabbah* (1961, 3:375), and in the *Midrash on Psalms* it is written, "The salvation of the Holy One, blessed be He, depends upon the salvation of the people of Israel" (1959, 1:179). And the salvation of the people of Israel depends upon their capacity for memory and recovery. Yet where the memory is ever present, the recovery is ever yet to be. The task, then, is ever upon them.

Thus, I end the search into the Holocaust memoir not with closure or conclusion but with hope by opening up another level of memory and recovery. And it is appropriate that I end the wrestling with this Jewish memory by invoking a sacred word from Jewish tradition, *vedok*. Rabbi Steinsaltz explains: "One of the great talmudic commentators, the Maharsha, often ended his commentaries with the word *vedok* (continue to examine the matter). This exhortation is an explicit admission that the subject has not been exhausted and that there is still room for additions and arguments on the question" (1976, 273). And so I say, *Vedok*.

Works Cited

Index

Works Cited

Abraham ibn Ezra. 1943. *The Commentary of Ibn Ezra on Isaiah.* Translated by Michael Friedlander. New York: Feldheim.

Améry, Jean. 1977. *Jenseits von Schuld und Sühne.* Stuttgart: Klett-Cotta.

———. 1980. *At the Mind's Limits.* Translated by Sidney Rosenfeld and Stella P. Rosenfeld. Bloomington: Indiana Univ. Press.

Appelfeld, Aharon. 1979. *First-Person Essays.* Jerusalem: Zionist Library.

Aristotle. 1972. *De memoria et reminiscentia.* Translated by Richard Sorabji. In *Aristotle on Memory,* edited by Richard Sorabji, 47–60. Providence, R.I.: Brown Univ. Press.

Aron, Milton. 1969. *Ideas and Ideals of Hasidism.* Secausus, N.J.: Citadel.

Augustine. 1961. *Confessions.* Translated by R. S. Pine-Coffin. New York: Penguin.

Bachya ibn Paquda. 1970. *Duties of the Heart.* Translated by Moses Hyamson. 2 vols. New York: Feldheim.

The Bahir. 1979. Translated with commentary by Aryeh Kaplan. York Beach, Maine: Samuel Weiser.

Bakhtin, Mikhail. 1981. *The Dialogic Imagination.* Translated by Caryl Emerson and Michael Holquist. Austin: Univ. of Texas Press.

———. 1984. *Problems of Dostoevsky's Poetics.* Translated by Caryl Emerson. Minneapolis: Univ. of Minnesota Press.

———. 1986. *Speech Genres and Other Late Essays.* Translated by Vern W. McGee, edited by Caryl Emerson and Michael Holquist. Austin: Univ. of Texas Press.

———. 1991. *Art and Answerability.* Translated by Vadim Liapunov. Austin: Univ. of Texas Press.

Benjamin, Walter. 1974. "Über einige Motive bei Baudelaire." In *Gesammelte Schriften,* vol. 1, pt. 2, 605–53. Frankfurt: Suhrkamp.

———. 1977. "Zum Bilde Prousts." In *Gesammelte Schriften,* vol. 2, pt. 1, 310–24. Frankfurt: Suhrkamp.

Bergson, Henri. 1929. *Matter and Memory.* Translated by N. M. Paul and M. E. Dowson. New York: Macmillan.

————. 1954. *The Two Sources of Morality and Religion.* Translated by R. Ashley Audra and Cloudsley Brereton. Garden City, N.J.: Doubleday.

Buber, Martin. 1965. *Between Man and Man.* Translated by Ronald Gregor Smith. New York: Macmillan.

————. 1969. *The Legend of the Baal-Shem.* Translated by Maurice Friedman. New York: Schocken.

————. 1970. *I and Thou.* Translated by Walter Kaufmann. New York: Charles Scribner's Sons.

Camon, Ferdinando. 1989. *Conversations with Primo Levi.* Translated by John Shepley. Marlboro, Vt.: Marlboro Press.

Campbell, Joseph. 1959. *The Masks of God: Primitive Mythology.* New York: Viking Press.

Cohen, Elie. 1971. *De Afgrond.* Amsterdam: Monteau.

————. 1973. *The Abyss: A Confession.* Translated by James Brockway. New York: W. W. Norton.

Dante. 1954. *The Inferno.* Translated by John Ciardi. New York: New American Library.

Delbo, Charlotte. 1965. *Aucun de nous ne reviendra.* Geneva: Editions Gonthier.

————. 1968. *None of Us Will Return.* Translated by John Githens. Boston: Beacon Press.

Des Pres, Terrence. 1976. *The Survivor: An Anatomy of Life in the Death Camp.* New York: Oxford Univ. Press.

Donat, Alexander. 1978. *The Holocaust Kingdom.* New York: Holocaust Library.

Dresner, Samuel H. 1960. *The Zaddik.* New York: Abelard-Schuman.

Dribben, Judith. 1969. *And Some Shall Live.* Jerusalem: Keter Books.

Emerson, Ralph Waldo. 1965. *Selected Writings,* edited by William H. Gilman. New York: New American Library.

En Jacob. 1916–21. Translated by S. H. Glick. 5 vols. New York: Hebrew Publishing.

Ezrahi, Sidra DeKoven. 1980. *By Words Alone: The Holocaust in Literature.* Chicago: Univ. of Chicago Press.

Fackenheim, Emil L. 1970. *God's Presence in History.* New York: Harper and Row.

————. 1978. *The Jewish Return into History.* New York: Schocken.

————. 1987. *What Is Judaism?* New York: Macmillan.

————. 1989. *To Mend the World: Foundations of Post-Holocaust Jewish Thought.* New York: Schocken.

————. 1990. *The Jewish Bible after the Holocaust.* Bloomington: Indiana Univ. Press.

Fénelon, Fania. 1976. *Sursis pour l'orchestre.* Paris: Stock.

————. 1977. *Playing for Time.* Translated by Judith Landry. New York: Atheneum.

Ferderber-Salz, Bertha. 1980. *And the Sun Kept Shining.* New York: Holocaust Library.

Florensky, Pavel. 1970. *Stolp i utverzhdenie istiny.* Westmead, Eng.: Gregg International.

Foley, Barbara. 1982. "Fact, Fiction, Fascism: Mimesis in Holocaust Narratives." *Comparative Literature* 34: 330–60.

Foucault, Michel. 1965. *Madness and Civilization.* Translated by Richard Howard. New York: Pantheon.

Frankl, Viktor E. 1962. *Man's Search for Meaning.* Translated by Ilse Lasch. Rev. ed. Boston: Beacon Press.

Friedländer, Saul. 1978. *Quand vient le souvenir.* Paris: Éditions du Seuil, 1978.

———. 1980. *When Memory Comes.* Translated by Helen R. Lane. New York: Avon.

Gersonides. 1984. *The Wars of the Lord.* Translated by Seymour Feldman. 2 vols. Philadelphia: Jewish Publication Society.

Geve, Thomas. 1981. *Youth in Chains.* Jerusalem: Rubin Mass.

Ginsburgh, Yitzchak. 1991. *The Alef-Beit: Jewish Thought Revealed through the Hebrew Letters.* Northvale, N.J.: Aronson.

Halevi, Jehudah. 1924. *Selected Poems.* Translated by Nina Salaman, edited by Heinrich Brody. Philadelphia: Jewish Publication Society.

Hart, Kitty. 1982. *Return to Auschwitz.* New York: Atheneum.

Heimler, Eugene. 1959. *Night of the Mist.* Translated by Andre Ungar. New York: Vanguard.

Heschel, Abraham Joshua. 1955. *God in Search of Man.* New York: Farrar, Straus, and Giroux.

———. 1962. *The Prophets.* 2 vols. New York: Harper and Row.

———. 1981. *The Sabbath: Its Meaning for Modern Man.* New York: Farrar, Straus, and Giroux.

Jabès, Edmond. 1977. *The Book of Yukel and Return to the Book.* Translated by Rosemarie Waldrop. Middletown, Conn.: Wesleyan Univ. Press.

———. 1990. *From the Desert to the Book.* Translated by Pierre Joris. Barrytown, N.Y.: Station Hill.

Jackson, Livia E. Bitton. 1980. *Elli: Coming of Age in the Holocaust.* New York: Times Books.

Jaspers, Karl. 1959. *Truth and Symbol.* Translated by J. T. Wilde, W. Kluback, and W. Kimmel. New Haven, Conn.: College and Univ. Press.

Kaplan, Aryeh. 1990. *Innerspace.* Brooklyn, N.Y.: Moznaim.

Ka-tzetnik 135633. 1958. *House of Dolls.* Translated by Moshe M. Kohn. New York: Pyramid.

———. 1971a. *Kokhev ha'efer.* Tel-Aviv: Hamenora.

———. 1971b. *Star of Ashes.* Translated by Nina De-Nur. Tel-Aviv: Hamenora.

———. 1987. *Tsofen: E. D. M. A.* Tel-Aviv: Hakibbutz Hameuchad.

———. 1989. *Shivitti: A Vision.* Translated by Eliyah De-Nur and Lisa Herman. New York: Harper and Row.

Kazantzakis, Nikos. 1960. *The Saviors of God.* Translated by K. Friar. New York: Simon and Schuster.

———. 1963. *The Rock Garden.* Translated by R. Howard and K. Friar. New York: Simon and Schuster.

Kessel, Sim. 1972. *Hanged at Auschwitz.* Translated by Melville Wallace and Delight Wallace. New York: Stein and Day.

Kielar, Wieslaw. 1980. *Anus Mundi*. Translated by Susanne Flatauer. New York: Times Books.

Kierkegaard, Soren. 1941. *Repetition*. Translated by Walter Lowrie. Princeton, N.J.: Princeton Univ. Press.

Kitov, Eliyahu. 1973. *The Book of Our Heritage*. Translated by Nathan Bulman. 3 vols. New York: Feldheim.

Klein, Gerda Weissmann. 1957. *All but My Life*. New York: Hill and Wang.

Lacan, Jacques. 1968. *The Language of the Self*. Translated by Anthony Wilden. Baltimore, Md.: Johns Hopkins Univ. Press.

———. 1977. *Écrits*. Translated by Alan Sheridan. New York: W. W. Norton.

Langer, Jiří. 1976. *Nine Gates to the Chassidic Mysteries*. Translated by Stephen Jolly. New York: Behrman House.

✓ Langer, Lawrence. 1975. *The Holocaust and the Literary Imagination*. New Haven, Conn.: Yale Univ. Press.

———. 1982. *Versions of Survival: The Holocaust and the Human Spirit*. Albany, N.Y.: SUNY Press.

———. 1991. *Holocaust Testimonies: The Ruins of Memory*. New Haven, Conn.: Yale Univ. Press.

Leitner, Isabella. 1978. *Fragments of Isabella*, edited by Irving Leitner. New York: Thomas Crowell.

Lengyel, Olga. 1972. *Five Chimneys*. London: Granada.

Lerner, Lily Gluck. 1980. *The Silence*. Secaucus: Lyle Stuart.

Levi, Primo. 1961. *Survival in Auschwitz*. Translated by Stuart Wolf. New York: Macmillan.

———. 1965. *The Reawakening*. Translated by Stuart Wolf. Boston: Little, Brown.

———. 1975. *Il sistema periódico*. Torino: Einaudi.

———. 1985. *The Periodic Table*. Translated by Raymond Rosenthal. New York: Schocken.

———. 1986a. *I sommersi e i salvati*. Torino: Einaudi.

———. 1986b. *Moments of Reprieve*. Translated by Ruth Feldman. London: Michael Joseph.

———. 1988. *The Drowned and the Saved*. Translated by R. Rosenthal. New York: Vintage Books.

———. 1989. *La tregua*. Torino: Einaudi.

Levinas, Emmanuel. 1969. *Totality and Infinity*. Translated by Alphonso Lingis. Pittsburgh, Pa: Duquesne Univ. Press.

———. 1978a. *Existence and Existents*. Translated by Alphonso Lingis. The Hague: Martinus Nijhoff.

———. 1978b. "Signature." *Research in Phenomenology* 8: 175–89.

———. 1981. *Otherwise Than Being or Beyond Essence*. Translated by Alphonso Lingis. The Hague: Martinus Nijhoff.

———. 1982. *L'au delà du verset*. Paris: Éditions de Minuit.

————. 1985. *Ethics and Infinity.* Translated by Richard A. Cohen. Pittsburgh, Pa.: Duquesne Univ. Press.

————. 1986a. "Bad Conscience and the Inexorable." In *Face to Face with Levinas,* edited by Richard A. Cohen, 35–40. Albany: SUNY Press.

————. 1986b. "Dialogue with Emmanuel Levinas (with Richard Kearney)." In *Face to Face with Levinas,* edited by Richard A. Cohen, 13–33. Albany: SUNY Press.

————. 1987a. *Collected Philosophical Papers.* Translated by A. Lingis. The Hague: Martinus Nijhoff.

————. 1987b. *Time and the Other.* Translated by Richard A. Cohen. Pittsburgh, Pa.: Duquesne Univ. Press.

————. 1988a. "The Paradox of Morality." Translated by Richard A. Cohen. In *The Provocation of Levinas: Rethinking the Other,* edited by Robert Bernasconi and David Wood, 168–80. London: Routledge.

————. 1988b. "Useless Suffering." Translated by Richard A. Cohen. In *The Provocation of Levinas: Rethinking the Other,* edited by Robert Bernasconi and David Wood, 156–67. London: Routledge.

————. 1989a. "Ethics as First Philosophy." Translated by Sean Hand and Michael Temple. In *The Levinas Reader,* edited by Sean Hand, 75–87. Oxford, Eng.: Basil Blackwell.

————. 1989b. "Ideology and Idealism." Translated by Sanford Ames and Arthur Lesley. In *The Levinas Reader,* edited by Sean Hand, 235–48. Oxford, Eng.: Basil Blackwell.

————. 1989c. "Prayer without Demand." Translated by Sarah Richmond. In *The Levinas Reader,* edited by Sean Hand, 227–34. Oxford, Eng.: Basil Blackwell.

————. 1989d. "Revelation in the Jewish Tradition." Translated by Sarah Richmond. In *The Levinas Reader,* edited by Sean Hand, 190–210. Oxford, Eng.: Basil Blackwell.

————. 1990. *Nine Talmudic Readings.* Translated by Annette Aronowicz. Bloomington: Indiana Univ. Press.

Lewinska, Pelagia. 1968. *Twenty Months at Auschwitz.* Translated by A. Teichner. New York: Lyle Stuart.

Lubetkin, Zivia. 1978. *B'yamiy kliyon v'marad.* Tel-Aviv: Hakibbutz Hameuchad.

————. 1981. *In the Days of Destruction and Revolt.* Translated by I. Tubbin. Tel-Aviv: Hakibbutz Hameuchad.

Luzzatto, Moshe Haim. 1990. *The Path of the Just.* Translated by Shraga Silverstein. 3d ed. New York: Feldheim.

Maimonides, Moses. 1956. *The Guide for the Perplexed.* Translated by M. Friedlaender. New York: Dover.

————. 1967. *The Commandments.* Translated by Charles B. Chavel. 2 vols. New York: Soncino.

————. 1990. *The Existence and Unity of God: Three Treatises Attributed to Maimonides.* Translated by Fred Rosner. Northvale, N.J.: Aronson.

Meed, Vladka. 1948. *Fun beyde zaytn geto-moyer*. New York: Workmen's Circle.

———. 1973. *On Both Sides of the Wall*. Translated by Benjamin Meed. Tel-Aviv: Hakibbutz Hameuchad.

Mekilta de-Rabbi Ishmael. 1961. Translated by Jacob Z. Lauterbach. 3 vols. Philadelphia: Jewish Publication Society.

Michelson, Frida. 1973. *Ya perezhila Rumbulu*. Tel-Aviv: Beit Lohamei Getaot.

———. 1979. *I Survived Rumbuli*. Translated by Wolf Goodman. New York: Holocaust Library.

Midrash on Psalms. 1959. Translated by William G. Brauche. 2 vols. New Haven, Conn.: Yale Univ. Press.

Midrash Rabbah. 1961. Translated and edited by H. Freedman and Maurice Simon. 10 vols. London: Soncino.

✓ Mintz, Alan. 1984. *Hurban: Responses to Catastrophe in Hebrew Literature*. New York: Columbia Univ. Press.

The Mishnah. 1988. Translated by Jacob Neusner. New Haven, Conn.: Yale Univ. Press.

Müller, Filip. 1979a. *Auschwitz Inferno: The Testimony of a Sonderkommando*. Translated by Susanne Flatauer. London: Routledge and Kegan Paul.

———. 1979b. *Sonderbehandlung*. Munich: Steinhausen.

Nachman of Breslov. 1973. *Rabbi Nachman's Wisdom*. Translated by A. Kaplan, edited by Z. A. Rosenfeld. New York: A. Kaplan.

———. 1983. *Advice*. Translated by Avraham Greenbaum. Brooklyn, N.Y.: Breslov Research Institute.

———. 1984. *Tikkun*. Translated by Avraham Greenbaum. Jerusalem: Breslov Research Institute.

———. 1986. *The Aleph-Bet Book*. Translated by Moshe Myhoff. Jerusalem: Breslov Research Institute.

Nachmanides. 1971–76. *Commentary on the Torah*. Translated by Charles B. Chavel. 5 vols. New York: Shilo.

✓ Neher, André. 1981. *The Exile of the Word*. Translated by D. Maisel. Philadelphia: Jewish Publication Society.

Newman, Louis, ed. 1963. *The Hasidic Anthology*. New York: Schocken.

Nomberg-Przytyk, Sara. 1985. *Auschwitz: True Tales from a Grotesque Land*. Translated by Roslyn Hirsch. Chapel Hill: Univ. of North Carolina Press.

———. N.d. *Lydzi w Oswiecim*. Manuscript E/1448. Yad Vashem Archives, Jerusalem.

Nyiszli, Miklos. 1960. *Auschwitz: A Doctor's Eyewitness Account*. Translated by Tibere Kremer and Richard Seaver. New York: Fawcett Crest.

Ortega y Gasset, José. 1969. *Some Lessons in Metaphysics*. Translated by Mildred Adams. New York: W. W. Norton.

Pascal, Blaise. 1966. *Pensées*. Translated by A. J. Krailsheimer. New York: Penguin.

Patterson, David. 1991. *In Dialogue and Dilemma with Elie Wiesel*. Wakefield, N.H.: Longwood Academic.

Perl, Gisella. 1948. *I Was a Doctor in Auschwitz*. New York: International Univ. Press.

Pesikta de Rab Kahana. 1975. Translated by W. G. Braude and I. J. Kapstein. Philadelphia: Jewish Publication Society.

Pirke de Rabbi Eliezer. 1970. Translated by Gerald Friedlander. New York: Herman Press.

Pisar, Samuel. 1979. *Of Blood and Hope*. Boston: Little, Brown.

Plato. 1961. *The Republic*. Translated by P. Shorey. In *The Collected Dialogues*, edited by E. Hamilton and H. Cairns, 575–844. Princeton, N.J.: Princeton Univ. Press.

"Protocol of the Wannsee Conference, January 20, 1942." 1981. In *Documents on the Holocaust*, edited by Y. Arad, Y. Gutman, and A. Margaliat. Jerusalem: Yad Vashem.

Rabinowicz, Harry M. 1988. *Hasidism: The Movement and Its Masters*. Northvale, N.J.: Aronson.

Rashi. 1972. *Commentary on the Torah*. Translated by M. Rosenbaum and A. A. Silbermann. 5 vols. Jerusalem: Silbermann Family.

Rawicz, Piotr. 1975. *From Bergen-Belsen to Jerusalem*, edited by Emil L. Fackenheim. Jerusalem: Institute of Contemporary Jewry.

Rosenfeld, Alvin. 1980. *A Double Dying: Reflections on Holocaust Literature*. Bloomington: Indiana Univ. Press.

Rosenzweig, Franz. 1955. *On Jewish Learning*. Translated and edited by N. N. Glatzer. New York: Schocken.

———. 1972. *The Star of Redemption*. Translated by William W. Hallo. Boston: Beacon.

Rubinstein, Donna. 1982. *I Am the Only Survivor of Krasnostav*. New York: Shengold.

Saadia Gaon. 1976. *The Book of Beliefs and Opinions*. Translated by S. Rosenblatt. New Haven, Conn.: Yale Univ. Press.

Sandberg, Moshe. 1967. *Shanah l'ayn kayts*. Jerusalem: Yad Vashem.

———. 1968. *My Longest Year*. Translated by S. C. Hyman. Jerusalem: Yad Vashem.

Sassoon, Agnes. 1983. *Agnes: How My Spirit Survived*. Edgeware, Eng.: Lawrence Cohen.

Schneerson, Menachem M. 1986. *Torah Studies*. Adapted by Jonathan Sacks. 2d ed. London: Lubavitch Foundation.

Sefer Yetzirah: The Book of Creation. 1990. Translated with commentary by Aryeh Kaplan. York Beach: Samuel Weiser.

Sforno. 1987. *Commentary on the Torah*. Translated by Raphael Pelcovitz. 2 vols. Brooklyn: Mesorah.

Shapell, Nathan. 1974. *Witness to the Truth*. New York: David McKay.

Shapira, Kalonymus Kalman. 1991. *A Student's Obligation*. Translated by Micha Odenheimer. Northvale, N.J.: Aronson.

Steinsaltz, Adin. 1976. *The Essential Talmud*. Translated by Chaya Galai. New York: Basic Books.

————. 1980. *The Thirteen Petalled Rose*. Translated by Yehuda Hanegbi. New York: Basic Books.

————. 1984. *Biblical Images*. Translated by Yehuda Hanegbi and Yehudit Keshet. New York: Basic Books.

————. 1985. *Beggars and Prayers*. Translated by Yehuda Hanegbi. New York: Basic Books.

————. 1988. *The Long Shorter Way*. Translated by Yehuda Hanegbi. Northvale, N.J.: Aronson.

Szmagelewska, Seweryna. 1947. *Smoke over Birkenau*. Translated by Jadwiga Rynas. New York: Henry Holt.

Tillich, Paul. 1957. *The Dynamics of Faith*. New York: Harper and Row.

Tillion, Germaine. 1973. *Ravensbrück*. Paris: Éditions du Seuil.

————. 1975. *Ravensbrück*. Translated by Gerald Satterwhite. Garden City, N.Y.: Doubleday.

Topas, George. 1990. *The Iron Furnace*. Lexington: Univ. Press of Kentucky.

Trepman, Paul. 1978. *Among Men and Beasts*. Translated by Shoshana Perla and Gertrude Hirschler. New York: Bergen Belsen Memorial Press.

Vinocur, Ana. 1972. *Un libro sin título*. Montevideo: Ediciones Juventa.

————. 1976. *A Book without a Title*. Translated by Valentine Isaac and Ricardo Iglesia. New York: Vantage.

Vrba, Rudolf, and Alan Bestic. 1964. *I Cannot Forgive*. New York: Bantam.

Wardi, Charlotte. 1986. *La génocide dans la fiction romanesque*. Paris: Presses Universitaires de France.

Wells, Leon W. 1978. *The Death Brigade*. New York: Holocaust Library.

Wiesel, Elie. 1958. *La Nuit*. Paris: Éditions de Minuit.

————. 1960. *Night*. Translated by Stella Rodway. New York: Hill and Wang.

————. 1964. *The Town beyond the Wall*. Translated by Stephen Becker. New York: Avon.

————. 1966a. *The Gates of the Forest*. Translated by F. Frenaye. New York: Holt, Rinehart, and Winston.

————. 1966b. *The Jews of Silence*. Translated by Neal Kozodoy. New York: Holt, Rinehart, and Winston.

————. 1968. *Legends of Our Time*. New York: Avon.

————. 1970a. *A Beggar in Jerusalem*. Translated by Lily Edelman and Elie Wiesel. New York: Random House.

————. 1970b. *One Generation After*. Translated by Lily Edelman and Elie Wiesel. New York: Pocket Books.

————. 1973a. *Ani Maamin: A Song Lost and Found Again*. Translated by Marion Wiesel. New York: Random House.

————. 1973b. *The Oath*. Translated by Marion Wiesel. New York: Avon.

————. 1973c. *Souls on Fire*. Translated by Marion Wiesel. New York: Vintage Books.

―――. 1974. *Zalmen or the Madness of God.* Adapted for the stage by Marion Wiesel. New York: Random House.

―――. 1976. *Messengers of God.* Translated by Marion Wiesel. New York: Random House.

―――. 1977. *Dimensions of the Holocaust.* Evanston, Ill.: Northwestern Univ. Press.

―――. 1978. *A Jew Today.* Translated by Marion Wiesel. New York: Random House.

―――. 1981. *The Testament.* Translated by Marion Wiesel. New York: Summit.

―――. 1982a. *Paroles d'étranger.* Paris: Éditions du Seuil.

―――. 1982b. *Somewhere a Master.* Translated by Marion Wiesel. New York: Summit.

―――. 1985. *Against Silence: The Voice and Vision of Elie Wiesel,* edited by Edited by Irving Abrahamson. 3 Vols. New York: Holocaust Library.

―――. 1987. *Twilight.* Translated by Marion Wiesel. New York: Summit.

―――. 1988. *The Six Days of Destruction.* Translated by C. Lander and E. Friedlander. Oxford, Eng.: Pergamon.

―――. 1990a. *Evil and Exile.* Translated by Jon Rothschild. Notre Dame, Ind.: Univ. of Notre Dame Press.

―――. 1990b. *From the Kingdom of Memory.* Translated by Marion Wiesel. New York: Summit.

―――. 1991. *Sages and Dreamers.* Translated by Marion Wiesel. New York: Summit.

―――. 1992. *The Forgotten.* Translated by Stephen Becker. New York: Summit.

Wiesenthal, Simon. 1970. *Die Sonnenblume: Von Schuld und Vergebung.* Hamburg: Hoffmann and Campe.

―――. 1976. *The Sunflower.* Translated by H. A. Piehler. New York: Schocken.

Wittgenstein, Ludwig. 1922. *Tractatus Logico-Philosophicus.* Translated by C. K. Ogden. London: Kegan Paul, Trench, Trubner.

―――. 1979. *Notebooks 1914–1916.* Translated by G. E. M. Anscombe, edited by G. H. von Wright and G. E. M. Anscombe. 2d ed. Chicago: Univ. of Chicago Press.

Young, James. 1987. "Interpreting Literary Testimony: A Preface to Rereading Holocaust Diaries and Memoirs." *New Literary History* 18: 402–23.

―――. 1988. *Writing and Rewriting the Holocaust.* Bloomington: Indiana Univ. Press.

Zalman, Schneur. 1981. *Likutei Amarim Tanya.* Translated by Nissan Mindel. Brooklyn: Kehot.

The Zohar. 1984. Translated by Harry Sperling and Maurice Simon. 5 vols. London: Soncino Press.

Zyskind, Sara. 1978. *Ha'atarah sh'avdah.* Tel-Aviv: Hakibbutz Hameuchad.

―――. 1981. *Stolen Years.* Translated by Margarit Inbar. Minneapolis: Lerner.

Index

Abel, 156, 201, 202
Abraham, 19, 42, 80, 119
Abraham ibn Ezra, 164
Adam, 105, 143
Amersfoort, 111
Améry, Jean, 54, 67–68, 70
Appelfeld, Aharon, 163
Aristotle, 8, 13, 104
Augustine, 13
Auschwitz, 2, 7, 21, 28, 70, 71, 137; emergence from, 177, 187–88; and God, 18–19, 20, 103, 199; and humanity, 23, 150, 165, 178; and idolatry, 5; and silence, 122, 124, 182; and time, 130; as world, 117, 124, 144, 190

Babi Yar, 195
Bachya ibn Paquda, 66, 90, 191
Bakhtin, Mikhail, 3, 14, 15, 16–17, 29; on the child, 39; on God, 107; on human presence, 113; on rebirth, 206; on silence, 132; on the soul, 174; on truth, 210
Belzec, 137
Benjamin, Walter, 14, 15
Bergen-Belsen, 188
Bergson, Henri, 13, 15, 60
Bialik, Chaim Nachman, 79
Bible, 24. See also Torah
Birkenau, 48, 51, 86, 92, 94, 113
Borowski, Tadeusz, 5
Buber, Martin, 127; on the Good, 52; on the other, 109, 182, 190; on prayer, 76, 130

Buchenwald, 3, 25, 26, 88
Bühler, Josef, 52

Cain, 113, 143, 155–56
Campbell, Joseph, 201
Caro, Joseph, 53
Célan, Paul, 5
Chelmno, 110, 137
Christendom, 110
Cohen, Elie, 111, 115, 141–42, 148
confession, 149–50
Covenant, 8, 30, 41, 80, 167, 213
Cracow, 188
Creation, 41–42, 129; and Auschwitz, 124
Czerniakow, Adam, 83

Dachau, 56, 93, 106, 115, 172
Dante, 6, 62, 74, 118
Delbo, Charlotte, 39, 54–55, 67, 74; on bearing witness, 200; on indifference, 110, 112; on language, 136, 137; on liberation, 180; on the movement of return, 154; on responsibility, 114; on the "there is," 125; on time, 129
Des Pres, Terrance, 1, 3–6, 27
DeVore, Irven, 4
divine image, 105–6
Donat, Alexander, 63–64, 79, 91, 129; on the child, 85, 97; on the face, 116; on identity, 166, 171, 172, 177; on liberation, 185, 194; on the loss of humanity, 112–13; on madness, 117; on responsibility, 147–48; on the "there is," 127
Dribben, Judith, 21, 44, 77, 165